From Budapest to Psychoanalysis

This book follows the personal and professional journeys of three Jewish women from Budapest, originally classmates in the same high school. The book shows how they and their families were marked by the Shoah, and explores the impact of the social, cultural, and political milieu in which they travelled upon their development as psychoanalysts.

Following an introduction by the Hungarian psychoanalyst, Judit Mészáros, who gives a broad historical review of Hungarian Jewry during the Shoah and the Soviet era, the three authors provide autobiographical accounts of their own psychoanalytic evolution and interconnectedness. They describe their motivations for emigrating from Hungary, their early struggles to fit in and their eventual acculturation. The authors explore their coming of age as clinicians in their adopted homelands and explain how their theoretical orientation and clinical styles were shaped by their respective analytic environments, their training experiences, and their own personal histories. They offer clinical vignettes to illustrate their respective psychoanalytic perspective. The book closes with an afterword from American psychoanalyst, Adrienne Harris, who contemplates the authors' immigration experiences alongside her own.

Replete with personal, cultural, and political history, this book will prove both informative and fascinating for psychoanalysts, psychotherapists as well as the general public.

Veronica Csillag is a faculty member and a training and supervising analyst at the Manhattan Institute for Psychoanalysis, a faculty member at the National Institute for the Psychotherapies, and an associate editor of *Psychoanalytic Dialogues*. She is the author of several psychoanalytic papers, which were published in a variety of journals. She is in private practice in New York City.

Katalin Lanczi was born in Budapest and emigrated to the UK in 1980. She is a Fellow of the British Psychoanalytical Society, a training and supervising analyst of the British Psychoanalytic Association and the co-director of the European Psychoanalytic Film Festival. She lectures and teaches widely, and is in private practice in London.

Julianna Vamos was born in Budapest and studied in Paris (Sorbonne Paris 5) for a PhD in clinical psychology and psychopathology. She is a psychoanalyst and member of the Société Psychoanalytique de Paris (SPP).

Psychoanalysis in a New Key Book Series

Series Editor: Donnel Stern

When music is played in a new key, the melody does not change, but the notes that make up the composition do change: change in the context of continuity, continuity that perseveres through change. Psychoanalysis in a New Key publishes books that share the aims psychoanalysts have always had, but they approach these aims differently. The books in the series are not expected to advance any particular theoretical agenda, although to this date most have been written by analysts from the Interpersonal and Relational orientations.

The most important contribution of a psychoanalytic book is the communication of something that nudges the reader's grasp of clinical theory and practice in an unexpected direction. Psychoanalysis in a New Key creates a deliberate focus on innovative and unsettling clinical thinking. Because that kind of thinking is encouraged by exploration of the sometimes surprising contributions to psychoanalysis of ideas and findings from other fields, Psychoanalysis in a New Key particularly encourages interdisciplinary studies. Books in the series have married psychoanalysis with dissociation, trauma theory, sociology, and criminology. The series is open to the consideration of studies examining the relationship between psychoanalysis and any other field – for instance, biology, literary and art criticism, philosophy, systems theory, anthropology, and political theory.

But innovation also takes place within the boundaries of psychoanalysis, and Psychoanalysis in a New Key therefore also presents work that reformulates thought and practice without leaving the precincts of the field. Books in the series focus, for example, on the significance of personal values in psychoanalytic practice, on the complex interrelationship between the analyst's clinical work and personal life, on the consequences for the clinical situation when patient and analyst are from different cultures, and on the need for psychoanalysts to accept the degree to which they knowingly satisfy their own wishes during treatment hours, often to the patient's detriment. A full list of all titles in this series is available at: https://www.routledge.com/Psychoanalysis-in-a-New-Key-Book-Series/book-series/LEAPNKBS

'It is not often that we have the opportunity to see how theory emerges from lived experience, but this is what this book offers. Three women have gathered here to tell us about the confluence of their personal and psychoanalytic journeys from post-WWII Hungary to the West; stories that are then reflected upon by two other women psychoanalysts. These are stories of hope and action, of potential and the ability to realize it, but also of deep awareness of the burdens of history and of the political and social forces that drive our lives through it. Ultimately, this is a book about the power of ideas, and of making sense of life's overwhelming riddles together to keep us going. A deep reading, and psychoanalytic adventure.'

Eyal Rozmarin *is a co-editor of the book series* Relational Perspectives in Psychoanalysis, *and associate editor of the journals* Psychoanalytic Dialogues *and* Studies in Gender and Sexuality

'Three women in three voices present their remarkable journeys from Budapest to psychoanalysis. This original book has the texture of a fabric woven with different threads. History with a capital "H" has impacted their individual and generational trajectories. They journey through different countries, as well as through languages. Their ability to mobilize themselves towards singular and creative orientations is a testimony to their perseverance and vitality. In the background, psychoanalysis proves to be an endless resource.'

Armelle Hours *is a psychiatrist, psychoanalyst and member of the SPP IPA and GLPRA*

'This is an enthralling book that has emerged from a dialogue between three classmates from Budapest who became psychoanalysts in three different cultures. In addition to being drawn into the personal journeys of each of the three women, the book also reflects developments in contemporary psychoanalysis that are at once diverse and overlapping. The three essays address the role of the tragic history of the Hungarian Shoah in the formation of the writers' identities, their struggles to come to terms with the traumatic past of their families and their process of mourning. The essays illuminate the psychoanalytic identity of each, revealed in their theoretical and clinical approaches. This is a remarkable contribution to the field and is likely to be of interest to clinicians and the general public alike.'

Anne Patterson *is the editor of the New Library of Psychoanalysis book series, Routledge*

'Budapest, along with Vienna and Berlin, was a centre of psycho-analysis from 1900 until the Second World War, when many psychoanalysts managed to escape to Britain, America and France. These are the countries where the three authors of this book – all second-generation survivors of the Shoah in Hungary – practice today. Nearly half a million Hungarian Jews were sent to be murdered in Auschwitz, and antisemitism has continued to mark the recent history of Hungary. The authors, who met as students in grammar school in Budapest, all went on to become psychoanalysts. This deeply moving book is a celebration of their capacity to survive intergenerational trauma and migration and of the role that psycho-analysis has played in their blossoming.'

Rosine Perelberg *is the president of the British Psychoanalytical Society; she has published* Psychic Bisexuality: A British-French Dialogue; Murdered Father, Dead Father: Revisiting the Oedipus Complex; Sexuality, Excess, and Representation; *and the podcast 'The Shoah and Contemporary Antisemitism' for the International Psychoanalytic Association*

'Three Hungarian immigrant women recall and examine their personal and psychoanalytic journey in this stimulating book of origins and on-going transformations. They movingly affirm that the making of a psychoanalyst is inseparable from personal and profes-sional maturation. Through writing this book they re-find each other and connect with a deep understanding of themselves. The book beautifully shows the authors' diversity and similarity, the powerful ingredients of any New Beginning.'

Giselle Galdi *is Editor in Chief of the* American Journal of Psychoanalysis *and a training and supervising analyst at the American Institute for Psychoanalysis*

From Budapest to Psychoanalysis

Three Portraits and their Analytic Frames

Veronica Csillag,
Katalin Lanczi, and
Julianna Vamos

Edited by Veronica Csillag

Routledge
Taylor & Francis Group

LONDON AND NEW YORK

Cover image: Margit Híd by Luca Korodi

First published 2023
by Routledge
4 Park Square, Milton Park, Abingdon, Oxon OX14 4RN

and by Routledge
605 Third Avenue, New York, NY 10158

Routledge is an imprint of the Taylor & Francis Group, an informa business

Introduction chapter translated by Thomas Williams

British Library Cataloguing-in-Publication Data
A catalogue record for this book is available from the British Library

Library of Congress Cataloging-in-Publication Data
Names: Csillag, Veronica, 1955- author. | Lanczi, Katalin, 1955- author. | Vamos, Julianna, 1954- author.
Title: From Budapest to psychoanalysis : three portraits and their analytic frames / Veronica Csillag, Katalin Lanczi and Julianna Vamos.
Description: Abingdon, Oxon ; New York, NY : Routledge, 2023. | Includes bibliographical references and index. | Identifiers: LCCN 2022014123 (print) | LCCN 2022014124 (ebook) | ISBN 9781032307695 (hbk) | ISBN 9781032307701 (pbk) | ISBN 9781003306542 (ebk)
Subjects: LCSH: Women and psychoanalysis--Hungary--Budapest--History--20th century. | Women psychoanalysts--Hungary--Budapest--History--20th century. | Jewish women--Hungary--Budapest--History--20th century.
Classification: LCC BF173 .C8346 2023 (print) | LCC BF173 (ebook) | DDC 150.19/50943912--dc23/eng/20220701
LC record available at https://lccn.loc.gov/2022014123
LC ebook record available at https://lccn.loc.gov/2022014124

ISBN: 978-1-032-30769-5 (hbk)
ISBN: 978-1-032-30770-1 (pbk)
ISBN: 978-1-003-30654-2 (ebk)

DOI: 10.4324/9781003306542

Typeset in Times New Roman
by MPS Limited, Dehradun

Contents

Acknowledgments

Many people contributed to the development and completion of this book and am grateful to them all. Here I will only mention those who have been directly involved.

First, I wish to thank Adrienne Harris, my teacher and mentor of many years, who also graciously agreed to write the Afterword.

I thank my fellow authors, Katalin Lanczi and Julianna Vamos. In addition to writing their own chapters, they contributed countless ideas and critiqued every aspect of this volume. The final text is the result of very close collaboration among the three of us as well as with Adrienne Harris and Judit Mészáros, who wrote the Introduction and who also merits special thanks.

The editor of this series, Donnel Stern, has been a source of endless support. Without his encouragement, this book may not have ever seen the light of day. Thank you!

I am grateful to Routledge Senior Publisher, Kate Hawes and the members of her editorial and production team, most especially to Georgina Clutterbuck, who was practically holding my hand through this entire process.

My colleagues and friends at the Manhattan Institute for Psychoanalysis and in the larger analytic community, including my former analysts and supervisors as well as my own patients, supervisees, and students, all shaped me as a clinician, thinker, and writer. You have my gratitude.

Finally, let me take this opportunity to thank friends and family, especially my partner, A. L., who listened to my ideas and survived my bad moods and limited availability without much retaliation or abandonment.

Veronica Csillag

My co-authors have stimulated my thinking throughout the writing of this chapter: I owe them a great deal as I do to my patients.

Special thanks to friends and colleagues Pina Antinucci, Michael Brearley, Don Campbell, Rachel Chaplin, Sally Cowley, Jeffrey Murer, Anne Patterson, Jenny Roberts; their help was invaluable throughout the process of writing. I am indebted to my clinical discussion group for their help in thinking about confidentiality and to a reading group of historians and psychoanalysts who contributed to my understanding of the historical background and the aftermath of the Shoah. With gratitude to my analysts Drs H. and G. and all my supervisors, among them most especially to Caroline Polmear, Vic Sedlak, Don Campbell, and Irma Brenman-Pick. Above all my love and thanks to my husband and brave editor, Stephen Wilson, without whom this project and, indeed, the whole psychoanalytic project, would not have existed.

Katalin Lanczi

In the process of contributing to this book, I received a lot of help, big and small, in direct and indirect ways. I thank Veronica Csillag for introducing the idea, and I am grateful for the extensive dialogue with my co-authors while elaborating on our professional destinies.

Many thanks to my colleagues from the SPP and from other analytical societies for reading my chapter, asking questions, making comments, pushing me forward and helping me elaborate and fine-tune my thoughts.

Special thanks as well to my friends all over the world, for the conversations we have had about this project. I am grateful for the help I have received from several people for my English writing. I thank each and every one of them.

Last but not least, I am indebted to my patients, both babies and adults, with whom this unique passionate analytical experience has been taking place.

Julianna Vamos

Contributor biographies

Adrienne Harris is a faculty member and supervisor at the New York University Postdoctoral Program in Psychotherapy and Psychoanalysis and at the Psychoanalytic Institute of Northern California. She is an editor of Psychoanalytic Dialogues, and Studies in Gender and Sexuality. She is co-editor of the Book Series Relational Perspectives in Psychoanalysis, and editor of the International Psychoanalytical Association (IPA) ejournal, Psychoanalysis Today.

Judit Mészáros is professor honoris causa at the Eötvös Loránd University, training and supervising analyst of the Hungarian Psychoanalytical Society (affiliated with the IPA) and staff member at the European Psychotherapy Training Institute, Budapest. She has written scores of papers, and edited and authored many books. She is curator of exhibitions on Ferenczi and the Budapest School of Psychoanalysis in London and Budapest.

Chapter 1

Introduction

The individual in a historical context

Judit Mészáros

The life paths of the authors begin with common historical roots formed by the socio-political events of twentieth-century Hungary – specifically, Jewish assimilation into Hungarian society, the anti-Semitism that culminated in the Holocaust, and the Stalinist and post-Stalinist periods in the countries of Eastern Europe. It is this historical fabric in which the authors' families are embedded. It pervades the authors' early years from their birth to their experiences in school and with their peers to their emigration from Hungary. Their lives have fateful similarities: all three authors' mothers went to the same Jewish girls' grammar school in Budapest before the Second World War. The three authors were classmates in the same English programme at a strongly competitive grammar school in Budapest. Despite their fundamentally different personalities, they formed a friendship and, during their university years or shortly thereafter, all three defected. All three found themselves and their chosen vocation in the same field, psychoanalysis. Today they practise and teach as psychoanalysts in three cities on two continents: Paris, London and New York. Can this all be a coincidence?

It is certainly an honour as a fellow psychoanalyst in Budapest to have been requested by the authors to write this introduction about the period before they emigrated, and I am reminded of a story that likewise ties the threads together. The Budapest-Fasori Grammar School has produced a number of world-renowned alumni, including John von Neumann, the mathematician who laid the theoretical foundations for the computer and emigrated to America, Edward Teller, the nuclear physicist and father of the hydrogen bomb, who

DOI: 10.4324/9781003306542-1

also left for the United States, John Charles Harsányi, the Nobel Prize-winning US economist, and Eugene Paul Wigner, the Nobel Prize-winning US physicist. Is this all a coincidence? Americans have asked, what is it in that neighbourhood that that school should have produced so many ingenious mathematicians and physicists? So they went there and studied the place. Perhaps it was something that they had all eaten or drunk. Perhaps it was the water? Might there have been something in it that affected the functioning of the brain? No – it was not the water! It was the school's outstanding teachers, many of them Fellows of the Hungarian Academy of Sciences, truly great figures, who had a powerful impact on their talented students. Beyond this, there was something else: history, which forced them to emigrate.

The authors were born in the mid-1950s, just a decade after the Second World War, members of the second-generation Holocaust survivors. The war and the socio-political events in Hungary that followed impacted the individual, including members of the generation of survivors, like a roller coaster: given the forces of the external world, one endeavoured to control one's own impulses, while also maintaining a balance. Just when one thinks one has found stability, one suddenly feels disoriented, not knowing which way is up and which way is down, what is true and what is false, how something can be both appealing and repugnant, at once "a left-leaning liberal, sympathetic to socialist ideology but critical of the establishment" (Csillag, p. 31) how to separate the negative phenomena, the anachronistic contradiction of a dictatorship taking shape under an umbrella of promising ideologies (e.g., all people are equal). One struggles for a state of internal balance in a sphere of cognitive and affective dissonance.

The authors were born in a period of ten years (between 1945 and 1956), which defined a total of four-plus decades (1945–1989). They came into a world where they had to come to terms with the deep contradictions between the informational and emotional messages relayed in verbal communication, where the content and symbolism of open communication differed from that of the non-verbal sort. They were socialised in a climate in which far too much was not as it appeared. What motives lie beneath the surface, forming and sustaining this double-bind communication?

Hungary was allied to the Third Reich in the Second World War. The country was occupied by the Germans in mid-March 1944 and liberated by Soviet troops little more than a year later. The liberation of the capital (in February 1945) represented a chance for survival for Budapest's Jewry, who had lived through the threat of deportation and the mass murders committed by Hungary's fascist Arrow Cross. Soon, however, the country's liberators would also become its occupiers. By 1948, Hungary found itself under a Stalinist regime within the Soviet zone of occupation. The multiparty system came to an end, and, like other countries within the Soviet sphere of influence, Hungary was dependent on the U.S.S.R. from the perspective of public administration, policymaking, the economy, scholarship and culture.

All three authors are part of the second generation of Holocaust survivors. The trauma of the survivors had an effect on the following generations throughout the world, independent of the form of government – whether democratic, autocratic or dictatorial; for the most part, there were clear signs of survivor syndrome and transgenerational phenomena (Wardi, 1995). Beyond that, Hungary, a country that had joined the Soviet bloc, faced particular challenges with its origins in a mix of the historical shock people there had experienced and the pathogen of the political present. This is the main root of the authors' common fate.

In the second half of the nineteenth century, Hungary opened its doors to Jewish communities beset by the pogroms of the Eastern European region. Around the turn of the century, many Jews in Hungary, who were facilitating modernisation and the rise of the middle class there, changed their Jewish-German names to Hungarian-sounding ones to express their allegiance to their adopted country. Several decades later (from the late 1930s), however, a name change like this came to symbolise the struggle to survive. Assimilation represented hope: is there a place in this country for the Jewish diaspora. Hungary's reform-minded, assimilationist Neolog Jews built what was then the largest synagogue in Europe at the end of the nineteenth century. It had a capacity of 3000 and even featured a traditionally Christian liturgical instrument. The violin of escape had been replaced by the pipe organ, which symbolised the intention to remain. In contrast to the houses of worship concealed in the inner courtyards of houses, the synagogue, with its Moorish style that was visible from far off,[1] demonstrated the wishful fantasy that those who had come here imagined their future and those of their descendants in this country. The Neolog Jewry were prepared to assimilate. Just think of the various cultural signs of this intention, e.g., the architecture, the naming practices and the bilingual (Hungarian-Hebrew) prayer books.

The political anti-Semitism that arose after the First World War was therefore incredibly disillusioning, culminating as it did in laws that deprived Hungarian Jews of their rights on both an economic and social level and, ultimately, in mass murder. Exclusionary and anti-life phenomena motivated by anti-Semitism were present in Hungary long before the German occupation in the form of the numerus clausus law in the early 1920s, which placed limits on the percentage of Jewish students at university, in the fascist Scythe Cross movement in the 1930s (Papp, 2014), in forced labour camps in the 1940s and in the mass murder of Hungarian Jews at Kamianets-Podilskyi in 1941.[2] Like one of the authors, many have asked the question: Was assimilation an illusion? Was Hungarian society a truly welcoming one? And if so, to what extent? In terms of its world view, was this country open to accepting a value system from another culture? Or was it really only an "imagined assimilation" (Fenyves, 2010)? Did the country primarily need the adopted people's ability to create economic value, thus resulting in a tolerant attitude among those who opened the doors in prosperous times? In contrast, in lean times and under tense social conditions, was it possible for an unreflective tension to lead to destruction in the shadow of a growing exclusionary ideology of seeking an enemy and creating a scapegoat (as expressed in such commonplaces as "this problem is somebody else's fault" and "they're the ones to blame").

When the Germans occupied the country, Eichmann commandos, whose task it was to eliminate Hungary's Jewry, numbered no more than 65, while the Gestapo in Budapest consisted of 33 men (Ungváry, 2015). It is in this historical context that the Hungarian authorities themselves (the gendarmerie, the police and public administration), with the cooperation of the Hungarian populace (neighbours reporting on neighbours), arranged or actually brought about the deportation and destruction of nearly half a million (437,000) Hungarian Jews, along with Hungarian Roma and non-Jewish leftists, in the space of only a few months. The plundering of Jewish possessions involved active Hungarian participation. A clear example of this is the designation of "yellow-star houses". After Jews were forcibly moved from the countryside in the spring of 1944, the Hungarian authorities set up what were called "yellow-star houses" in the capital (Nádor, 2015).[3] One Jewish family was forced to move into one room each within 2000 designated blocks of flats. This served three aims: Jewish movable and immovable property could be immediately accessed and appropriated, deportation was made easier through collection points, and, most importantly, the "yellow-star houses" marked strategically important areas near a railway station and bridges, which, given the siege of Budapest, offered up those who were fated for destruction anyway. While Regent Miklós Horthy suspended the deportation of the Budapest Jewry under international pressure, the fascist regime of Arrow Cross leader Ferenc Szálasi that followed Horthy's overthrow set up the Budapest ghetto in the final days of the war (November 1944) and issued a decree that made it possible to seize all (movable and immovable) Jewish property. This occurred at a time when parts of Europe had already been liberated and the eastern half of Hungary itself was already occupied by Soviet troops, so the outcome of the war was beyond doubt.

Those who survived the Holocaust, returned and still did not emigrate had to carry on with their lives in a place from which they had been sent to their deaths, where their flats or houses had been looted and where those who were staggering home from the concentration camps were received with horror – Hungary not having sent a single vehicle to the concentration camps after the liberation (Fenyves, 2015). *1945* (Török & Szántó, 2017) is an excellent film about the Hungarian population's fear of the return of Jewish survivors, the sense of terror that they would come back and demand what their neighbours had stolen. The film, to which Lanczi also refers, uses the power of the image and the tools of dramaturgy to enable one to experience what the word, the language of memoirs and interviews, seems to be less able to convey – at least emotionally.

It is no surprise that the surviving Jewry saw the Soviets as liberators and were filled with hope at the idea of communism, one of egalitarianism, which stood in contrast with fascism, a system of destruction based on religion, ethnicity and/or politics. According to Lanczi, "my father ... believed fervently that he was helping to build a new world, in which discrimination and prejudice will cease to exist" (p. 110). Survivors were happy to offer their skills to the Soviet-style regime, which was in dire need of people who had not compromised themselves under the previous authority. Careers in public administration and law enforcement, which had shut them out before, were thus open to them now. However, this led to unpredictable consequences (Karádi, 1992). They instantly found themselves trapped insofar as the Soviet-style dictatorship required those who joined it to completely forsake their previous life/identity, whether it be tied to religion or background (including class, nationality and ethnicity). Lanczi observes that "there was no more talk about the Shoah and the word 'Jew' had disappeared from the public domain" (p. 104). The communist party and the sectors of power demanded that members of Jewish descent in fact silence, deny and repress their life so far. Each attempted to satisfy this impossible requirement in their own way: through identification or through the secret and dangerous maintenance of a dual identity. This writer clearly remembers visiting her grandparents for the Jewish holidays as an elementary schoolgirl. She entered a house of worship built in the inner courtyard of a building, but then, before she opened the door, she cautiously looked around to see if anyone noticed her. Hungary was well-known as a country of neighbours reporting on neighbours. This was also observed by its occupying German commanders. Based on their accounts, there were simply no mass reports from neighbours in any other country.

The trauma of the Holocaust was therefore rendered impossible to work through because of the political consequences of the new regime. At the same time, anti-Semitism had not ended. It appeared openly in the form of incidents that flared up in the countryside in the years immediately after the war (Standeinksy, 2007), it emerged in the streets and at the universities for a few days during the 1956 Revolution, and it bubbled to the surface in the form of references and metaphors for decades like an underground stream (Mészáros, 1998). It took some time for this writer to understand why at one of the clinics at the medical university in Budapest in the 1980s certain patients were referred to as "a child of old parents". This was a vitriolic reference to children of Holocaust survivors who had tried again after their earlier children had been murdered. While one did not hear anti-Semitic references in everyday conversation from the 1960s to the 1980s, they were present in social situations and returned with renewed vigour as open anti-Semitism in politics and emerged in public discourse after the regime change of 1989 (Szántó, 2012). Based on the latest research, 36% of Hungary's adult population is anti-Semitic, with anti-Semitic feelings identifiable in the thinking of over half (56%) (Hann, 2021).

Becoming aware in several steps

How did I find out I was Jewish?

The phenomenon was so common that it became the object of a study in social psychology in the 1980s (Erős et al., 1985). The trauma of the generation of survivors had been silenced for decades. Unfinished sentences, questions left unanswered, non-verbal gestures and irrational fears (of gas water heaters, gas cookers and travel by train, as we learn from the authors' own experiences), losses that have not been worked through, "a sense of subtle gloom" (Lanczi, p. 108) and an atmosphere of secrets and taboos formed a constant in the lives of the next generation (Kestenberg, 1989; Mészáros, 1997; Virág, 1984). The social environment and the individual psychological processes were so complex and contradictory that they could only begin to be explored many decades after the Shoah.

Like so many of their contemporaries, the authors did not have the experience of being born into a religious Jewish family or even one that carried its roots naturally. Instead, they somehow found out later – between the ages of 6 and 11 in this case. There were some whose parents told them at a key moment, others who learned through their schoolmates under the influence of their parents' prejudices and still others who came to terms with their Jewish descent in a chance situation – between two floors in the lift – as Vámos described so powerfully. All of this was independent of whether their parents came from a religious or assimilated Jewish family, whether they were atheists or not, and whether they had become party members under the communist regime or not. There was the empty space in their families caused by the deportations – grandparents, aunts, cousins and grandchildren "did not come back" (a typically euphemistic expression for deportation) – the experience of the labour camps or the ghettos, and the powerful helplessness and vulnerability which was often intermingled with feelings of shame and guilt. The parents of those born after the Shoah attempted to protect their children. They thought there was such a thing as a tabula rasa. Meanwhile, the trauma reached their children through unconscious manifestations and societal conflicts. Csillag tells us that "at the age of six, I was searching for friends. There was this cool girl … . I asked to be friends. She said she'd think about it. The next day she told me that we could not possibly be friends because I was Jewish. I was familiar with the word but did not fully comprehend its meaning. I did realise, however, that it had to be something truly awful. When I returned home that afternoon, I asked my mother if, in fact, I was Jewish. She looked me in the eye and said 'no'". As Lanczi recalls, "Aged four, I become friendly with a little girl in kindergarten. For some unfathomable reason, neither her parents nor mine encourage the relationship. I feel hurt and baffled; very unusually, my parents do not give an explanation. Only many years later do I realise … There was mutual recognition between the two families: we were on two sides of history" (p. 98). Why are there no words? Why is there no one who will come out and say it?

The iron curtain

As with the other countries in the Soviet bloc, the citizens of Hungary saw the end of freedom of movement in the direction of Western civilisation as of 1949. The relationship between the two superpowers, the United States and the Soviet Union, was marked by great tension and accompanied by the division of Europe into East and West after the Second World War. Countries that had suffered losses during the war but had ended up within the Soviet power structure received no aid under the US Marshall Plan, thus slowing recovery after the war. The emergence of a Stalinist dictatorship in Hungary also changed the structure of the economy, with nationalisation launched and private property and market economy eliminated. The state party seriously hamstrung expression of opinion and freedom of movement. It put an end to the free flow of culture and made it difficult if not impossible to maintain personal and professional ties with the Western world. The age of the Cold War had started. The authors' generation was born into a country where, in conjunction with the bliss of free education and free healthcare, all instruction was placed under an ideological umbrella, with Russian language learning having become compulsory from primary to higher education. It was a country where the independent learning of Western languages was the only option available to most, at least until grammar school – within the confines of the contemporary environment and culture.

Many university-educated parents – and this holds true for Jewish parents in particular – placed a strong emphasis on the next generation possessing competitive knowledge and learning some world language because one never knew when medical or engineering skills or indeed any convertible knowledge or qualifications in the arts might save one's life – and, of course, all of this had to be achieved with excellence. This notion imbued parents' need to protect their children so deeply that it remained with them even after they had emigrated: when the university-educated mother of one of the authors learned that her daughter would become a psychoanalyst, she said, "But will you gain an internationally accepted qualification?" (Lanczi, p. 126).

The happiest barracks – the 1960s

All three authors started primary school in the early 1960s under a relatively soft dictatorship after the death of Stalin in 1953, the crushing of the 1956 Revolution and the retribution that followed. Culturally, it was known as the 3T period, in which creative works and their creators were classified as "támogatott", "tűrt" or "tiltott" – that is, the authorities would either back them, abide them or ban them. These fell along a continuum between being socialist realist and/or supportive of the regime at one end and being seen as anti-Marxist and/or undermining the system at the other. The doors were thus open to a wide range of literature, theatre, fine arts and contemporary music – and this included the Beat period produced by the

Silent Generation in the West, whose music and culture eventually managed to sneak under the Iron Curtain. The number of copies of works by American, British and French authors in translation increasingly surpassed those of Soviet/Russian ones in Hungary. Kerouac's *On the Road* and Ginsberg's *Howl* were some of the significant works by the Beat Generation that became available in translation, while the contemporary Hungarian music scene had been infiltrated by bands not usually associated with the Beats in the West, such as the Beatles and the Rolling Stones. These books and records became symbols of an avant-garde youth in Hungary in the 1960s. The way they dressed, wore their hair and behaved in general set in motion changes whose effects could be felt for decades not only musically, but also culturally and socially. Rock and beat bands (no relation to Beat writers) often clashed with police, but they mobilised a generation of teens and twenty-year-olds. More and more bands appeared, including hard rock and even blacklisted groups among them (Romsics, 2017). Dissidents used metaphors and veiled references when they spoke in public. The metaphors in song lyrics naturally testify to this as well. Messages critical of the regime could clearly be read between the lines. In fact, this dual communication reached the level of art. As with all good jokes, it was in the tension between the dictionary meaning and the symbolic meaning that the essence of the message could be found and, indeed, where the strong dissident message of oh so innocent-sounding lyrics lay. When the most beautiful young woman in a faraway land boldly rejects the old king's marriage proposal, adding that she would rather leave and never return in Illés and Bródy's (1969) "Valahol egy lány" (Somewhere a girl), it was resoundingly clear to anyone truly listening what was being communicated. There were naturally consequences to these kinds of lyrics. For example, the album *Jelbeszéd* (Sign Language) was banned not long after its release and did not see the light of day until it was put out again in 1983.

Those creative works that the authorities did not "abide" were still disseminated in samizdat publications produced in ordinary flats and through avant-garde cinemas in people's homes (cf. Csillag, p. 41), while Radio Free Europe[4] and the Voice of America – whose broadcasts it was long forbidden to receive – reached an audience critical of the regime or simply open to the rest of the world. At the same time, the soft dictatorship of the 1960s made it possible to produce a number of works of literature, cinema and fine art that are still considered world-class.

After starting school, the authors soon found themselves part of the Young Pioneer movement. While membership was not compulsory in principle, it was nearly impossible to avoid. Those who did were marginalised in the community of children. The movement was a significant means of instilling communist ideology, but it was also a forum for community experiences, sport and leisure-time activities (e.g., theatre groups, after-school activities tied to the arts, humanities or sciences, and summer camps), as well as for nurturing talent and forming communities. Having adopted various formal motifs from the pre-war scouting movement (e.g., the use of a uniform and the group structure), the Young Pioneer movement inculcated an ethos of country, party and proletarian internationalism. One could later move on to the Young Communist League in high school and at university. A person who wished to enter university or apply for a passport was at a disadvantage without being a member.

However, the neo-Marxist movements at American and Western European universities in 1968 also found adherents among Hungarian students. Associating with the cults of Mao Zedong or Che Guevara could even result in expulsion from university. The crushing of the Prague Spring in 1968 – when Warsaw Pact troops from the Soviet Union and its satellites invaded what was then Czechoslovakia – had a powerfully sobering effect. The only question was when one would lose the illusion of purity with regard to leftist ideology. Indeed, the authors reflect on the invasion – "I became totally disillusioned about the political system I lived in" (Csillag, p. 38) – and their personal experience – "I was, myself, going through a political crisis and a process of disillusionment in the Communist Youth movement at the school" (Lanczi, p. 24). As Rainer (2004) puts it, "What followed was the loss or emptying of a buoyant 'critical' thinking, a 'primitive turn' of leftist theory. From the perspective of a lifetime, I would say the decade can truly be characterised as follows: a 'change' in 'way of life' or 'lifestyle' or a cultural revolution of 'the 1960s'" (p. 11).

Apropos of creative works that authorities banned, abided or backed, it is worth turning to the special "human view" (Ignotus) of psychoanalysis, which the authors chose as a means of self-knowledge and later as a model for their professional life. Psychoanalysis in pre-war Hungary had the power to form the culture (Erős, 2011; Mészáros, 2014). It could be found not only in conversations in cafés among the educated public, but also in modern literature and art. However, all autocratic/dictatorial regimes, such as the Stalinist dictatorship, stood in opposition to the central message of psychoanalysis, the efforts to liberalise the individual (Damousi & Plotkin, 2012). From the late 1940s in Hungary, psychoanalysis was banned as the "home psychology of imperialism", with the renowned Hungarian Psychoanalytical Society having dissolved itself (in 1949) and having ceased to exist as an orga-nisation. Only a few in Budapest continued practising psychoanalysis underground during a period that lasted until the mid-1960s (Mészáros, 2012). In the late 1960s and early 70s, only the most discerning teachers raised the issue of psychoanalysis in education. According to Lanczi, "An important link with my future career choice emerged in my passion for the inter-war poet Attila Jozsef (1905–1937). It was through studying him that I first encountered psychoanalysis, which he linked in an original way with his interest in Marxism" (p. 115). Until the mid-1970s, one heard nothing about psychoanalysis in psychology training at university.

A recruitment and surveillance system

The 1960s and 1970s in Hungary was a period in which an alternative culture was taking shape, with beat and rock bands playing concerts, house parties and the samizdat literature of the counterculture. A strong identity-shaping effect was the common denominator of the various groups involved. Members of a group identified with the group norms in their outward appearance, language usage (slang) and ideals and gave voice to their world view in numerous ways. The authors also had strong ties to various alternative cultures. They found that liberation is not the same as freedom, that breaking boundaries is a source of other problems, and that simply rebelling against something is not enough. This situation is coloured by the fact that if one has an anticipatory vision, it is often idealised, leading to inevitable disappointment. Reality is already very complicated indeed if one's idea of what is to come is not idealised. It poses en-ough of a challenge just to cope with obstacles for which one cannot prepare in advance. For Vámos, the group became a source of indispensable experiences: a reference group, a "chosen family". As Vámos describes it, "In the group, we were sometimes hard on each other, we contended with competition, rivalry, envy. But the secret of small-group dynamics, the "chosen family", the belonging together was stronger than the pain. ... We learned how to think together, to elaborate our ideas freely, even in a dictatorship. Without being aware of it, I perceived that public discussions are better avoided. I became conscious of the danger we faced from being under surveillance, as some of my friends were" (p. 171). There were groups that represented values that lasted a lifetime, such as the one surrounding Ferenc Mérei. The beginning of Vámos's immigration story speaks to this. She chose Paris. After spending a year in America, she returned to the French capital and continued her studies at the Sorbonne, just as Mérei had once done. Mérei was a Marxist while criticising the regime at the same time (for which he was sentenced to prison). He was a social psychologist who knew about child psychology and who, after being freed on amnesty (in 1963), established a clinical workshop at the National Institute of Psychiatry and Neurology in Budapest, better known as "Lipót". His charismatic personality enabled him to become a model with whom others could identify, and his expertise made it possible to establish links to other trends in psychology, including Moreno's psychodrama, which he introduced in Hungary.

None of this took place under cloudless skies, however. The Ministry of the Interior established the III/III group as part of the political police, whose task it was to keep domestic dissidents under surveillance and neutralise them. They generally used blackmail to recruit their informers, who reported on groups of their own peers. A system of informants was developed, which permeated the civil sphere: it was there at the workplace, the university, rock concerts and house parties. Those who had been recruited included colleagues, friends and family members – even fathers and mothers – whose activities came to light after the regime change in 1989 (Esterházy, 2002; Forgách 2015; Ungváry & Tabajdi, 2008). No one could feel safe. The government or party headquarters would step in and force dissidents to remain silent or to leave the country, as was the case with the students of philosopher György Lukács (Ágnes Heller,

György Márkus and Mihály Vajda) in the early 1970s and with the avant-garde theatre affiliated with Péter Halász – which would later become Squat Theatre.

Emigration

Hungary has seen a number of noteworthy waves of emigration in the twentieth century – in 1919–1921, 1938–1941 and 1956 – where the push side in the push-pull dynamic can be attributed to socio-political factors first and foremost. On the push side of the first wave of emigration (1919–1921), we see anti-Semitism, political retribution and a post-war economic crisis (Frank, 2009). The majority of those who left the country during the two exiles (the second being between 1938 and 1941) were scientists, writers, artists and other highly educated people as well as those who wished to study. Most of them were of Jewish descent. Many later capitalised on their knowledge in other countries and on other continents, for example, members of the Budapest School that had formed around Sándor Ferenczi, whom the authors encountered in their psychoanalytical training as British, American and French psychoanalysts of Hungarian descent (Mészáros, 2014). Those who studied at universities abroad while still young naturally enjoyed greater chances of integrating. There was another characteristic of the emigration of the university-educated in the period between the two world wars after Hitler came to power: for the most part, there were supportive organisations and host institutions, universities and professional communities that aided immigrants, forced as they were to leave behind their homeland, native language and life thus far, in integrating as soon as possible into their host country.

Those in the first wave of emigration who were of Jewish descent and had resettled elsewhere in Europe were compelled to emigrate once more. The majority of Hungarians found refuge in the United States, Canada, Australia and Israel (Szondi & Seres, 2011). The literature deals more with those who were forced to leave their homeland than with those who could not leave for whatever reason – personal or professional – or who did not wish to emigrate in spite of their poor social well-being. From a certain perspective, those who left and those who stayed behind all lost out. Those who left in the hope of a better, more secure life left behind their country, native language and culture, their relationships with family and friends, indeed, their whole social network, as well as their former lives. Those who stayed behind lost those who left, their family members, friends and professional contacts, as well as a part of their past – and soon their hopes for the possibility of a better, more secure life. All the challenges notwithstanding, those who left arrived in a more democratic, economically more stable, more prosperous world, where their individual efforts produced measurable results.[5] Those who stayed behind found themselves under a new dictatorial regime. During and immediately after the 1956 Revolution, nearly 200,000 people left the country – for political and economic reasons – both university-educated and non-university-educated alike. They resettled in 35 countries with the aid of the U.N. Refugee Fund, the majority of them in Austria, Germany, Switzerland, France and Great Britain as well as the United States and Canada.

Writers and scholars who had emigrated for political reasons to Western Europe, the United States and Canada established significant groups and publications, with which they endeavoured to establish contact with Hungary's democratic dissidents and to relay their views to the population of Hungary. According to Borbándi (2006), "it was refreshing to see that Hungarian émigrés do not think the same way, that numerous variations of opinions flourish, and that they succeed in resisting any efforts to unify their behaviour. It thus became a real alternative to present-day Hungary, where a central will reigns supreme and an independent way of thinking or expression of opinion or individual stance is impossible on a number of issues. The power of Hungarian émigrés is their diversity, pluralism and opportunity to make democratic choices" (p. 256).

Emigration occurred sporadically in the 1960s and 1970s, but the efforts of young university-educated people – Christian, Jewish, religious or atheist – to leave the country stood out. The winds of the counterculture movements of Western Europe and the United States could be felt here as well. The triumph of freedom – through the hippie culture from America (in the late 1960s) and the student revolts in Paris (in 1968) – represented a powerful buoyant force and a true cultural revolution. For example, in Paris, school uniforms were eliminated (while Hungary saw some passionate individual efforts in that regard – who was wearing what under their school smock?), even as Nazism was starting to be dealt with in Germany (Mitscerlich 1975). The seeds of the counterculture found fertile soil in the socialist bloc. The winds of freedom hit the young generation in the "happiest barracks". The push and pull forces had their effect. I believe there is no well-known high school class or university year from that time that did not produce defectors. The authors from the outstanding English programme at Fazekas Grammar School in Budapest testify to this: all three of them left the country either at the beginning of their university studies or after completing them. Importantly, all three of them were also influenced by something other than their longing for the free world conveyed to them by the avant-garde groups. This was the realisation of their parents' unfulfilled dreams of emigration. As Vámos points out, "Before my birth, emigration was in the landscape" (p. 167). The parents' wishes lie dormant, and their children make them a reality. There are messages and motives involved that emerge unconsciously, just as there are completely conscious manifestations. One of the author's parents actually sent her to America, making no secret of their intention that she should "stay there". The parents of the other two authors sought opportunities to emigrate either before or after the war but changed their minds under emotional pressure. Later, when one of the authors' parents attempted to defect in 1949 after the borders had been closed, they were arrested and put in prison. I think that it is no coincidence that many – and two of the authors are representative of them – sought the chance to emigrate without it being classified as defection. That is, they wanted no legal consequences for those they would leave behind at home or for themselves: passports being withdrawn or a years-long ban on returning home. Despite certain divergent "technical solutions" – marrying a foreign citizen (out of love or merely out of convenience) – all three of them left the country with their parents' knowledge, which (in conjunction with their own individual freedom struggles) represented an enormous source of psychological support. Their otherwise not particularly easy situation was therefore not further burdened by the guilt of "you abandoned your ageing parents". At the same time, all three authors also made their parents' unfulfilled wishes a reality. However, this is an unconscious transgenerational burden, a process that influenced self-development, with which they had to struggle later in order to find their own, freely chosen identity, autonomous life and inner freedom.

This book can be seen as an experimental one. As training analysts, teachers and practising psychoanalysts/psychotherapists, the authors offer the reader an insight into the story of their lives, their emotions and the dilemmas they have faced. In doing so, they have taken a risk. Indeed, anyone in the public eye will always be taking some degree of risk, but writing authentically about one's personal experience most certainly exposes one to risk. These authors have accepted the risk in order to demonstrate the process through which they have become who they are now.

Translated by
Thomas Williams

Notes

1 The Dohány Street Synagogue was completed in 1859. It represented a stage of assimilation. It was a site of cultural events then, as it is today. After its completion, statesmen, writers and artists were among those invited, for example, on the occasion of the celebration of "Jewish–Hungarian Brotherhood" in December 1860.

2 The Hungarian authorities immediately deported Jews who had escaped from Germany, Austria and what was then Czechoslovakia as well as those in areas that had been re-annexed to Hungary in 1941 as part of a revision of the Treaty of Trianon, which had established the terms of peace with Hungary after the First World War. Jews who could not prove their Hungarian citizenship were deported to an area in the Soviet Union then occupied by the Germans. The majority of the 23,600 Jewish women and men who were executed in Kamianets-Podilskyi (Kam'yanets'-Podil's'kyi in present-day Ukraine) on 27–28 August 1941 were from Hungary. They were murdered not only by German police and the SS, but also by Hungarian soldiers and the Ukrainian auxiliary police.

3 The decree on the yellow-star houses designated 2639 buildings on 16 June 1944 with one room apportioned to each family. The decree was issued by the mayor of Budapest even after the Americans had landed at Normandy (on 6 June 1944), an event which marked the beginning of the end of the war.

4 Radio Free Europe (RFE) is a United States government-funded organisation that broadcasts and reports news, information and analysis to countries in Eastern Europe, Central Asia, the Caucasus and the Middle East where it says that "the free flow of information is either banned by government authorities or not fully developed". During the Cold War, RFE was broadcast to Soviet satellite countries (including the Baltic states). RFE was founded as a source of anti-communist propaganda in 1949 by the National Committee for a Free Europe (https://en.wikipedia.org/wiki/Radio_Free_Europe/Radio_Liberty).

5 Emigration is always an indicator of social discontent. Approximately ten per cent of the present-day population of Hungary – about one million people – live and work in other countries: mostly Austria, Germany and Great Britain. As we have seen repeatedly throughout history, it is the layer of society with the most schooling, the university-educated and skilled labourers, as well as the most at-risk minority (the Roma today) that has left the country.

References

Borbándi, Gy. (2006). *A Magyar Emigráció Életrajza 1945–1985*. Országos Széchényi Könyvtár Budapest, Magyarország 2006. https://mek.oszk.hu/03400/03472/03472.pdf

Damousi, J. and Plotkin, M. B. (eds.) (2012). *Psychoanalysis and Politics: Histories of Psychoanalysis under Conditions of Restricted Political Freedom*. Oxford University Press Inc.

Erős, F., Kovács, M., Lévai, K. (1985). Hogyan jöttem rá, hogy zsidó vagyok? Interjúk. *Medvetánc, 2–3*, 129–144.

Erős, F. (2011). *Pszichoanalízis és Forradalom*. Budapest: Jószöveg Műhely Kiadó.

Esterházy, P. (2002). *Javított Kiadás - Melléklet a Harmonia Caelestishez*. Budapest: Magvető Kiadó.

Fenyves, K. (szerk.) (2015). *A holokauszt és a családom*. Budapest: Park Könyvkiadó.

Fenyves, K. (2010). *Képzelt asszimiláció? Négy zsidó értelmiségi nemzedék önképe*. Budapest: Corvina.

Forgách, A. (2015). *Élő kötet nem marad*. Budapest: Jelenkor Kiadó.

Frank, T. (2009). *Double Exile. Migrations of Jewish-Hungarian Professionals through Germany to the United States, 1919–1945*. Bern, European Academic Publishers, Peter Lang AG.

Hann, E. (2021). Medián Közvélemény- és Piackutató Intézet felmérése. https://telex.hu/belfold/2021/07/20/median-felmeres-a-magyar-felnott-lakossag-36-szazaleka-tekintheto-antiszemitanak

Karádi, V. (1992). A Shoah, a rendszerváltás és a zsidó azonosságtudat válsága Magyarországon In: M. M. Kovács, M. K. Yitzhak, F. Erős (szerk.), *Zsidóság-identitás-történelem*. Budapest: T-Twins Kiadó.

Kestenberg, J. S. (1989). Transposition revisited: clinical, therapeutic and developmental considerations. In: P. Marcus, A. Rosenberg (eds), *Healing their wounds: psychotherapy with holocaust survivors and their families* (pp. 67–89). New York: Praeger.

Mészáros, J. (1998). Anti-semitism and Jewish identity in Hungary between 1989–1994. In: J. S. Kestenberg & C. Kahn (eds.), *Children surviving persecution. An international study of trauma and healing* (pp. 90–103). Westport, Connecticut, London: Praeger.

Mészáros, J. (2012). Effect on dictatorial regimes on the psychoanalytic movement in Hungary before and after World War II. In: J. Damousi and M. B. Plotkin (eds.), *Psychoanalysis and politics. Histories of psychoanalysis under conditions of restricted political freedom* (pp. 79–108). Oxford University Press.

Mészáros, J. (2014). *Ferenczi and beyond: exile of the Budapest School and solidarity in the psychoanalyic movement during the Nazi years.* London: Karnac.

Mészáros, J. (1997). The return of the repressed. In: *The annual of psychoanalysis. (ed. by the Chicago Institute for Psychoanalysis)*, 25.

Mitscherlich, A. (1975). *The inability to mourn: principles of collective behavior.* New York: Grove

Nádor, É. (szerk.) (2015). *Csillagos házak. Emberek, házak, sorsok/Yellow-star houses: people, houses, fates Budapest, 1944.* Budapest: Nádor és Társa Tanácsadói Iroda.

Papp, B. (2014). *A kaszáskeresztesek és Dévaványa.* Budapest: Gondolat Kiadó.

Rainer, M. J. (2004). A "hatvanas évek" Magyarországon. Politika történeti közelítések. In Rainer M. J. (szerk.). *Hatvanas évek Magyarországon.* Budapest: 1956-os Intézet.

Romsics, I. (2017). *Magyarország története.* Budapest: Kossuth.

Standeinksy, É. (2007). *Antiszemitizmusok.* Budapest: Augmentum Kiadó.

Szántó, T. G. (2012). Az antiszemita nyelv legitimmé válása a közéletben. Interjú Kovács Andrással. Szombat, Az antiszemita nyelv legitimmé vált a közbeszédben | Szombat Online (utolsó hozzáférés: 2021.07.19).

Szondi I., Seres, A. I. (2011). Tengerentúli magyarok. In: *Acta Universitatis Szegediensis: forum: acta juridica et politica*, (1)2, 169–200 http://acta.bibl.u-szeged.hu/29294/1/juridpol_forum_001_002_169–200.pdf

Török, F. and T. Szántó, G. (2017). 1945. Film directed by Török, F.

Ungváry, K., Tabajdi, G. (2008). *Elhallgatott múlt. A pártállam és a belügy. A politikai rendőrség működése Magyarországon, 1956–1990 [Silenced Past. The Party State and the Ministry of the Interior. The Operation of the Political Police in Hungary, 1956–1990].* Budapest: Corvina 1956-os Intézet.

Ungváry, K. (2015). Előszó. In É. Nádor (szerk.), *Csillagos házak. Emberek, házak, sorsok./Yellow-star houses: people, houses, fates Budapest, 1944.* (pp. 10–23). Budapest: Nádor és Társa Tanácsadói Iroda.

Virág, T. (1984). Children of the Holocaust and their children's children: working through parent trauma in the psychotherapeutic process. *Dynamic Psychotheraphy: The Journal of the Postgraduate Center for Mental Health, 2*(1), 47–60.

Wardi, D. (1992). *Memorial Candles.* London and New York: Routledge.

Chapter 2

Trialogue

Veronica Csillag, Katalin Lanczi, and Julianna Vamos

This book will follow the journeys, literal as well as psychic, of three Jewish women from Budapest, Hungary, from the same high school, same class (academic as well as social, more or less). They all have (second generation) baggage from the Shoah as do all Jewish people in Hungary. These three women left Hungary in the mid-seventies and early eighties, before the collapse of the Soviet empire, for personal as well as political reasons.

Julianna Vamos went to Paris, Katalin Lanczi to London, Veronica Csillag to New York. Sooner or later they found their way to psychoanalysis, to deal with the personal and historical catastrophes they had to contend with. They have come of age as clinicians in their adopted homelands and their theoretical orientation and technical preferences were shaped by their respective analytic environments, their specific training experiences as well as their personal histories.

We are so different yet so much alike. Let's start from the beginning. Not only were we classmates in high school, but our mothers also attended the same high school, the Jewish High School for Girls in Budapest, though they studied there at different times. This coincidence is rather remarkable as our families come from different experiences and identifications of Jewishness and did not know of one another until after the three of us met in high school.

The Jewish High School in Budapest between the two World Wars was a special place. In 1919, a short-lived socialist-communist revolutionary experiment – with progressive as well as brutally oppressive features – took place in Hungary. This was followed by a

DOI: 10.4324/9781003306542-2

home-grown fascist regime, referred to as the "White Terror." This new extreme right government persecuted communists, leftists as well as Jews, for good measure. Within this heterogeneous group, there were outstanding intellectuals, and university professors, who were no longer allowed to keep their prestigious jobs and were forced to seek employment elsewhere. Many of them ended up teaching at the Jewish High School and became highly revered teachers of our mothers.

Trialogue

Veronica: I met Katalin when I was 11 or 12 at a math competition for sixth graders in the 8th district of Budapest. I was drafted into participation almost accidentally, by my math teacher who noticed that math came rather easy for me and I enjoyed solving problems. I did reasonably well. That was the highlight and pretty much the end of my math career.

Katalin and I took to one another right away and became quasi friends, occasionally bumping into one another at various events in Budapest.

Katalin: Well, I do remember clearly meeting Veronica for the first time at the math competition. There was immediately a kind of connection and I think we met a few times afterwards until we finally found ourselves at the same school and eventually, at 16, in the same form.

I don't think I understood the connection then. Of course, our friendship has evolved over more than five decades and especially during our time together at university … but I am jumping ahead. At the time I think there was a sense of something familiar, a link. With hindsight, being Jewish must have been part of it.

I don't think we ever talked about this during the school years, did we? Not until the university years and, to be frank, I am not sure we did all that much then either. I suspect this came later when, in 1982, I was visiting Veronica in New York, from London.

Veronica: Fast forward a couple of years: Time to go to high school. Ambitious as I was, I wanted to go to the best. Fazekas was regarded as the most rigorous. I applied and was accepted into its intensive English program.

Mihaly Fazekas High School in Budapest, reprinted with kind permission of Béla Garamvölgyi

Mihaly Fazekas High School in Budapest, reprinted with kind permission of Béla Garamvölgyi

Katalin: Perhaps at this point it would be helpful for our readers to understand the place our school, Fazekas, in the labyrinths of Hungarian education in the 1970s. It had a junior school, largely a neighborhood establishment, which I joined at age 10. The secondary school had a three-form entry: general, language, and math. The three groups were selective to varying degrees, the math track particularly so. The gen ed admissions gave some preference to the students from the lower school. As such, in spite of the academic rigor and certain hierarchies, there was also a social mix.

I started in the math class and at 16 I transferred to the English class, where I joined Julianna and Veronica.

Julianna: By the age of 16, when all three of us found ourselves in the Fazekas High School, I had already been in five different schools. This was quite unusual in stable Budapest, in the 60s and 70s. I joined Fazekas and along with Katalin, I entered the class Veronica attended from the beginning. Unlike them, I did not realize until much later what a selective, elite establishment it was.

Veronica: After my sophomore year, I spent two months in London, to study English. It was a weird experience. As my command of English was good enough, I was placed in a class with people significantly older than me, college students mostly. They went pubbing after classes, whereas I, Miss Goody Two-Shoes back then (this changed later) returned home to the care of my very proper English landlady, in whose backyard I spent the afternoons running laps whenever I was not studying the hundreds of new words I came across each day.

I always had a theatrical bent. The rage in the London theater world back then was *A midsummer night's dream* directed by Peter Brook. I decided that I had to see the performance, come what may. Tickets, however, had already been sold out for the summer, so I bought one for September, which meant that I would not get back to Hungary until after the start of the school year. Devil may care: I will catch up. The performance was mesmerizing and proved to be one of the most amazing theatrical experiences of my life!

The day after the show, I took the train to Dover, got on the ferry, and then on another train halfway across Europe. When I went back to school I realized that there were three transfer students added to our class, GL, the son of the music teacher, gorgeous and brilliant, who was expelled from another high school for disrespect; Julianna, one of our protagonists, who was also removed from her school due to misbehavior, and whom I found sitting in the chair I used to occupy, next to my then quasi-boyfriend. Serves you right for the arrogance of going to the theater instead of back to school! I was intrigued by her. She was said to be very smart but I was annoyed that she took my seat. The third newcomer was Katalin, who was done with being a math wiz and wanted to engage in a serious study of English instead.

This is where our story really begins.

Julianna: Each of us had different survival strategies. At least that is how I see it now: I was a student with a minimal presence whose mind was elsewhere. But I have a vivid after-school memory: Veronica's mother took her and me to see the aforementioned *Midsummer Night's Dream* performance in Budapest when the Royal Shakespeare Company came on tour. It was unforgettable.

Veronica and I have another theatrical link. I attended the performances of the underground avant-garde apartment theater that later, in New York, morphed into Squat Theater. After they left Hungary, they spent a year in Paris before moving overseas. I hung out with them a lot. They were one of the most creative groups of people I ever knew. Veronica got involved with them later, in New York. We share the love for their radical art.

Katalin: I was, myself, going through a political crisis and a process of disillusionment in the Communist Youth movement at the school. It was around this time that I first heard about psychoanalysis. We were studying the outstanding inter-war Hungarian poet, Attila Jozsef, who had an analysis in the 1930s. He also tried to synthezise Marxist ideas and Freudian psychoanalysis.

Julianna seemed to belong to rather exalted circles; in her group, there were Western records and jeans and there were parties with cool boys. They read books I was not familiar with. Members of this group were clever, chic, and, most importantly, counter-cultural. I felt on the margins ... perhaps the story of my life, both personal and professional.

I remember Veronica getting very involved with acting and alternative theater groups and Julianna beginning to talk about psychology, a subject that was not covered at school. I think Veronica and Julianna were much closer to one another than I was to either of them.

I struggled to keep up with the English classes for a while as I had to catch up with two years of intensive teaching. This, and some adolescent crises, kept me occupied. I did go to one or two memorable alternative theater performances but I did not much understand what it all meant and, in any case, I was already – as I still am – much more interested in cinema and, the family heritage: classical music.

Julianna: Psychoanalysis was part of life for the adults who took me under their wings, they couldn't imagine life without it. As my parents took me to a psychologist at the age of 8, I felt they were open to it. Then, after high school, came the essential question of what to study. My wish was to get into university and choose psychology, but mostly because of the challenge it represented. I was very happy when I got in, and I studied for a year in Budapest but without much conviction. Then I left Hungary. I didn't have any contact with Veronica and Katalin for quite some time. It took a few years in Paris to become seriously interested in psychology. Though I was in analysis from the beginning of my emigration.

Katalin: My relationship deepened with Veronica at University where we were in the same study group and we prepared for exams together, often well into the night.

I have a vivid memory of Veronica visiting me a few days before I left Hungary. I had this "special" passport, which allowed me to leave legally and she wanted to see it, hold it, marvel about it.

Our paths diverged and I had little contact with Julianna. We knew about each other and from time to time tried to meet but somehow this never happened, even though we often visited each other's cities. Then one day I heard from psychoanalytic colleagues that they had met someone called Julianna, also from Hungary, at a Paris conference and that she in fact knew me! But really it is the preparation for this book that brought us together again. Veronica and I were in contact in the early part of our emigration but then not for a while. When we met again, at Lake Balaton during a summer holiday in 1997, it was the first time we spoke about psychoanalysis and I discovered that Veronica was now working as a psychotherapist.

Veronica: Our friendships and professional affiliations went through various iterations. Julianna and I developed an electric connection early on: we would discuss existential matters but also boys and sex. Then at the age of 19 she left. We did not meet again until we were both mothers and on our way to psychoanalysis. Katalin and I became intimate friends during our university years, then we both left, stayed in close touch for a few years, and then drifted apart. (This was before the internet and cheap phone calls, we mostly corresponded by what we now call snail mail.) As Katalin said, we reconnected in 1997, during a summer vacation at Lake Balaton, Hungary, and have cultivated a strong friendship ever since.

Julianna: I have one very precious memory of an important event. Veronica came to Paris with her son and their visit coincided with the moment my daughter had her Bat Mitzvah in 2004. I hoped to transmit to my children something of the Jewish heritage, beyond the deadly force of the Shoah. To have her/them with us was an experience of continuity which made that moment even more meaningful. Veronica and Tamàs were like family. That very year the Shoah Museum in Budapest had my grandparents' name on the wall and Rebecca's name was written in the community journal of our liberal community after her Bat Mitzvah. I felt we were victorious over destruction. We survived, we would not be exterminated. Moments like this made emigration worth the trouble. I would never have proposed studying Talmud Torah to my children in Budapest.

Veronica: I have been thinking about developing this book for a long time. It has been percolating for many years. How come, I was thinking, that out of a class of 40 the three of us left (others did too, that group was not a bunch of happy campers) and became psychoanalysts, having made our choices largely independent from one another's influence? There was a story there, a connection deeper than I had previously recognized.

First, I tried to convince Katalin to join me in this project. Her response was an adamant "no." No writing, no exposure, no more heroic achievements for her. Live a little. Then I approached Julianna at the 2018 Ferenczi Conference in magical Florence. She did not need much convincing; she was smitten right away.

Julianna: Feeling very inspired by the book project, I have lived with it since we decided to write it. Veronica and I met at the International Sandor Ferenczi conference in 2012 in Budapest. It was our first professional exchange in shared territories. It was meaningful. Then in 2018, we met up again in Florence at another Ferenczi conference called "Ferenczi in our time and the renaissance of psychoanalysis." I was giving a talk. And so was Veronica. The conference was held in an impressive Florentine palace, Convitto della Calza, next to the Porta Romana, a 14th-century former convent. In its beautiful garden, Veronica told me about her idea of a book and I was immediately enthusiastic.

Katalin: When Veronica first mentioned the project, I was disinclined, to say the least. I have always been extremely reluctant to publish clinical material with all the dilemmas of confidentiality and I was even more reluctant to write about my personal journey. Everything now available online, I was concerned about my patients' access to such material and its impact on them. Above all, I no longer felt the drive to push myself – my free time better spent, I argued, with family pursuits, such as looking after my grandchildren.

Veronica: Julianna and I joined forces and with some additional help from her husband and colleagues, we dragged Katalin into this endeavor, practically against her will, kicking and screaming. So here we are.

Katalin: Indeed. In fact, buoyed by this process, I got inspired to embark upon other rewarding writing projects. Writing this book has been a challenging and exciting process, though it has also stirred up some difficult dynamics – some of which remind me of my youth. Our psychoanalytic identities are different, our conceptualization of the impact of the Shoah varies, our politics diverge somewhat – negotiating these differences led to creative tensions and, I hope, a book that will be of interest to others.

Julianna: To think about our analytical journey in this project was an opportunity to look at the big adventure of emigration and growing. Becoming, being, relating as old school comrades and new colleagues, as psychoanalysts from three different traditions. We immersed ourselves in it and we keep on thinking about it together.

Veronica: Writing my chapter was a deeply gratifying experience. I have been thinking about my life as well as my psychoanalytic credo for some time. As a result, the text came out gushing. There was little resistance, and clearly, not much censorship. It has everything but the kitchen sink. The editing process has been more of a challenge. The goal has been to articulate our, at times, divergent ideological, professional perspectives while maintaining respect for one another's opinions in these politically turbulent times.

Epilogue

It has been quite a journey. Rich, inspiring yet at times painful and overwhelming. We could have known, and in fact, did know, that autobiographical self-disclosure would elicit vulnerability. No matter how much we have all benefited from long years of analyses we couldn't escape repetitions, unconscious cracks, and failures while considering unresolved or only partially resolved early experiences. Unsurprisingly, reconnecting to our Shoah heritage also contributed to some fraying of nerves and to tension arising in the creative process. Another appearance of intergenerational transmission. The varying sense of our Jewish identity, the many and complex differences in our characters, our divergent ideological, professional perspectives, our identifications with our cultural milieux also required navigational skills not always readily at our disposal.

Much of the writing took place during the Covid 19 pandemic, which was a traumatic time for each of us as we faced our losses in three very different countries.

In spite of our recognition of the risks involved in undertaking this project, when trouble arose in the interpersonal field, it caught us seemingly unawares and caused us much suffering, to each their own. Still, with so much growth and a deeper understanding of ourselves and one another having taken place, the outcome seems to have justified the effort.

Chapter 3

The theater of the psyche

Veronica Csillag

> *the art of losing's not too hard to master*
> *though it may look like (Write it!) like disaster.*
> Elizabeth Bishop, 2008, p. 166[1]
> *Walker, there is no path. The path is made by the walking.*
> Antonio Machado, 1912

The socio-political framework

My ex, P, used to be an actor. He was a founding member of the now-defunct Squat theater, the avant-garde troupe exiled from Budapest, Hungary in the late 70s. After we became a couple, several years after my arrival at these American shores, he told me that he chose to come to New York with his ensemble so that he could present a red rose to a lady on stage as a token of love, not as a political gesture. Back then the color red did not represent the rabidly reactionary electorate of several US states but the Communist Revolution, which, by my formative years, had degraded into a largely dysfunctional totalitarian regime, if it was ever anything else.

While I thought that his comment was witty, and I imagined myself to be his leading lady being offered the red rose on stage, it was hardly a surprise. I grew up surrounded by politics. My parents would have their political discussions, mostly disagreements, shouting matches, right at the dinner table. They could never agree on anything.

Mother was a left-leaning liberal, sympathetic to socialist ideology but critical of the establishment, reluctant to fall in line with rules and regulations. Father was a proponent of Social Darwinism, survival of

DOI: 10.4324/9781003306542-3

the fittest, the weak can perish. He advocated internment camps for deplorables and undesirables, a set whose definition evolved from day to day, but invariably included "good-for-nothing intellectuals" and pretty much everyone on the left side of the political spectrum. Apparently, he was way ahead of his time. His hatred was primarily directed at my mother but I also felt attacked. The tragic irony of father's pre-occupation with sending groups of people off to camps is that as a Jew, two decades earlier, he himself was conscripted into forced labor.

My family is Jewish but we were not observant by any stretch of the imagination. We never kept the Jewish holidays, there was not even any mention of them. We celebrated Christmas though. There were Christmas trees with real candles and ornaments, Christmas music – Heilige Nacht and all – candies and gifts. Still, my mother could not bring herself to serve the traditional fish dinner on Christmas Eve and snuck in a chicken soup dish – ohne the matzo balls – as a nod to her Jewish heritage.

Both of my parents came from educated families or at least educated fathers. My maternal grandfather was an attorney, while my paternal grandfather was a dermatologist. According to family lore, he had a distinguished career and was among the first in his field to recognize that diseases of the skin were for the most part local manifestations of underlying states of internal morbid conditions. Grandfather himself grew up in a village (Berettyoujfalu), in a poor family with a dozen or so children. Given his outstanding intellect and impressive school performance, the local Jewish community sent him to the capital, to study medicine. They paid for his education. Whether out of gratitude or a sense of obligation, or both, he helped out various members of that community for the rest of his life.

My maternal grandmother was supposedly observant, which in-furiated my grandfather, a thoroughly secular man, to no end. Still, there was enough Jewish affiliation in mother's family to send her to the Jewish "Gymnasium," the Jewish High School for Girls, if for no other reason than because of the outstanding quality of the education it provided. My mother claimed to have been one of the best students in her class, of which she was very proud. She seemed to be equally proud of having failed Hebrew.

The Jewish High School in Budapest between the two World Wars was a very special place. In 1919 a short-lived socialist revolution took place in Hungary. This was followed by a home-grown fascist regime, referred to as the "White Terror." This new extreme right government persecuted communists, leftists as well as Jews, for good measure. Within this heterogeneous group there were outstanding intellectuals, university professors, who were no longer allowed to keep their prestigious positions and were forced to seek employment elsewhere. Many of them ended up teaching at the Jewish High School. One of them, Dr. Jozsef Turoczi-Trostler, professor of Germanistics, was my mother's idol. He instilled in her a life-long passion for literature and German culture. Later, during the Nazi occupation, this love became a source of deep internal conflict for her.

My first encounter with my Jewishness came in elementary school. I was a bit feral. I never went to nursery school, kindergarten. At home I had a brother, eight and a half years older. Other than that, I was rarely in the company of other children. In my mother's family there was only one child my age, all the countless cousins having been murdered in the war. There were some relatives with children on my father's side but out of envy and contempt and what have you my mother could not stand my father's relatives so there was not much contact.

So, when I started school at the age of six, I was searching for friends. There was this cool girl, fast-talking, well-groomed, Andrea. I asked to be friends. She said she'd think about it. The next day she told me that we could not possibly be friends because I was Jewish. I was familiar with the word but did not fully comprehend its meaning. I did grasp, however, that it had to be something truly awful. When I returned home that afternoon, I asked my mother if, in fact, I was Jewish. She looked me in the eye and said "no." This happened in the 1960s, not in 1944: Jews were not being deported, and even the "enemies of the people," former landowners, industrialists, anticommunists, liberals, etc., were not routinely deported or imprisoned anymore. Still, out of fear, I assume, my mother found it necessary to deny our Jewish identity and contribute to the muddle regarding ethnicity, in general, and Jewishness, in particular, in acceptable discourse.

This question brings me to what I see as the unspoken perverse pact, (Stein, 2008; Harris, 2019) between the surviving Jewry and the Soviet-style State after WWII, according to which Jews could finally participate in the public sphere and could even gain positions of power as long as they kept quiet about their Jewish identity, the Holocaust, and especially about the complicity of the wartime Hungarian regimes as well as a large segment of the Hungarian population in their systematic extermination. Some of the surviving Jews were more than willing to participate: devastated and grief stricken, they were only "happy" to stay silent. For many the horror was simply unspeakable. Others were eager to put their wartime experiences of persecution aside and return to some semblance of normalcy as well as to the long-cultivated illusion of full emancipation and assimilation.

This destructive pact got ever-so-complicated over time. For Jews the Soviet invasion was liberation and escape from certain death. For Hungarians it meant that their country lost the war and was in ruins. It also meant the loss of territories granted by the Vienna Awards during the war, an award from Hitler for Hungary's loyalty to the Axis powers. With the entire population of the country having been thoroughly traumatized, there was no room for retrospection and a rational discussion regarding the question of responsibility.

Many of the surviving Jews lived in the capital, were non-observant and quasi-assimilated to begin with. They tended to be educated and held left-leaning views or were outright communists or communist sympathizers, as communist ideology held out the hope to end class and also national and ethnic differences as well as affiliation, thus also to end antisemitism. No more Jewish identity = no more antisemitism. This state of affairs did not generate much goodwill in the rest of the population, most of whom regarded the Soviet power and the communist takeover with much suspicion or outright hostility. Worse, during the most oppressive period of the totalitarian Stalinist epoch (1948–1953) the four prominent leaders of the party and state apparatus, the so-called four-in-hand, were all Jewish. These four people had just returned from the Soviet Union, where they fled to escape the persecution of Jews as well as of Communists. Other positions of power were also awarded to those of Jewish descent, if for no other reason, because they often had the required professional/educational qualifications and were not implicated in the preceding bloodbath. Nevertheless, the Party leadership gradually moved away from promoting Jews into positions of power and, when possible, replaced them with nationalist-leaning Hungarians (Kovacs, 2008), many of whom with antisemitic sentiments.

Subscription to the new communist ideology further allowed the surviving Jews to avoid the question of responsibility: if rampant antisemitism was the direct result of capitalist exploitation and class system, they did not have to feel that they lived in a hostile environment, populated by neighbors who shipped their loved ones to be exterminated like vermin. "It is better to be a sinner ruled by God than to live in a world ruled by the Devil" (Fairbairn, 1952, pp. 66–67).

Lest it appears that I might be blaming the victim, let me clarify that when I talk about the perverse pact, I use the term similarly to the way Harris (2019) discusses the concept with regards to racism and white colonial power: The main features of the perverse pact are dissociation and amnesia, and with that the disavowal of hatred and hostility. While the oppressed might be an unwitting participant and may get degraded in the process, the onus of responsibility always rests with the perpetrator (Csillag, 2020). There is no moral equivalency, the perverse pact is not between the oppressor and the oppressed, it is lived out consciously and unconsciously *within* the dominant culture and in the individual consciousness of the oppressor. It is a pact "around refusals to know what is in plain sight. The perverse pact is both engaged and denied" (p. 2).

The perverse pact corrupted most if not all, and was most likely designed, at least on the part of Hungarian gentiles – unconsciously, perhaps – with the very purpose of this corruption: if the Jews were willing to deny their identity in exchange for an otherwise livable life, civic participation, and a modicum of power they were no better than Judas Maccabeus or the Hungarians who sent the Jews to their death, cooperating with the Eichmann Commando with record speed, therefore no one needed to feel guilty. Instead, there were fake news, profound deceit, complete with the false cheer of the manic defense (Meszaros, 2010).

Jewish-Gentile relations did not significantly improve during and after the 1956 uprising. While there were few antisemitic atrocities reported during the revolutionary days and there was significant support for the revolution among Jewish intellectuals, many ordinary Jews were scared: the revolt evoked fears of pogroms and persecution. Thousands left the country, others were secretly praying for the impending Soviet invasion, even if they had already been bitterly disappointed by the values and especially the practice of the so-called socialist system (Kovacs, 2008).

The long history of entrenched native antisemitism, complete with charges of blood libel and occasional pogroms was followed by the systemic disavowal of Jewish identity and the projection of all blame on the Germans and the recurrent depiction of Hungarians as comparable victims. This sequence initiated moral slippage in the service of the evasion of truth and the taking of responsibility. It contaminated the public sphere and poisoned the mind (Layton, 2019; Grand, 2019).

I grew up in this era of obfuscation. My unfortunate parents were tortured, deformed souls who could never come to terms with the Shoah or its aftermath. They reenacted their experiences in their sadomasochistic, over-sexualized marriage. No doubt, they adored my brother and me, still, they were too undisciplined and self-indulgent to take proper, thoughtful care of us. They mismanaged my hip dysplasia, which went undiagnosed until the age of one and a half when a stranger pointed out to my mother that I walked funny, in spite of the fact that my father was an accomplished physician; They missed my brother's strep infection, which ultimately resulted in a severe kidney disease that nearly killed him when he was eight because parents were too busy cultivating their own affairs to pay attention to his deteriorating condition. Their total inability to explain our Jewish affiliation was yet another omission. Truth be told, this was not a unique situation: Apparently, until the 1990s it was quite common for Hungarian Jews not to be able to reckon with their Jewish identity and therefore to communicate about it with their offspring.

The author as a child in 1956

The author's mother

The author's father

Political awakening

In my early childhood, I did not comprehend my parents' political disagreements and acrimonious fights. They were mostly just frightening noise. My actual introduction began when my brother was preparing for his entrance examination to law school. (In Hungary, students apply to law school directly from high school, circumventing college.) As he was too busy studying for his high school finals and was cramming for the exam, he did not have much time left to follow current events, which could have easily come up in his interview process. So, he asked me, at the ripe old age of barely ten (in exchange for some pocket money, the original source of which must have been our parents), to watch the nightly news on our newly acquired first-ever black-and-white television set and give him a brief summery at the end of the day. I was quite traumatized by the daily footage of the Vietnam War and the violence in Cyprus even if, or especially because, I could not really place these events in a historical, socio-political context.

I distinctly remember the moment of my actual political awakening. It happened on Wednesday, August 21, 1968. I was 13. The previous day, August 20, was a national holiday, traditionally, and now again St. Stephen's Day, commemorating the king who orchestrated the conversion of the Hungarian tribes to Christianity, as well as the Festival of the New Bread (the harvest, in plain English), and which, in Soviet times was officially referred as the Day of the Constitution. As such, my family and I spent the day in our country home, on the Danube, some 40 kilometers from Budapest. We had a splendid time. On our way home we stopped the car in the hills of Buda to watch the annual fireworks. It was a clear night; it was a great spectacle. We were all content. In a rare instance of agreement my parents pronounced that life in Hungary was not so bad after all: the Soviet system was now tamer, more user-friendly, or as it was referred to back then, imported from the phraseology of the Prague Spring, it was socialism with a human face.

The next morning we woke up to the news that during the night the Soviet Union, with political and military support from the Warsaw Pact countries of Bulgaria, East Germany, Poland, and Hungary, invaded Czechoslovakia to stop and reverse the Prague Spring, the liberal reforms implemented earlier in the year, such as the guarantee of free speech and freedom of the press, under the pretext of defending the people of Czechoslovakia from bourgeois ideology and anti-socialist forces and prevent a "counter-revolution."

My parents were appalled and profoundly disturbed. Whatever happened to socialism with a human face? The invasion was a blatant interference in the internal affairs of a supposedly sovereign country and a prime example of Soviet imperialism. Until that time my political alignments, to whatever degree I had any, given my age, were driven by identification, mostly with my mother. This time though I was actually listening to my parents' reasoning and started on a long journey towards political consciousness. After the start of the school year, in early September, I discussed the impact of the invasion with a couple of classmates. I had an epic fight about the events with a boy, who previously seemed like an intellectual ally in a not particularly impressive school. A few decades later he became a major political figure and a member of the cabinet.

Still, it was not for quite some time, not till the last couple of years of high school that I became totally disillusioned about the political system I lived in. The enlightenment came through exposure to the ideas of some mostly older youth, immersed in the then blossoming counter-culture. I was reading widely and indiscriminately: Chekhov, Tolstoy, Dostoyevsky, Thomas Mann, Camus. Dino Buzatti's existentialist masterpiece, *The Tatar Steppe*, about a military officer wasting his entire life waiting for the final battle with the barbarians, only to fall ill when they eventually arrive, left a lasting impression on me even if I did not fully comprehend the text. Another influential experience, which I understood even less, was the Marco Ferreri movie, *Dillinger is dead,* also a contemplation on existential dread and vacuity. So went my education and coming of age.

I joined a theater company when I was 16. I went to subversive, avant-garde performances. It was at one of those events, at a performance of *The Killers of the Skanzen,* in January 1972 that I first saw the ex, father of my son, on stage. I was mesmerized. The play ended with a red dragon swallowing up everything and everyone in its way. While the group, the Kassak Studio Theater, which later, in New York City morphed into the internationally acclaimed Squat Theater, denied the obvious political symbolism, the work was censored and the troupe was officially banned. They went underground and continued to perform in the home of one of the founders, Peter Halasz. A few years later they left Hungary. They came to New York via Paris and Amsterdam.

Nachträglichkeit

I visit Hungary practically every year. A few years ago, I arranged my travels in a way that I could attend my 40th high school reunion. I was looking forward to catching up with old friends, Katalin and

Julianna among them, and I was also curious enough about how others, most of whom I had not seen or heard of for decades, evolved. Some people had not changed at all, others I barely recognized. I was taken aback by the heavy toll time had taken on some of my former classmates. A couple of them had died. Still, it was an informative and friendly enough event until it was not. A few hours into the reunion, by which time a good amount of alcohol had been consumed, the genie came out of the bottle: a group of buzzed men began to air their political sentiments: first they expressed their suspicion and hostility regarding refugees and immigrants, then their hatred and contempt toward the Roma, whom they referred to as "gypsies," a term now considered dated and discriminatory. I left their table before the antisemitic slurs would surely emerge. I was disgusted but not particularly surprised. At that juncture I was approached by someone else, a woman, I'll call her Emma. She said that she wanted to share with me something that had been weighing on her for all those years.

Let me provide some context before I summarize what Emma had to say. At my high school, having been a highly selective one, most of the students were planning to apply to and be accepted at various colleges and universities. I was one of the top students in my class (even if I have to say so myself), I had stellar grades plus I ranked high – in the top ten – in a national competition. While I was nervous about admissions, I had a very good chance of getting accepted to the highly competitive program I applied to.

In addition to academic excellence, a student needed a letter of recommendation from their school to be accepted. What Emma told me was that in the Spring of our senior year there was a meeting organized by our headmaster, a kind and fair man. Several classmates participated, among them one member of the hate-mongering, racist coalition at the reunion. I'll call him Alex. Reportedly, at this meeting it was discussed who should and who should not be recommended for admissions to higher education. According to Emma, when it came to my evaluation, Alex suggested that I should not be allowed to attend college/university because of my subversive political views – i.e., my critical stance regarding the State's interference in every aspect of its citizens' lives – as well as my Jewish ethnicity, and the assumption of cosmopolitan leanings. Ethnicity – it was because I was neither religious nor had a particularly well-developed Jewish identity back then. I just happened to be born Jewish. Whether or not Emma's recollections were correct, whether or not Alex said exactly what was reported, this story, just as a first memory frequently does, captures quite well the spirit of the milieu which I grew up in.

Oh, brother

My brother, Adam, is eight and a half years older than me. In my early childhood, we were not particularly close. What good is a small girl to an adolescent boy? When I became a teenager though, I started hanging out with him and his friends, who noticed that I was morphing into a bona fide female. As their advances were typically polite and respectful, they were welcome. I enjoyed my new status as well as my increasing independence and broadening horizons.

The last year of high school was stressful. I did not attend classes because I had a small role in a performance. Instead, I had to take exams in each and every mandatory subject, of which there were many, from math through English, through history, to physics (at which I sucked [and now I actually, understand why: my spatial skills are very limited]). I had to take all the exams in one day. By the end I could barely walk or talk, and definitely not at the same time. Then there were the Baccalaureate exams, and the university entrance exams, written as well as oral. National competition in English. And boys. One boy, in particular. Well, two.

By May, I was exhausted. My brother was away in Belgium, on a scholarship. I missed him. On the day of his scheduled return, I went to meet him at the train station. As I was a couple of minutes late, when I did not see him, I assumed that he had already left. Disappointed, I went home, to my mother. (My parents had separated two years earlier, I lived with my mother, Adam with father.) I told my mother what had happened. And then I looked up at her. Her eyes were red, she had been crying. She said that she just got off the phone, Adam had called and told her that he was not coming back. He would defect and move to West Germany.

This was a big, depressing loss for me and especially for my mother. She was inconsolable. Not that she was ever a big drinker but she enjoyed a glass of wine here and there. She would never be able to consume alcohol again since whenever she tried, she burst into tears and would not be able to stop crying. There were consequences for me as well. As an immediate family member of a dissident or defector I would not be able to travel outside of the Socialist block for years, five at the very least, and my university admissions would once again be in jeopardy. My only hope was that admissions decisions would be made before the authorities realized that my brother was gone. And that's exactly what must have happened as I was admitted and in September I enrolled. This was 1973, not 1953. Once a student was registered, they would not be kicked out over a family member who had defected. Still, this was the beginning of a new phase, exciting in some ways and desperate and depressing in many others.

#MeToo: Nachträglichtkeit

I married young. I was not yet 19. I married my first sexual partner, C. He was a poet and a writer and a literary thinker. I loved him or at least liked him well enough but that is not the reason why I married him. We got married because his mother would never stop nagging us about living together "in sin." And it was also a good gig even though we did not have a wedding. We got two witnesses from the registrar's office and informed our parents after the fact. It was fun to tell people, especially that one other boy, that I was married. Nobody else was. We were playing adult. For a while we had a lot of fun. Much sex, literary explorations, founding a samizdat journal (first banned, and later published as an anthology, without any credit to me), movies, adventures, political involvement. Nevertheless, not surprisingly, the marriage did not last. We had different preferences, habits, aspirations. Much later I came to the painful recognition that we also had/have different moral standards. Or rather, in certain areas he had none. More about that later.

As our relationship deteriorated, we both strayed. Soon after we finally separated, I threw myself into the Budapest counter-culture sex scene. Which was something. Profoundly corrupt, promiscuous. I realize that this adjective has fallen out of favor and is now regarded as not politically correct but I can't think of another term to describe the situation. People were sleeping around with no restraint. Sleeping with their best friend's husband, boyfriend, wife, girlfriend, there wore orgies and sex parties. Having had a modicum of common sense, the latter two I skipped. The more the merrier. Well, for me and many of my female fiends it was not all that merry in the end. We thought that we were voluntarily participating in the exercise of free love. There was some of that for sure, and it was exhilarating. But there was also a lot of exploitation of girls and young women by boys and young and not-so-young men within an intellectually vibrant and politically progressive subculture, which sadly, remained fundamentally patriarchal, in spite of its stated commitment to the contrary. Being in a relationship with the most attractive guy was the best, whether or not he remained faithful. Anyway, there were only so many of those. Sleeping around was considered the next coolest thing. What most of us did not realize at the time was that we were initiated into this ethos by our male counterparts. It was a cult with not one leader but many. And these shenanigans took place in the otherwise most progressive intellectual circles in Budapest. I'd venture to say that a lot of the guys who were having sex with an acquaintance in the bathroom while their wives or girlfriends would be preparing food for their friends at a house party, did, and still do, consider themselves "feminists." An apocryphal anecdote will well illustrate the situation. One of my schoolmates at university, back then an up-and-coming and now a prominent member of the intellectual elite, supposedly said after surveying the field at a concert of classical music: "All the women I have ever slept with are here. Sadly, all I ever will fuck are here too."

Far be it from me to suggest that casual sex is not for females. But I, and many of my friends, inexperienced, barely out of childhood could not get much emotional satisfaction or even sexual pleasure out of these shallow predatory encounters.

We (or at least I) were outdoing the men at their own game without realizing that it was still their game. I am not crying rape or sexual misconduct after 40 plus years, and, in fact, when I was, a few times, inappropriately propositioned I was able to push back and refuse to oblige. Occasionally, I would even exercise the power of "no" even when action was well underway. Luckily, no one ever tried to rape me or murder me. Which is terrific but it is also keeping the bar rather low, isn't it?

Under surveillance: Betrayal

After 1989, when the Soviet empire collapsed and then crumbled, the files of the Secret Police, the so-called III/III dossiers, were made available to the public, specifically to citizens who were under surveillance. Upon consideration, immediate family members could also gain access. For the uninitiated, throughout most of their existence, the Soviet Union and its satellite states operated a very elaborate secret police system, the primary aim of which was – beyond protecting national interest from foreign interference – to monitor their citizens and their political and cultural preferences so that any dissident views could be squashed. Until the 50s this was a brutal enterprise costing millions their lives or freedom. By the 70s, at least in Hungary, political dissidents were not killed, were rarely jailed but their existence could be made miserable, their jobs taken away, their career prospects destroyed. Informants were either recruited from a circle of personal friends of the targeted individual or from the ranks of those who could easily infiltrate their social milieu.

When I reconnected with my first ex-husband, C, during one of my visits back to Hungary he told me that there were rumors that we, too were under surveillance because of the aforementioned samizdat journal we had been working on during the late 70s. It occurred to me that like many others, I too could ask to see my file but I decided against it. I had no desire to be confronted by how I was perceived by hostile eyes. Also, that period was over and done with. Then, several years ago I learnt that in his new docu-novel, his preferred genre, about the story of said surveillance, C published parts of my file, which included notes by informants as well as by government investigators. Many of the reports were printed verbatim, with full names quoted and all. C wrote the book without as much as telling me, let alone asking for my permission even though some years earlier, when we talked about his work, I specifically requested that he not write about me. This was a torturous experience: the informants were friends, thankfully not close ones though. One of them was originally just a mere acquaintance, who befriended me and then romantically approached me primarily if not exclusively, for the purpose of reporting on me. I was by no means his only victim, he, Gusztav Habermann alias Laszlo Algol alias Zoltan Pecsi had other, better known and more established "clients" than I was. Even though I had not realized that I was as important as that, I was not entirely surprised by this revelation, and, in fact, I felt betrayed by C more than by the informants. They did not much matter but C and I were really close once. After the book was published, I tried to explain to him my perspective but he did not comprehend it. He insisted that the state and the informants bore all the blame, he did nothing wrong. After that I cut ties with him altogether, we are no longer on speaking terms.

The reports were mostly mundane, not revealing much of interest. I feature in them as Anna. They were disturbing in their ordinary factuality: what I was wearing, where I shopped for my groceries. Some were funny, there was a recurring phrase, an "epitheton ornans" of sorts in their description of me: The reports frequently mentioned that I was wearing a long, flowing skirt, had a pocketbook slung around my shoulder, and was holding a shopping bag in my left hand. They noted what bus route I would take to return home after a day spent at the library but they did not follow me there or into the grocery store. My diet, I suppose, did not pose a national security risk. While these days I walk around with a red backpack instead of a shopping bag, some things have not changed, I still have a pocketbook slung around my shoulder but I doubt that anyone gives a damn. I am described as depressed and desperate, which was, in fact, a mostly accurate assessment. But at least they gave me credit for editing the journal, which is more than what I can say about C and the friend we started the project with.

Emigration

When I was 24 or so, I was seduced by and then fell deeply in love with a brilliant and highly accomplished man, Z. Unfortunately, as I found out over the years, he was also emotionally and morally bankrupt. There was a short period of bliss, mutual devotion and then after about a year he moved on as he did a few times earlier and several more times later. I had been naive and tender, and I was heartbroken. So much so that my parents, worried about my well-being, wanted to send me on a voyage, as if we still lived in the 19th century. Sending me to a psychotherapist would have made more sense but in the 70s Budapest psychotherapy was not much in vogue. Arrangements were made for a trip to the United States instead, which was overdue anyway, given that I was engaged in American studies. I was not really in the mood to travel, I was profoundly depressed, I could care less about New York City and the rest of the country. In the end, I agreed to go but informed my parents that if I liked it there, I might not return. They said: "Fine. Go, just go. Get the hell out of here."

Perhaps this is a good place to explain that my parents spent much of their adult life planning to emigrate. They wanted to leave in the early 40s when they realized the extent of the persecution of Jews but by then it was too late. They wanted to leave in 49, after the dictatorial Communist takeover but once again by that time the borders were closed. Then they wanted to leave in 56 but in the end, they were afraid and were also reluctant to leave behind three aging parents. Then they wanted to leave in 68 as well. My mother and brother got exit visas to travel to Western Europe and the plan was that during their trip my father and I would go to the former Yugoslavia. (Entire families were not allowed to travel together to the West, with the – not at all unreasonable – assumption that many of them would not come back. One person, at least, always had to stay behind as hostage.) So, the crazy idea my parents concocted was that my mother and brother would defect while my father would find someone to smuggle us into Italy by boat. I was 13 and knew nothing about this plot. I only found out about it much later. I am not sure what happened exactly but we all returned to Hungary. I think my parents got cold feet again. There was one other time my parents were considering (illegal) emigration. I believe it was in 1973. This time someone reported us to the Ministry of Internal affairs and our exit visas were invalidated. As we later learnt the person who initiated the report was very close to the family. Talk about betrayal! For all I know there may have been additional plans as well, ill-conceived or otherwise, but none other was brought to my attention.

By 1980, my brother was gone and living in West Germany for seven years. It was only a little while earlier that the rest of us were given exit visas to travel West and my brother was allowed to visit. Pained as they were about his absence and my impending departure, they did not object. They were genuinely convinced that life in Western Europe and the United States was better than within the Soviet bloc, and they also experienced vicarious gratification from us finally actualizing their lifelong dreams. My brother and I thought that we were acting out of free will but in reality, we were sent on a pluperfect errand to carry out our parents' ambitions. These errands are freeing and exciting as well as oppressive and confining, binding us to the preceding generations. (Apprey, 2014). In the end, after much struggle, immigration worked out for me. Alas, not so much for my brother, who in spite of his many talents and outstanding intellect, did not achieve professional re-cognition or financial stability.

There were other factors as well prompting me to leave Hungary. I was disenchanted professionally, I was writing literary reviews and translating fiction as well as poetry. While the work was, in part, gratifying, it was also tedious and lonely. I could not imagine myself sitting at a desk, surrounded by dictionaries, for the rest of my life. I was also put off by the counter-culture scene, with all its back-stabbing and sexual morass. Close friends had already left, Julianna and Katalin among them. Katalin's departure preceded mine by only a few months. Another friend committed suicide. It was time for a new chapter.

The night before my flight to New York City via Berlin, where my brother and his then-wife lived, I visited with a few people, saying goodbye. It was late in the evening, on a balmy night in early September, when I was finally heading home. The city was lit up like a jewelry box: the bridges across the Danube, the Parliament, the Royal Castle were all gleaming. It was just beautiful. How could such a gorgeous town be so rotten, I was thinking. My heart sank. When will I see this place again, I wondered? Eventually, I did but not for another eight years, it turns out.

Fresh off the boat

Adam bought the plane tickets (round trip, fur alle falle) as they had to be paid in what was then referred to as "hard currency," not ruble-based funny money, and I had none of the former. After a week in Berlin, I arrived at JFK on September 16, 1980. I was going to be headquartered in the home of distant relatives of my father, an older, religious, Orthodox Jewish couple in Queens. I expected to stay with them for up to six months and go on expeditions to explore the rest of the country from there. We did not hit it off well. I came right in the midst of the high holidays, Rosh Hashanah and Yom Kippur. They were at shul all the time and I showed no interest in participating in any of the observances. Back then I barely identified as Jewish and I definitely had no religious inclinations. Quite the contrary. In spite of my anti-establishment political affiliations in Hungary, in many ways I was the product of my Socialist upbringing: atheist, lefty, egalitarian. I also had a gigantic chip on my shoulder: I knew everything better. I was opinionated, judgmental. While they were fasting away in synagogue on Yom Kippur, I was busy exploring Manhattan, the isle of sin. In about a week or so I walked all over the city, from Battery Park to Harlem, all by my lonesome. At night I visited friends of friends (I had not met a soul beforehand), and frequently ended up at the Squat Theater, watching a performance or a show in their music program and then stayed for the after-party. Sometimes I did not get home till two or three in the morning. They must have been horrified and I think that they were genuinely concerned for my safety. Out of reverence for my father, of which there was no shortage, they put up with me for a while but after a few weeks, they found a convenient excuse and asked me to leave.

And thus began the long series of adventures and experiments, trials and tribulations that comprised the first several years of my life in the United States; New York, really, a world in itself. My parents were right in sending me off, the change of air helped. My depression notwithstanding, I completely fell in love with New York and in less than a month I decided to stay. I applied for political asylum and naively assumed that having come from behind the Iron Curtain would make me automatically qualified. Times had changed though, and the liberalization of the Soviet bloc countries came with a hidden price tag: their citizens were no longer received with open arms all over the Western world. Luckily, some of my former political activities, however insignificant, were documented in the press and that helped my case. My application was accepted and eventually, in what seemed like an eternity, approved. I got a work permit (I still have my original Hungarian passport with the "EMPLOYMENT AUTHORIZED" stamp in it), and I was good to go or rather good to stay.

The Big Apple goes bananas over Kent III taste

I came to the United States with a master's level of education in English and Hungarian. I won competitions in English. I had no trouble conversing and reading. I had translated literary texts from English to Hungarian and these translations were published. In fact, one compelling reason that I came to the United States and did not try my luck in my beloved Italy was that I had what I assumed to be an excellent command of English and would have no problems with communicating or at least getting along. I was in for a surprise though, with the joke on me. First, I had to get used to the accent, but that was the least of it, it was part of the package.

My first job, one month in, well before I received my "EMPLY-MENT AUTHORIZED" stamp, was as a domestic, working for a stereotypical Jewish family on the Upper East Side. I was hired to provide child-care and light housekeeping. The housekeeping included some grocery shopping, to be executed after the unruly six-year-old was delivered to the front door. One afternoon we set out to the supermarket on the corner, with a shopping list in hand. The list contained the following articles:

Ivory
Brillos
Jarlsberg
Bagels
Yukon Gold
Yams

among other, more ordinary items, such as apples and oranges, peppers and tomatoes.

Junior and I marched over to the supermarket and I did my best to appear to be the informed adult (That was before psychoanalytic training: I do not care much anymore about being the subject who is supposed to know.) and I was desperately searching for the above goods. Somehow, I managed to stumble upon Ivory and Brillos in the local Gristedes but the nature of bagels (there was no such thing in Hungary back then) and Jarlsberg remained a mystery. After 20 minutes of futile search in the store, I turned to my companion for help. The six-year-old had no trouble enlightening me. He directed me to the bread and deli departments. I was humbled: I had thought that I had been an educated adult, fluent in English, and still, I failed at some really basic tasks.

A few weeks later, I had yet another, perhaps even more humiliating experience. Junior turned seven and he had a birthday party. The following day the apartment looked like a battlefield and there was a lot of cleaning to do. Mistress asked me to vacuum. This was well within the scope of my responsibilities so I took no offense. I found the vacuum and was very pleased with myself. Funny, how the definition of success evolves over time, isn't it? I plugged in the appliance and turned on the switch but nothing happened. I was puzzled. I tried another outlet. Nothing happened. Then another. Still nothing. Ashamed, frustrated, I finally called my employer. She not so patiently went through the motions with me and eventually informed me that there was a central light switch in the living room and that needed to be turned on to activate the outlets. Something else that did not exist in Hungary. These events might seem like much tedious and boring details but these were the contents of my experience of degradation as I transitioned from young intellectual to house maid.

The final blow that put me in my place was the billboard sign (well before internet): *The Big Apple goes bananas over Kent III taste.* I looked at it and suddenly I burst into tears. I had an advanced degree in English and I did not understand a word of that advertisement, if I even realized that that's what it was. Perhaps I should have known what the Big Apple was but I did not. I came to New York not to a big apple. I was a smoker then and I may have known about Kent but what was Kent III? Finally, how do you go bananas? Isn't banana a fruit?

Slumming (poverty)

As stated earlier, I was not in good shape when I arrived. I did not come with the hope of a better life, I escaped. I ran from historical, social, and personal calamity: a tradition of persecution, toxic love, and mostly private and public lies. Donald Trump did not invent fake news, he is simply a diligent student of Hitler, Goebbels, Stalin, and the like. I came with my useless liberal arts degree and did not really know what to do with myself in the wild, wild West. I did odd jobs like babysitting and house-cleaning. I made a lackadaisical attempt to enroll in a graduate program in English but my heart was not in it. Given that I had no other qualifications and practical skills – I was a lousy typist and a scaredy driver – I decided to pursue my childhood dream of acting. That was a dumb idea if ever there was one. Reportedly, I had some talent as a dramatic actor, still, I had a slight accent, which I was never able to shed, I am short, I cannot sing or dance, I am not cut out for an endless series of rejections, which is typically the lot of an aspiring performer. Few people are. But in this land of opportunity and entrepreneurship no one told me that I did not have a snowball's chance in hell. There was always an acting coach willing to work with me, there were always auditions to attend. Miraculously, I got a few roles throughout the years. In one production I played the mean-spirited, antisemitic, fascist sympathizer Elizabeth Nietzsche; in another Ms. Boerstecher, angel of death, proprietress of Palace Hotel Thanatos. Splendid fits. Needless to say, these jobs were either unpaid or were compensated by a small stipend. To make ends meet, I did what many self-appointed actors do in New York City and began working as a waitress (or server, as they are referred to these days).

I waited tables for several years. I worked in a diner, where I was propositioned by a pimp, a kosher restaurant, where the head-waitress stole our tips, a small Italian place near the United Nations, and eventually at Canastels, a then fashionable spot at 19th St. and Park Avenue South. It was an upscale drug dan and bordello, where reportedly, some of the waitresses were not wearing panties under their skirt. My career as a waitress ended when during a slow Sunday shift the Maître D of the night made fun of my short stature. By then I was fed up. While my forays into acting and waiting tables started as a free-spirited excursion, after several years it had morphed into an exercise in degradation. In response to the Maître D, I turned around, marched into the bathroom, took off my uniform jacket, threw it into the garbage can and walked out. I never looked back and never worked in a restaurant ever again. It was one of the most liberating moments of my life.

Subsequently, I spent a few years working as a proofreader and copyeditor while still taking on an occasional acting job. Finally,

I played in a couple of satisfying if not widely recognized projects. I believe it was this gratification which helped me, in part, to eventually disengage from this whole ill-conceived project. Eventually, but not before:

Implosion & catastrophic change

During this period, I managed to establish a love relationship with one and then another charismatic but rather dysfunctional man. Some people, those with good-enough alpha function, manage to learn from their experience (Bion, 1962). Back then I had not yet. One day I did, and then I moved on. But not for a long time. As a result, in spite of my meager income for over twenty years, starting in my late 20s, specifically, in 1984, I became the primary wage earner in my family unit, first as part of a couple, and then of another with P and then with him and a child.

A few years before the child came in 1992 there were some disastrous developments, compared to which economic hardship was a walk in the park. To provide perspective let me give an exact chronology here. On November 15, 1989, P's father died unexpectedly. On November 30, P attempted suicide. It was a near miss and he was subsequently hospitalized and was, upon discharge, hooked up to the psychiatric-industrial complex, which ultimately saved his life or destroyed him, depending on one's perspective. Then on December 15 (we are still in 1989), my father died of bladder cancer, which was supposedly under control and which was not supposed to kill him (until during one of my visits a few months earlier the urology professor informed me that it would). I was so worried about P's precarious mental state that I did not even go back to attend my father's funeral. (True, I traveled three times to Hungary earlier in the year, once just to be with my father. Now I have regrets though.) And then on December, 30, P's mother died.

We were beyond devastated, we were crushed, bludgeoned. Did not know what to do with ourselves. The next day, on New Year's Eve, we attended a small gathering at the home of one of the founders of the aforementioned Squat Theater, who happened to live a few blocks from us. We did not go to celebrate anything but to have company in our distress. We were praying for the year to finally end.

And when it did and the cold days of January 1990 froze our fresh wounds and after P was initiated into the world of psychotherapy and sufficiently and subsequently excessively medicated, it was time for me to assess my own situation. If I had my brains about, I would have been hatching gentle and compassionate exit strategies. But I was not, not yet, not for many years. I was hopelessly in love. I realized though that something was very wrong and after a couple of previous, half-hearted and short-lived attempts, the winter of my discontent finally sent me in search of serious psychotherapy. Unlike earlier times I did not have the energy or the wherewithal to interview clinicians and search for the best fit. I went with the recommendation of a friend in the field (another former Squat Theater affiliate). I got lucky. In spite of said friend's subsequent misgivings, R proved to be a terrific psychoanalyst, classical/object relations in theory, somewhat interpersonal in style. I lapped it all up. It was like this is what I had been waiting for all my life.

For me the whole endeavor was a revelation but really it was just a typical story. I started out deeply depressed, professionally stuck, barely making ends meet, romantically deflated. Questions arose. Just how much did P love me if he wanted to die? He loved me, he loved me not. I was turning 35, and not only was I childless I had not even figured out yet whether or not I wanted to be a mother. I was plagued by doubt and felt like a failure. The narrative in my head was still dominated by the notion that my parents, their flaws notwithstanding, had been dedicated to my wellbeing and provided me with a good upbringing, financial security, healthcare, education. Given all that, plus my innate talents, which were not negligible, if things were as bad as they seemed to be something had to be really wrong with me.

I find it difficult to reconstruct how I went from a tornado-just-hit-me, utterly miserable to less miserable and then eventually finding solidifying ground under my feet. Revealed in the analytic dialogue was that some of my despair was caused by not having been my own person and not having known who I was and what I wanted. At first it was hard to see because I have always been headstrong and as such often came across as purposeful. That was true in minor matters but not regarding major decisions. R thought that to no small degree I had lived a false existence, construed by my mother and in opposition to my father. (Apologies to my parents and to the parents of my patients, they tried and often did the best they could and often failed. Then tried again, failed again, failed better, failed worse. True, it is the parents' job to hold the environment but they don't always have a lot of options: socially, economically, psychologically.)

While I was trying to wrap my head around this false self business, two major developments occurred. In a relatively short period of time, a year and a bit, I came to decide that I could not continue wasting my talents and had to find a professional path regardless of what kind of impact it would have on my acting career. Given how excited and animated I was by the analytic process I wished to be a professional patient but understood that would have been an even more impractical choice than acting. So I decided to pursue the next best thing and try my hand at becoming a therapist. I looked at graduate programs. I wanted to get a doctoral degree in clinical psychology. Between my age and my financial limitations I ultimately decided that it would be yet another self-defeating project. I applied to social work school instead.

It was during this process of professional reorientation that I slowly began to realize that leaving the world of theater behind did not break my heart. I assumed that there would be a lot of grief but, in fact, there was not much left to mourn. I had stopped taking acting classes and going to auditions a while back. I had already moved on even though I had not known it yet. I did so because I had to, because apparently, acting was never a voluntary project, it was my mother's agenda. She was the original theater person, first a dancer, then an aspiring theater director, and eventually a dramaturg and a professor at the Hungarian Academy of Theater and Film Arts. From an early age, she trained me like a circus animal, to learn and recite poems for guests and events, then encouraged me to participate in competitions, join theater ensembles. In the end, acting fell off my shoulders like an old, ragged jacket. Years went by before I fully recognized that I did not miss any of it and I was, actually, relieved. In fact, I do not like theater much. There are exceptions but I find a lot of it dull and stale. Decades ago I did, I genuinely did, that was not just my mother's introjection, but that was in the late 60s, 70s, a time of great social and political upheaval across the globe, a kind of environment in which theater tends to thrive. We might be witnessing the beginning of a new golden age of theater for the same reason. Remains to be seen.

The other fundamental shift was about having children. After several months in treatment, I concluded that I wanted to have a child after all. Or at least, I did not want to miss out on the experience. It was not some cynical calculation: I became genuinely curious and excited about the whole process, from conception through childbirth, to raising a being till adulthood and beyond. This epiphany came about in the process of mourning my father's death. It was very difficult as he and I did not have a great relationship. On one hand, I trusted blindly that he would come and rescue me if I were in dire straits, I respected his work ethic and his professional achievements, on the other hand, I found his illiberal political views, particularly his misogyny (even though he made a bit of an exception for me), offensive. My father claimed to believe that a woman's most important function, especially a Jewish woman's function, was to procreate. Regardless of other aspirations and achievements, woman's job was to find and rope into marriage a good provider and pop out children, at least a couple. In deciding to have a child, my age was a significant factor, after all, at 36 I could not have waited a whole lot longer, and so was my father's death. Sadly, while he was alive and I felt pressured to produce an offspring, I simply could not or would not oblige. In retrospect, it is a big loss for all involved. I am sure that my father would have adored my son, my son would have been so lucky to have him, and I would have enjoyed their relationship.

According to Bion (1967) all change is catastrophic (Eigen, 1993), as it requires a shift from primary experience to actual thinking, from beta to alpha. In this process one's allegiance to one's principal affiliations are called into question and the loosening of the object ties brings on anguish, persecution, and guilt (Csillag, 2019). Layton (2019) summarizes Bion in this regard exceptionally well: "lying, rather than thinking, may become a customary way of defending against ... catastrophic change ... lies may be painful to live with, but they are less painful that the truth, which can threaten to annihilate the self and its bonds ... For both Bion and Freud ... disavowal, turning a blind eye to painful truths, is at the heart of perversion, repetition, and the inability to learn from experience" (p. 111). The catastrophic change I experienced was the reevaluation of my parents, most specifically my mother. R's presence allowed me to think thoughts that would have been too terrifying to contemplate on my own. I came to question my undifferentiated idealization of my mother. I was used to seeing her as the brilliant, charismatic victim of patriarchal oppression, and while this perception never fully changed, other aspects of her personality emerged: I came to realize that she was also possessive, narcissistic, shallow, and vain. I reconsidered the devaluation of my father, and was able to reconnect to some of the archaic love that had to have existed between us, and move beyond the prohibition on having children that developed in opposition to his demands. In my quest for a more authentic way of being in the world there was much gain but it came at a high price: In the process of finding "myself" (to the degree that there is such a thing) I lost them, my parents, as I had known them before. I grew up.

P.S.: R moved to California in 1995 to be near family. There were a couple of follow-up phone calls and then we lost touch. This was another loss in an endless series of losses to be absorbed. And now, just recently (on January 22, 2020, to be precise) I found out that, sadly, R, had developed Parkinson's and Alzheimer's in her not-so-old age and committed suicide. I completely understand the desire to be done under those circumstances and to leave while one still can maintain a modicum of dignity, still, this is a deeply disturbing development, which will take me a very long time to process. Darkness prevails.

Clearing in the clouds

In quick succession, I started social work school, got pregnant, had a child with my depressive and largely unemployed love partner, began my internships, all the while commuting within Staten Island and between Staten Island and Manhattan, without a car or even a valid driver's license. (While technically part of New York City, Staten Island is car country, public transportation is sporadic and unreliable.) We had NO money. It was all totally crazy: reading the required literature (and way beyond, having had access to the libraries at NYU and later at the Postgraduate Center for Mental Health was heaven, I was being a kid in the candy store), writing papers when my son napped and after he went to sleep at night, breastfeeding as I returned home in the evening before I even had a chance to take my jacket off.

The madness continued for a couple of decades and has only recently, with a solid private practice and a well-functioning and supportive partner, subsided, if. I was always reaching, always doing too much. Well before graduating I knew that I wanted to do psychoanalysis and psychoanalytic psychotherapy. I wanted to go into training right away but there was no way I could afford it. During graduate school, I did not even have health insurance. When I finally graduated, I was literally out of all funds, I had to find a full-time job. A few of my classmates, among them a close friend, started institute training straight out of social work school. I was green with envy. Or rather yellow, as you'd say it in Hungarian. (In Hungarian, as in French, envy is yellow, which makes a lot of sense to me: yellow as in jaundiced: Having liver or gall-bladder problems, how would someone not envy and hate the rest of the world?) And even more than envious, I was really sad. It seemed that all the questionable choices (they did not feel like choices, the decisions were automatic, overly and multiply determined, as psychological constellations tend to be) I had made were preventing me now, when I finally knew my heart's desire, to pursue my vision.

Partial compensation arrived in the form of a rewarding clinical position at the Jewish Board of Family and Children's Services, back then regarded as one of the best outpatient mental health operations in the New York City area, if not in the country. For many years it was an amazing experience. I had the opportunity of working with people from all walks of life and have them teach me about a wide range of psychic experiences, I was offered free training, on company time, no less. I had an Israeli supervisor, whose parents, having been deported to Auschwitz, were born in a DP camp in Germany. She taught me about historical traumatization and transgenerational transmission before it became the talk of town. She gave me books, papers, tapes of survivors' meetings. That was about when I realized that I myself was a second-generation victim/survivor even if my parents did not go to Auschwitz. My parents, my brother, as well as my own psyche, began to make sense.

Even though I was now gainfully employed, with my meager social worker income, we were poor. On account of his mental disability P qualified for food stamps and that was an important part of our food budget. In the grocery store, we shopped very cautiously. (I still do.

Old habits, waste not, etc.) We never ate out. My son wore hand-me-downs, I bought my clothes for pennies at the discount store next to my Jewish Board office. Eventually, I got a car, an eleven-year-old Honda Accord with over 100,000 miles, and relearned how to drive. It had manual transmission and when the clutch eventually gave out (as predicted), I burst into tears. The new clutch was going to cost $500. I did not have $500.

In spite of my marginal finances, I was more content than ever: I was with the person I loved and desired, however dysfunctional he was, we had a lovely boy, in spite of my relentless anxiety and quick temper I was being a better parent than I had ever expected to be, and finally, I was professionally productive. I had managed to get off the runaway train on track to nowhere I had been on. I escaped. Or so it seemed until ...

The theater of the real

When the World Trade Center was blown up on September 11, 2001 I was on my way to work at the clinic. No patients came. People in the office were getting hysterical. "America is under attack," was flickering on network television. After a few hours, I decided that rather than remaining there as a source of support – what support? - for my supervisees, perhaps I needed to rescue my nine-year-old son from what I imagined to be a similarly toxic environment at his school.

After I fetched him, we drove to the neighborhood deli and stood in line for half an hour to buy water and bread and matches in pathetically inadequate preparation for the unfolding apocalypse. Later, we walked down to the Staten Island waterfront, near the harbor. By this time, we were accompanied by his father, P, the ex, who spent the morning at home, watching the footage of the destruction of the World Trade Center countless times, getting sicker and sicker. On that incredibly "beautiful day," with blue skies and balmy temperatures, we watched the towers and an era burn to the ground. We were stunned. Life as we knew it came to a halt if not an end.

In the next few days, weeks, I tried to resume ordinary existence. With my private practice at Union Square and my home and my agency job on Staten Island, the commute became unbearable. For a while, there was no public transportation in downtown Manhattan so

I had to drive to my office, which took forever because of the congestion as well as all the police surveillance. Whatever were they looking for, I wondered. The investigation, the precaution is always after the fact, in response to a prior, unimaginable catastrophe. Millions of people each week have to take off their shoes at airport security (or at least had to until the current coronavirus pandemic, with most air travel on hold) because one person several years ago unsuccessfully tried to detonate a bomb packed into his shoes on route from Paris to Miami. It is like the story of the Maginot Line, the wall built by France after World War I to protect its borders from Germany. The French government at the time simply could not imagine that Germany, the country of Goethe, Beethoven, and Thomas Mann, would ever order its army to march into France through the Netherlands and Belgium after having invaded those countries despite their declared neutrality. Apart from historians and history buffs and perhaps the French, not many people know about the Maginot Line. For me, it has personal significance since I learned about it from my brother in my very early teens and dialogues of this sort ushered in my coming of age.

When public transportation was gradually restored, the subway downtown still did not run, so I took the bus. But the bus only went as far down as Fulton Street and I had to walk from there to South Ferry, about a mile, inhaling the toxic fumes of burnt rubber and plastic, and human flesh, multiple times per week. The same trip in the morning. After a couple of months, I was spent, exhausted. The mental space collapsed, anxiety prevailed. Whenever news of bloodshed or of a foiled terrorist attack were aired or printed in the media I would regress into a paranoid-schizoid state infused with dread and fury.

The destruction of the World Trade Center and the subsequent political events evoked in me fears I had deeply ingrained in me, rooted in my personal experiences as well as those of my parents and forebears going back to pogroms, persecution, and varying degrees of state-sponsored oppression, exploitation, and finally, genocide. These laws went from *numerus clausus,* limiting the number of students who could study at a university; to restrictions on practicing certain professions, such as law and medicine; to the mandate of wearing the yellow star and the forced relocation to the ghettos; to the cattle trains and the extermination camps.

During that period I had a dream. I dreamt about the summer house my parents bought when I was ten years old. From then on we spent most weekends and much of the summer in that house, over-looking the Danube and the remnants of a medieval castle on a nearby hill. It was a magical place and most of my fondest childhood memories are connected to my time spent there. There were flowers and cherries and raspberries in Spring and Summer; chestnuts and walnuts in the Fall; long dinners around the cast-iron stove in the Winter; there was local early romance and later trips there with boyfriends; there were hikes in the hills and long walks to an aban-doned quarry; there was swimming in the river and rowing in an ancient, leaky double skull. Sad to say, after my brother and then I left Hungary and our parents got old, the house fell into a state of disrepair, the garden was taken over by weeds, and the hillside, once an open slope, had a scattering of new houses on it. In my dream, the house burnt to the ground. We were about to have dinner when the fire broke out. We had time to evacuate but we were not able to save anything except some knives – the better to kill you with, my dear, a 'la Little Red Riding Hood – and other kitchen utensils. It was all very sad: the end of an era.

My psychoanalysis

It was not until 2003, nine years after graduating from social work school that I finally began psychoanalytic training. Getting there required very complicated mental math. While I was in a better fi-nancial situation by then, with a decent enough private practice, I was still struggling. P had completely fallen apart and with that so did our relationship. I had good friends but other than that I had little support. But my son was older and was more independent. Still, I had no idea how I would find the time and the money. We lived across the large and beautiful Silver Lake Park and as I would walk or run around the lake, which I did a few times most weeks, I would ru-minate about how I could square that circle. There was no obvious solution, all that contemplation eventually short-circuited itself: I came to realize that I would not be able to solve this puzzle in advance, and if I really wanted a psychoanalytic training, I just needed to jump in and figure it out as I went.

In the Fall, I enrolled at the Manhattan Institute for Psychoanalysis in New York City. Back then the Institute had a rather straightforward interpersonal bent, which did not particularly appeal to me but the institute's culture of relative openness and inclusiveness did. I also liked that I could meet the clinical requirements through my private practice, without having to take on several very low-fee patients, a common stipulation at many other institutes.

I never became a straight interpersonalist but I came to appreciate the Interpersonal tradition and it left a mark on me. I now consider myself a Relational analyst, probably closer to the Object Relations than to the Interpersonal edge. The Relational tradition began as a comparative psychoanalytic project and linked developments associated with a wide range of psychoanalytic theories. Its most fundamental sources are the British Independent School, the American Interpersonal Tradition, and the Intersubjective School (Bass, 2014). As such, the relational experience reconnects me to history and to my part identities both as a person and as a thinker: to Ferenczi and Balint, my Jewish Hungarian forefathers, to Winnicott, my first psychoanalytic love object, to Bion, my most enduring passion. It also keeps me in touch with the endlessly exciting Object Relations canon. Further, it was the process of writing and revising papers (Csillag, 2014, 2017) for the relational journal, *Psychoanalytic Dialogues,* that initiated my immersion in the more recent literature on the now blooming field of intergenerational transmission of trauma from Faimberg to Laub, Grand, Apprey, and way beyond.

For me, Sullivan's seemingly uncomplicated idea, namely that "we are all much more simply human than otherwise" (Sullivan, 1947, p. 16), is perhaps the most important message I absorbed from the American Interpersonal tradition. However self-evident this notion may seem at first, back in his day, in the rigidly-held psychoanalytic frame of mid-century American psychoanalysis dominated by ego psychology, it was a revolutionary idea. And in a way it still is. Interpersonal and Relational psychotherapy and psychoanalysis are a remarkably equalitarian business in a field that, in spite of its progressive origins, morphed into a highly hierarchical system, full of judgement. The equalitarian ethos is further strengthened by another interpersonal contribution: the recognition of the analyst's unavoidable participation in the clinical process. The most striking difference I see between clinical reports by Interpersonal and Relational authors and many practitioners of other persuasions is that of tone in their descriptions of clinical discourse. Regardless of similarities and differences of theory, I find that analysts not affiliated with the Relational movement tend to claim more authority and more power in the analytic encounter. Whether this is a reflection of the actual interaction or more a matter of writing style, I cannot say. This observation is obviously a gross generalization and is to be taken with a grain of salt. Still, reading papers by a diverse range of nonrelational authors and thinkers I otherwise admire, I often find that to varying degrees they write about their work as if they had supernatural powers and were performing magic, seemingly attributing all shifts in their patients, good or bad, to the transferential constellation and their interventions. By contrast, most Relational publications tend to sound more humble and more willing to consider factors other than the therapist-patient interaction in how the treatment unfolds. Some would contemplate psychoanalysis as a nonlinear dynamic system, in which small shifts may initiate chain reactions with significant consequences and outcomes are often unpredictable. This may not sound like science but it does not function without rhyme or reason (Seligman, 2014, p. 651). There is logic and a method to it.

There are other aspects of contemporary American psychoanalytic thought that appeal to me. In the past few decades, there has been much discourse about otherness. While this country is built on land stolen from the native inhabitants by violently coerced African slaves, it is also a nation of immigrants. Being different, coming from someplace else is embedded in the national DNA, right-wing protestations to the contrary notwithstanding. The mostly Jewish refugees who reached these shores just before, during or shortly after WWII were too traumatized to acknowledge much less elaborate on their immigration experience. But this has changed. The offspring of a previous generation of immigrants and the more recent arrivals, from all over the world, frequently from areas of great social and political turmoil, are none too shy about their journeys, physical as well as psychological. A lot of rich material has been written about the self-experience of otherness within and without the immigrant community (Eng & Han,

2000; Boulanger, 2004; Lobban, 2006; Gonzalez, 2017; Guralnik & Simeon; 2010; Khouri, 2012; Lijtmayer, 2001; Rozmarin, 2017; Saketopoulou, 2014, 2019).

The problem of the Other has been taken up and thoroughly investigated by philosophers and psychoanalysts, Levinas, Lacan, Laplanche among them. Recognition of the Other, without the historically customary inclination towards colonization, is accompanied by the subject's own acceptance of the inherently alien – because introjected or implanted – core of the self. These theoretical developments have been embraced by Relational psychoanalysis, and it has been wonderfully enriched by the incorporation of these concepts. The theoretical incorporation of the internal other has operationalized the process and internalization of the environment, human and non-human, and expounded their impact. In my mind, this development mitigates the long-standing antagonism between the intrapsychic and interpersonal/environmental camps. It is not one or the other: it is both. I do not assume that anyone, or at least anyone I read or talk to, would disagree with that in principle but I believe that Relational psychoanalysis has been singularly instrumental in the psychic elaboration of the unconscious internalization of the external: Relational psychoanalysis is evocative and exciting in its description of the movement from the outside in. Concepts from Bion, such as beta to alpha (from psychic rumble to usable mental properties); from Laplanche, implantation (the psychic translation of the parent, that is, the enigmatic other); from Althusser, interpellation (being called out and defined by the State); from Lacan, the encounter with the Real (the traumatic gaps in the symbolic order); are all suitable and evocative metaphors in this regard.

While I have always been drawn to the American ethos of egalitarianism, I had known even before my arrival at these shores that it was largely a myth. Democracy for the White elites; Native Americans, Blacks, Latinx, women, the poor, the sexually non-conform, etc., be damned. But I could not possibly fathom the ruthlessness and severity with which oppression and exploitation are practiced in these United States. Convincingly argued in theses that resonate with me, the unique brutality of American capitalism has its roots in slavery: universal social safety net would have to include Blacks, the descendants of slaves, and that idea is thoroughly reprehensible to a significant percentage of the US population. There are many who'd rather go without than see Black Americans thrive. In part, as a response to this extremely cruel sociopolitical reality, much of American intellectual life, in academia and increasingly more so in psychoanalysis, has taken a radically progressive turn in recent decades.

Relational psychoanalysis has incorporated social and political developments, a heightened recognition of race relations, the individual's embeddedness in the interpersonal as well as the biological field, intersubjective interconnectedness, contemporary feminism, queer theory, the reconceptualizing of gender (Mitchell & Harris, 2004). All of these developments are meaningful and alluring to me and I appreciate how we all struggle to maintain a psychoanalytic perspective without abandoning or denying the social dimension.

A few more words about the way I work. I'd say that I privilege what Ogden (2019) refers to as ontological as opposed to epistemological psychoanalysis. My focus is more on how to be in the world, how to live, how to immerse in an experience, how to play. I am less interested in the cause, the development, even though they are also supremely relevant. Ogden builds mostly on Bion and Winnicott, both of whom are dear and near to my psychoanalytic heart, in belaboring his ontological perspective and his dedication to "allowing the patient the experience of creatively discovering meaning for himself, and in that state of being, becoming more fully alive" (p. 661).

Partially inspired by my second analyst, who was rather loquacious (I wrote about my analysis with him at length elsewhere [Csillag, 2014]), over time I have become a much more conversational clinician than I was when I first embarked on this journey. I provide feedback, I give compliments, I make suggestions, I dispense information, I say "hell, no," when someone is about to self-destruct, embarrassed to admit, I even roll my eyes. I find that this style suits me, it helps engage my creative, contemplative, and playful side, it puts many a patient at ease, relaxes their defenses and then the story begins to flow. Obviously, this attitude does not work with everyone, every time, and I am prepared to take responsibility for being overly casual when that proves to be counterproductive. (As a matter of fact, I have gotten very good at apologizing and not just in a superficial way.) Even then though, patients tend to be grateful for the opportunity to air their grievances, which is typically experienced as much more important than the original slight or error that has occurred.

The author in 2006

Recipes: An evolution

What are recipes doing in a contemplative psychoanalytic memoir? While I do not consider myself a healer for fear of potential sentimental misinterpretation, psychoanalysis is considered a helping profession. As Ogden (2007) states, "Bion views his responsibility to be that of helping patients – a rather old-fashioned idea. If we do not believe that analysis is helpful, why are we spending our lives practicing it?" (p. 1195). But it is not only psychoanalysis that heals, food does too. Especially, old-fashioned chicken soup, the Jewish penicillin. Then there is the conversational part. There is a lot of talk about food in my work. While I have patients who don't know how to boil water, I have many others who are excellent cooks and like to discuss what they make. I used to bristle at the idea of talking about something as see-mingly superficial as food preparation. Not anymore. I listen carefully, and occasionally I add a recipe of my own. With some patients, such dialogues can contribute to holding and provide a feed (Csillag, 2020).

Mother's chicken soup

Place a whole small chicken in a large pot. Add an onion, a few garlic cloves, carrots, celeriac, kohlrabi, parsley root, salt, bay leaf, pep-percorns, and cover with cold water. Bring to a boil, skim off the scum, and simmer partially covered for a while. Perhaps an hour or a bit more. Rest, cool (refrigerate if you have an appropriate appliance, such as a refrigerator, which my family did not own until I was ten years old), scrape off surface fat, warm and serve in bowls. Eat and enjoy. Voila! The beauty of the recipe is that you can experiment with the kind and the amount of vegetables you use. Another is that it tastes great and cures all ills.

Modified chicken soup

In a large pot place a whole small chicken or a large chicken breast. Add an onion, a few garlic cloves, carrots, celeriac, kohlrabi or white turnip, parsley root or parsnip, a few slices of jalapeno peppers, salt, bay leaf, peppercorns, saffron (if you can afford it, turmeric otherwise) and cover with cold water. Bring to a boil, skim off the scum, and simmer partially covered for a while. Perhaps an hour or a bit more. Rest and cool. Discard onion, garlic, bay leaves, and peppercorn, if you are able to. Remove chicken, discard skin and bones, cut the meat into small pieces and store separately. Refrigerate. Scrape off surface fat. Reheat chicken and soup and serve in bowls. Eat and enjoy. Voila! The selection of vegetables is still a creative process. Delicious and cures some ills.

Batshit crazy chicken(ish) soup

This is the result of dark culinary experimentation. In a large pot place a pound or so of chicken feet and another couple of pounds of beef bones. If you survive this process without throwing up, add an onion, a few garlic cloves, one carrot, a couple of stalks of celery, a few slices of jalapeno peppers, salt, bay leaf, peppercorns, saffron (if you can afford it, turmeric otherwise), and cover with cold water. Bring to a boil, skim off the scum, and simmer partially covered for a long while. Hours. Rest, cool, and strain. Discard all solids. The remnants are gross and smell weird. If you are still not vomiting at this stage, refrigerate the broth. To prevent further nausea, take out the garbage immediately! Once the broth is chilled, scrape off surface fat, and make soup by cooking carrots, potatoes, parsley, and whatever else you are inspired to add to the liquid. Pour the soup into bowls. You may wish to add some noodles to the soup before you eat it. Voila! The selection of vegetables is still a creative process. It is still delicious and cures some ills but I don't think I will make it again any time soon because of the newly discovered:

Vegan variation

Whenever you use vegetables, collect (washed) skins, ends, unused parts (don't be shy, go bold) in a quart-size ziplock bag (think airport or sous vide, take your pick) and save scraps in the freezer. (I wish to acknowledge the contributions of one of my patients, whose identity shall not be revealed, for the development of this recipe.) Whenever the bag is full or when the mood strikes, whichever comes first, place the vegetable bits along with an onion, a few garlic cloves, one carrot, a few slices of jalapeno peppers, salt, bay leaf, peppercorns, saffron (if you can afford it, turmeric otherwise) in a large pot and cover with cold water. Bring to a boil, no scum to skim off, and simmer, partially covered for a while. Perhaps an hour or so. Rest, cool, and strain. Discard all solids. Not particularly appetizing but not much reason to throw up either. Once cold, there will be no surface fat to scrape off. Pour broth into containers and freeze. When the time to make soup comes defrost broth, select, creatively, some vegetables, carrots, potatoes, celery, and whatever else you are inspired to add to the liquid. Cook the whole concoction until the carrots and potatoes are soft but not mushy, about half an hour. Add chopped parsley when almost done. You may wish to serve some noodles, rice or otherwise, in the soup. Ladle the soup into bowls and eat. Perhaps offer some crusty bread to go with the dish. Voila! It is delicious even if it may not cure any ills. Excellent option in time of plague. Enjoy.

Impasse: Hauntology

> "Happy families are all alike; every unhappy family is unhappy in its own way."
>
> (Tolstoy, 1877, p. 1)

We are "not gentle creatures … " as Freud (1930, p. 111) pointed out. For confirmation all one needs to do is to glance at the front page of the newspaper.

Borrowing the phrase from Derrida, who, himself was building on the Communist Manifesto by Marx and Engels, and the work about psychic crypts by the Hungarian-French analysts, Maria Torok and Nicholas Abraham (1984), Alexander Etkind (2009) writes about hauntology, referring to the emergence of ghosts from the unacknowledged, unprocessed, unmourned tragedies and atrocities of the political past. The un-buried dead return and clamor for attention. They continue their existence as the dead-alive (Baranger, 2009). They emanate a black energy from the past, which then permeates the presence. In their book, *History Beyond Trauma,* Davoine & Gaudilliere (2004) assert that madness is the manifestation of traumatic history and that "when analyst and patient encounter each other in the war zone, all of both of their relatives and ancestors also enter this space (Gorney, 2004, p. 44).

My mother was a beautiful, witty, charismatic woman with impeccable taste. She would have her clothes made by the best tailors in town (and was hoping that I would follow suit, which I did not), and I was madly in love with her way beyond when it would have been healthy. She was also an anxiety-ridden, high-strung lady, who during my childhood would go around the house at night to make sure that all the lights and gas lines were turned off, and the apartment was not somehow going to burn down or blow apart, killing us all. When I was 7 or 8, long before I was familiar with the concept of *undoing* as a defense, I began to suspect that my mother was engaged in just that: I was terrified that beyond her obsessive preoccupation with keeping the family safe, she was secretly planning to kill herself as well as the rest of the family, while she was at it. I waited until everyone went to sleep and then began to check and recheck the stove, the lights, the front door, the markings of a full-blown obsessive-compulsive neurosis. How I was able to go to school and function the next day I cannot say.

Where did these terrors come from? As far as I know, my mother never attempted suicide or even threatened to kill herself but many years later I found out that my maternal grandmother did. That was before the other, catastrophic traumas came to the fore: Mother, seven months pregnant, marching from the Budapest ghetto, in line to be shot into the Danube by the Hungarian Arrowcross, the home-grown Nazi organization in the winter of 1944 and then let go by a German soldier, a member of the occupying force, on account of her obvious pregnancy; the shrapnel wound in her thigh just a few weeks later, resulting in sepsis and the stillbirth of a brother-to-be who never was. I wish I had expressed more empathy towards her suffering but it was difficult as she herself dismissed it, she told me her tale of woes as if it were entertainment, a good story. The recurrent narrative was always that my immediate family was spared, "only" my uncle was deported and taken to a concentration camp. My mother's response to any inquiry was dismissive: She would insist that "he was not murdered, he simply died of typhoid fever." There you have it, he just slipped out of this world and onto the next, under the watchful eyes of law-abiding German guards and dutiful, if de-humanized kapos.

Then there was the preoccupation with gas and being poisoned by cooking gas. In all fairness, it was not just the camps and the gas chambers, and the Nazis. When I was 6, I "fell in love" for the first time, in the purest way only a six-year-old can manage, with a boy in my apartment building. The romance was going well, he liked me as well. We played, we talked. Then, to my disappointment, one day he did not show up for our play-date. Later my parents told me that he had suffocated due to a gas leak. I was devastated. This subject was never ever discussed again.

I consider myself a good-enough psychotherapist/psychoanalyst yet I talk and write about impasse and failure more often than about anything else. I am intrigued by situations when, in spite of bad chemistry, the treatment dyad agrees to embark on the analytic journey, and by others when after what seems to be decent enough progress the treatment bogs down, and acknowledged and less con-scious hostilities permeate the relationship.

I think much about patients who get under my skin: Working through an impasse or, at the very least, finding an acceptable exit strategy requires a lot of attention. Also, one typically learns more from one's mistakes than from one's accomplishments. Beyond that, I am simply drawn to the dark side, to begin with, that is where I tend to reside. I am willing to delve into challenging situations, involve myself with scary, unstable, and/or unsavory characters in- and outside of the office. While I experience much emotional calamity as a result, luckily, I never suffered any physical or legal harm. Tongue in cheek, I would often say that I am totally dedicated to the death drive. What do I mean? I hate Pollyanna, false cheer. I am with Bion with regards to acknowledging and tolerating versus evacuating painful emotions and mental states.

Much of this attitude, I would imagine, stems from over 2000 years of persecution: I am the descendant of frightened, intimidated forebears, forever on the run, with a packed suitcase by the door, and with the corresponding suspicion, resentment, and hate. The denial of this hate, any hate, leads to sentimentality and that has no use in psychotherapy or in parenting (Winnicott, 1949).

Two vignettes

"God keep me from a therapy that goes well," as Sullivan famously quipped (Levenson, 2017). That sounds witty. In reality though, the majority of treatments I conducted went well and resulted in significant growth for patient and therapist alike. Needless to say, there were misunderstandings and hurt feelings and resentment, conflict, anger and rage, missed sessions, and all those other trying interpersonal constellations abundantly familiar to all clinicians. Most of the time these painful developments could be worked through and gained from. What allows the dyad to deal with and grow from such challenging situations is the increasing ability of the participants to tolerate and eventually perhaps modify their destructive tendencies, more specifically, frustration, rage, envy, and the like. This process leads to increased acceptance of the blows to one's grandiosity, the attendant shame and losses, and finality in general.

"When I first talked to you on the phone, I was afraid that you might be too sweet, phony, sugary, like a lot of Americans are, in a "How are you? Very well, thank you," kind of way. But after our first session, I started to worry that it might be the opposite, that you might be too harsh, like my mother." Thus began the four-year-long three-times-per-week psychoanalysis of Ronja, a Finnish performer, who started to see me when she was in her mid-twenties.

Ostensibly, she was seeking help with marital distress after she found out that her husband of just a few years, an American native (disambiguation: not a Native American) had cheated on her, just as her father had cheated on her mother and subsequently, abandoned the family. The marital discord was the trigger but as we know, and as the Symingtons (1996) so articulately state, most people do not know or are reluctant to say why they are seeking psychoanalysis. "The symptom then is the cover story for the analysis. It sounds all right if I say: 'I am having analysis because of my asthma', or:.. 'I am having analysis because I was depressed after my marriage broke down.' This sounds more respectable than saying: 'I am having analysis because I am not able to think,.. or: ' I am having analysis because I have made a fuck-up of my life.'" (p.4).

While Ronja was very much caught up in the ontological dilemma of what to do with herself, her life, and how to figure out what kind of a person she was and wanted to be (Ogden, 2019), she had not made a fuck-up of her life, she was too young and too emotionally sturdy for that but she was on her way. There was much she needed to sort out. She had a lot of ambivalence about her husband. She was resentful of her mother whom she described as intrusive as well as highly critical and dismissive. She felt abandoned by her exciting but unavailable father. Immigration was fraught with disappointment: while she loved New York she missed the slower pace of her home-land, she missed the familiarity, the food, she missed the snow. She missed the financial security, however limited it had been. She also struggled professionally. In childhood, she was regarded as somewhat of a prodigy but after puberty she experienced less success. In New York, with its glut of performers, she had difficulty getting paid jobs. To her escalating frustration, frequently she made it to the last round of the audition cycle only to be weeded out in the end.

Ronja grew up in Finland, in a small town on the Arctic Circle. With her pale complexion and hair so blond it was practically white she actually looked the part. She was an only child. Her parents di-vorced as she was entering adolescence, after her mother had found out about her father's philandering. With the divorce, her connection to her fun-loving, dare-devil of a father, who, in questionable judg-ment, would take her on steep ski-slopes and to dangerous dodgem car races, weakened. Mother-daughter relationship suffered as well: with the loss of father's engagement, mother became increasingly more critical, domineering and possessive. Without having been aware of the psychological implications of these developments, Ronja fled: first to Helsinki, then to London, from there to Los Angeles, and ultimately, to New York.

You can run but you can't hide. When the escape project inevitably implodes and when the pluperfect errand one has been sent on by one's forebears (Apprey, 2014) catches up – and perhaps, one finds oneself at crossroads with a stranger, who, long after the murder, proves to be one's father, and whose killing one spent one's entire life attempting to avoid and if poking out one's eyes and wandering into exile in the wilderness is not a reasonable option – humbled, one might seek out psychotherapy and psychoanalysis. As did I and as did Ronja.

In her analysis, there was much dialogue about two European immigrants working together. There was a lot of camaraderie and intuitive understanding as well as puzzlement and occasional mis-understanding. A few examples: According to local custom, whenever Ronja got sick, her mother would feed her blueberry soup, which she hated. She had to pass a snow-driving test to get a driver's license. It makes sense but it has never occurred to me that in some countries you have to prove your driving skills in the snow to be allowed on the road. With repulsion, she recalled having had to eat porridge for breakfast, which sounded strange to my 21st-century Americanized ears. People talk about eating oatmeal, not porridge in my world. For Ronja, this word may just have been part of her British usage, on account of her studies in England. For me, having spent the past forty years in the United States, the word conjured up images of abandoned and abused children in Dickensian orphanages. To my mind, this communication painted her childhood experiences with the stark hues they deserved, and it also reinforced our connection as Europeans, familiar with the sinister world of 19th-century practices of English childrearing, reportedly teaming with abuse and humiliation.

Both the camaraderie and the puzzlement can be viewed as mani-festations of what Marianne Goldberger (1993) terms the bright spot, the presumption of an instinctive understanding of the patient based on circumstantial similarities, in this case, our shared European origin. While the bright spot may degrade into a blind spot and lead to countertransferential enactment, it can also foster emotional intimacy and deepen the treatment, as it happened between Ronja and me.

Well-illustrated by her comments from one of her very early ses-sions quoted above, in Ronja's treatment, the negative maternal transference was set up almost immediately. She worried about my gaze, my opinion, my judgment. She expected to be found lacking as she did growing up. Just a few weeks into her treatment, she had a dream about sitting on a toilet and taking a shit with an older woman looking on. She felt terribly self-conscious in the dream as well as in recounting the story. Yet, she also enjoyed and was relieved by the process of narration: she liked being the subject of inquiry and the irony of producing such an obvious transference dream was not lost on her. She had a sufficient amount of good-enough experiences to have developed reflective capacity and thus ride the analytic waves, however stormy, rather well.

There were difficult developments though. As she began to detail the harsh, at times even sadistic emotionality of her mother, her yearning to be loved and nurtured began to emerge with force. After a particularly intense session about her increasingly needy dependence on me, she called me to let me know that we would have to have a phone session instead of an in-person one as she developed violent diarrhea and would not be able to leave the house. As we explored whether the runs were a somatic representation of her need to evacuate and the reluctance to face me, she acknowledged how confounded she was by the intensifying intimacy between us. She was sad and insecure. I acknowledged her discomfort and, worried that the pace of the analysis may have accelerated beyond Ronja's endurance, I asked if there was anything I could do to help her bear her distress.

In response, she said: "Just tell me that I am doing the right thing and that I am going to be fine." This is where I would typically freeze. I am better at it now but back then I really didn't do well with directives and demands for reassurance. She clearly needed me to say something but I was at a loss. Telling her that she needed me to convey my faith in her or that she was hoping that I had magical powers, seemed lame. I was trying to think but thinking was not happening, no miraculous solution presented itself. In the end, I came to acknowledge and own the absurdity of the situation in what turned out to be a playful manner. I said: "You are doing the right thing and you are going to be fine. There, does this help?"

She giggled. The tension eased. In retrospect I find that it was a successful case of containment: In spite of the pressure, I felt I was able to make light of the situation. On one hand, my use of humor revealed that I found her request for soothsaying unreasonable, on the other, it implied that I did not share her terror that her situation was as dire as that. What had been an unbearable emotional state became tolerable by my playful if awkward registration of the crushing material. My gesture signified that neither her greed nor her terror of it scared me off. Without being sentimental, I communicated that I had trust that we would manage.

From the description of my work, the reader might conclude that I am an incompetent or completely undisciplined therapist who promotes camaraderie, engages in cultural exchange, and provides reassurance. I do all that but not out of lack of discipline: In fact, I welcome these supposedly subversive and unorthodox conversations: in moments of micro-impasses, overbearing emotions, experiences of terror or vacuity, they can expand the space in which mental processing takes place.

By the time Ronja ended her analysis, she was in a much better place. She divorced her husband and after a while, she developed an amicable relationship with him. Her maternal introject, and with it, her nasty superego mellowed, she was less critical of herself, more content. She has made peace with her professional limitations and eventually, she decided to give up on being an experimental artist in the United States, where such endeavors do not often get financially rewarded and to move back to Finland, with its generous social safety net and an abundance of grants and stipends for creative types. We parted on a friendly, albeit bittersweet note, with the acknowledgment of loss. Loss of fantasies and aspirations, loss of time, and loss of our intimate connection.

Ronja's treatment ended many years ago. I'd like to believe that since that time my analytic style has become more nuanced and sophisticated. In some ways though it has not changed all that much. I listen with a keen ear to the historical, social, political register, to the stories of migration, immigration, and acculturation. I let the dialogue meander, and wonder at some seemingly insignificant details. I am content to explore the surface and trust that in the end, it will reveal its depth.

The emptiness of the emergency broadcast signal

"It is questionable to speak of failure when there is no consensus about the outcome of the experience ... The wish to prolong the analysis is akin to keeping someone alive who has long since been doomed. Failure? It is better to ... speak of 'the disillusions of psychoanalytic work'".

(Green, 2011, p. 51)

Teresa was a short and obese woman of Italian descent in her 30s. She lived with her mother and increasingly more dysfunctional sister, Cathy, in Queens. She came to see me in the midst of a severe bout of depression following the untimely and unexpected death of her alcoholic and philandering father, who had abandoned her and the family. She was an educated, smart lady, and was working in the art department of an advertising agency. She never had a serious relationship and was, in fact, still a virgin.

I immediately took a great deal of dislike to her. She emanated intense despair mixed with much rage and entitlement. All that hostility distorted her features, which, sad to say, were not particularly appealing to begin with. The worst of it though was her smell, which was not body odor but an artificial one. She was heavily doused in some cologne, an overly sweet, lily-of-the-valley scent I could not stand. Given my strong negative reaction, I probably should not have agreed to work with her but back then, nearly twenty years ago, I still had a lot of analytic grandiosity and assumed that I ought to be able to be of use to practically everybody. I also like a challenge. As I told my supervisor at the time: "I don't give up." Struggling financially, I also needed the money.

So, Teresa and I embarked on what turned out to be a three-year course of mostly twice-per-week psychoanalytic psychotherapy, which, in spite of some gains, such as professional advancement and increased income on her part, ended on a sour note, with frustration and disappointment for both participants.

There were good sessions, nay, periods, with friendly and productive dialogue yet the entire treatment was permeated by suspicion and hostility. The anger and dissatisfaction were mutual. I was taken aback by her narcissistic entitlement and rage: she was envious and critical of her colleagues; she was always trying to reel in the hottest boy, who, judgmental and perhaps even sexist as it may sound, seemed out of her league; she had a hostile-dependent relationship with her admittedly intrusive and dismissive mother. A case in point: she expected her mother to monitor her diet and help her to lose weight but became furious whenever her mother made a comment about her appearance.

She did not care for me either. She wanted less structure, more accommodation. She asked me to work around her ever-changing schedule and rearrange sessions accordingly. I did when I could (as is my general policy) but when I was not able to and still charged for a session, she was indignant. She also expected more hand-holding, more advice than I was able to provide. She may have also been resentful on account of my appearance. How could she have not? I am about her height but half her weight. As she frequently expressed envy and hatred towards women who were slimmer than her, I asked her a few times how she felt about the difference in our weight but she denied having any thoughts or emotions about the matter. It was the usual story, "it's different, you are my therapist." Eventually, perhaps in questionable judgment, I let the theme drop.

Teresa frequently complained about feeling horrible about herself, stupid and inefficient. Whenever her mother or her boss interfered with her independence, she felt stifled, and whenever they did not, she felt abandoned. The same with me. When I first suggested that she come twice a week, she felt coerced and entrapped. When I did not persuade her any longer, she assumed that I did not care about her anymore.

Two years into her treatment she had a dream. In the dream, her father was sitting at the kitchen table. He looked young. Mother and sister were present as well. Teresa was sitting across the table. In the dream, she confronted her father about his infidelity and eventual abandonment of the family. She said: "'I tore into him. I said 'how could you have done this to me and mommy and Cathy? I hate you. How dare you?' He was crying hysterically. I was feeling sorry for him. He looked like a failure. And he said, 'I am a failure.'"

Back then I missed the transferential implications that are abundantly clear now: I was the failure sitting across from her. I was failing her and she also experienced herself as a failure. We were a failed couple in an inevitably intertwined failing psychoanalytic encounter. Or to paraphrase Green (2011), who compares much analytic disappointment to "keeping someone alive who has long since been doomed," (p. 51), I was not ready to face the disillusions of psychotherapy and psychoanalysis and acknowledge what I knew quite well deep down, that I was of little use to her in the Winnicottian (1969) sense. I struggled to survive her pervasive envy and destructive attacks.

This dream brings to mind my own dream, recurring over a couple of decades about my own father. In my dream, I would be visiting

Budapest and would be trying to call him. The call was attempted near the end of my stay and was unsuccessful. I would try again and again and would not be able to get through. At times I would be able to arrange a brief visit with this very old man (my father was born in 1910) who was barely alive. Mostly, I would not be able to see him. I would leave the country with tremendous heartache, guilt, and shame. Then one night a few years ago, I dreamt that I called and we talked and I went to see him. He lived in a bright, spacious home, and we had a lovely time. I have not dreamt about trying to reach my father since that time. I have made peace, I guess.

Teresa often complained about being stuck with her mother and sister in their dysfunctional world. They kept pressuring her for financial and emotional support while constantly commenting on her diet and weight. She said that it was just like the sound of the TV monitor after hours or the emergency broadcast signal. Empty and unbearable at the same time.

Typically, I pride myself on being able "to boldly go where no man has ever gone before" (Star Trek), that is to tolerate pain and despair as they come, but I wondered then, and I still do if there was a part of her experience of unwantedness and lovelessness, manifest at first sight in her physical appearance, I did not want to share and unconsciously recoiled from. Unfortunately, with Teresa, the unwelcomness and the attendant death spell (Ferenczi, 1929), were largely dissociated and were cloaked in self-righteous rage and entitlement with tremendous shame under the surface, and could barely enter the dialogue. Speaking of shame: it's on me.

I was in training then and I kept discussing Teresa's case in supervision. But a few months later I found myself in a severe transferential quagmire with another patient and the focus shifted to that situation. After the crisis subsided, I suggested that we return our attention to Teresa. My supervisor, however, recommended that we continue with the second, very complex and intriguing case of a university professor with multiple Ivy League degrees. And thus, Teresa fell by the wayside, abandoned, once again passed over for someone more sophisticated, better looking, and definitely of a higher social class.

Our collaboration, such as it was, came to an abrupt end approximately a year after these sessions. One day she came to see me and announced that she was ready to move on, that is, to end her treatment with me. When I inquired how she reached that conclusion she acknowledged that the psychiatrist I sent her to, encouraged her to do so and, in fact, had already referred her to another clinician. (Needless to say, that was the last time ever that I referred anyone to that prescriber.) When it became abundantly clear that she was determined to leave I suggested that we have a termination phase of several sessions to complete our journey. She would have none of it. She left a couple of minutes before her session time was over and that was that. I was sad, disappointed, ashamed, indignant, disillusioned, and relieved.

November 2016

On November 9, 2016, the American public woke up to President Elect Donald Trump. That day was the 78th anniversary of Kristallnacht, the bloody pogrom against Jews throughout Nazi Germany in 1938, carried out by civilians as well as by paramilitary forces with the government's tacit approval. The apparent coincidence was pointed out to me by my first patient of the day, H, a Jewish-Japanese woman, who converted to Modern Orthodoxy in early adulthood, in part to create structure in what she experienced as a life lacking in reliable boundaries.

During a night of terror and tears followed by intermittent sleep, I received multiple emails of stunned horror from friends and family in Europe. They were wondering if Armageddon has finally arrived. I was anguished and horrified even if not completely surprised. You can never overestimate the forces of Beta, the Real, Satan, or what have you. Eventually, I dragged myself to work. I knew what I was in for but had no idea what impact my experience would have on me. Hour after hour I listened to my patients' despair and fear. It was a rainy day and someone quoted their six-year-old child having said in the morning, "God was crying." The child was referring to the election. Others stated that their children, their students were afraid that they, their parents, their friends would get deported. I had two meetings scheduled with colleagues that day, a peer group and a study group – where I am now designated as the "traumatized European Jew." There was more anxiety, tears, it was unbearable. By the end of the day, I was completely exhausted. I was ill, I had terrible diarrhea, which lasted several days. That was my body's way of evacuating what was indigestible.

For weeks I would listen to the fears and devastation of my patients. They were confused. Many got sick. Acne, eczema, colitis, all flared up. As the psyche is no longer able to cope with what's unbearable, the latter gets discharged directly into the body, which then begins to disintegrate.

The night after the election I had a nightmare: I see a guy on a tightrope. Very scary, he might fall. In the following sequence, I am the leading lady I always wanted to be but in an opera performance: The prima donna. The staging is chaotic, amateurish, people come and go behind the set. When it is my turn to sing the closing aria of the performance, I am frozen, I cannot do it, my throat is shut, I am unprepared. I forget the words and the tune. What a shame, what a disaster! The understudy will have to take over. I am heartbroken about the lost opportunity. The understudy does a poor job. She takes her time, gets overly dramatic in places. Performers and audience members are getting irritated and bored, they want to go home. A male performer whispers in my ear: "I need to catch my train. When will this ever stop?" When the show finally ends, I depart. As soon as I walk out to the street, I realize that it is raining and I left my umbrella at the theater. I return to the theater. Then I wake up.

The dream takes us back to the stage, where this essay started and where the personal, the professional, and the political intermingle. When I woke up, I thought that the man on the tightrope was both Hillary Clinton, who fell, and Donald Trump, who would. And indeed, he was in free fall through his entire endless term, very nearly taking the country down with him. It was super scary. And the fear is just barely subsiding. My inability to sing my part refers to having been frozen, shut up, speechless. The performance took a bad turn. The understudy – Trump – did an abysmal job, she was slow to catch up and was overly dramatic. People were anxious and they wanted to leave (the United States). Eventually, I also got out but later I realized that I didn't have my umbrella to protect me from the unfolding disaster and I returned. I gasped for air and woke up to realize that I was stuck in a time machine!

Now, years later, this dream reads in a vastly different way. We are way past the awful unfolding of the Trump presidency. We have all fallen off the tightrope – which is exactly where we had been as a nation and perhaps as a species, trying to keep up our high wire act – right into hell, into the hell of social and racial injustice, climate catastrophe, and the criminally mismanaged coronavirus epidemic, with its mounting death toll and economic devastation.

My dream catapulted me back to earlier eras: to Budapest in the1970s and its totalitarian regime, to New York in 1980 when Reagan got elected, to 2000 when Bush did, back to September 11, 2001, to March 19, 2003, when the Shock and the Awe bombardments of Iraq began. Worse, I was brought back to an experience before my time, to Nazi-occupied Hungary and I could not and still cannot get out. We are in the domain of hauntology, the realm of the dead-alive. Yolanda Gumpel (1998) states that social violence brings on psychic devastation. She terms radioactive identifications or radioactive nucleus the "unapproachable, nonrepresentable remnants of the memories of social violence that remain 'radioactive,' and under whose influence other, related material, is also rendered radioactive and unrepresentable" (p. 363). The radioactive fragments "lie scattered about – hidden in images, nightmares, and symptoms," and remain embedded in the psyche and continue to exert their noxious influence, especially, if they are evoked by subsequent social violence. The disturbing developments of the last several years, including but not limited to the 2016 presidential election, the attempts to delegitimize the 2020 one, the murder of George Floyd, followed by the ever-elusive promise of racial awakening, the rise of QAnon, the insurgency at the US Capitol, the resurgence of violent anti-semitism, all contextualized by inaction on climate change and the rouge abuses of sovereign power in the most current axis of international evil, Pyongyang, Moscow, Warsaw, Budapest, Minsk, etc., have reactivated all and every manner of horror and trauma my family and friends, my patients and I ever experienced so that we have now been in an endless groundhog day loop of a horror show, the nightmare from which there is no waking up. What has been unfolding globally is what Bion (1982) would have perhaps termed evacuation as opposed to a modification of frustration, and is a global disaster.

Tissue issue

On Friday, May 3, 2019, before my practice hours, I went for a routine breast imaging study. The sonogram revealed what appeared to be a small cluster of benign cysts in my left breast. According to protocol, fur alle falle, I was to have a repeat sonogram six months later. Which I did, on Friday, November 15, 2019. When she was finished with the exam, the sonographer informed me that there was no change in the size of the nodule. All was well or at least so I was led to believe. I wasn't terribly worried to begin with: in spite of my well-developed hypochondriasis and general terror of doctors' visits and diagnostic exams, somehow, irrationally, in spite of the statistics, I had concluded years earlier that breast cancer was not in the cards for me. I was convinced and I kind of still am, that it would be some gastrointestinal cancer to ultimately kill me, as it did three of my four grandparents.

I was relieved though, especially since a close friend, O, was only a few weeks earlier diagnosed with invasive lobular carcinoma and was having a couple of rounds of surgery followed by chemotherapy and radiation. Given my assumptions, I was surprised and moderately annoyed when a few days later I received a phone call from my gynecologist's office with the message that the imaging showed abnormality and I needed to have a biopsy done. Why? What was the abnormality if the size has not changed? The nurse's assistant did not know the answer, she just kept repeating that there was an abnormality. What kind of abnormality, I asked, with increasing irritation. Finally, I was able to talk to a nurse who did not have an answer either but at least acknowledged the validity of my question. She agreed to contact the radiologist and find out. She called two days later and informed me that while the size of the cluster had not changed, its cellular structure did: it morphed into a complex cystic nodule with angular margins. I am no doctor but I immediately understood that the angular margin part was bad news. I would have to schedule a needle biopsy. I took the first available appointment, on Wednesday, November 27, the day before Thanksgiving. The procedure, I was reassured, would be "nothing." Local anesthesia, a little pressure, some discomfort, no heavy lifting or strenuous exercise for a day. Well, that is not exactly how the events unfolded. The three needle punctures were, indeed, not a big deal but a few minutes later my breast began to hurt. A little and then a lot, and then I was in excruciating pain. My breast was hot and hard and it was growing. The radiologist took one look and immediately realized that I was developing a gigantic hematoma. It took three people and 15 minutes to ice the area and bandage me up to stop the internal bleeding. A little while later, I was on my way to my office, where I had a full day of work scheduled ahead of me, as I had assumed that the procedure was "nothing." The pain was relentless and the bandages were so tight that I could barely breathe. I was miserable. By mid-afternoon, I decided to cancel my last patient. I went home and took to bed. All night I kept icing my breast.

My left breast remained hard as rocks and extremely tender for weeks. On Thanksgiving day it turned bright red and then black and blue and eventually purple and yellow before it resumed its customary hue.

To her credit, the butcher lady, Dr. N, who, it seems, punctured a blood vessel or two during the biopsy, took it upon herself to call me in the afternoon the day after Thanksgiving, long after everyone else stopped working. She did not want me to have to wait till she returned from vacation a week later to find out the results. The moment I heard her voice I realized that she was not delivering good news. Yes, there were cellular changes, she confirmed but I did not have cancer. The pathology indicated atypical ductal hyperplasia, a precancerous condition. The nodule had to come out.

On Monday, November 25, I began to contact surgeons. I knew whom to call because O had done her due diligence and kindly shared her findings with me. I wanted to see a female doctor, as did she, since we both felt done with men poking around in women's bodies. The first piece of good news in that sequence was that her doctor, almighty head of breast surgery at Mount Sinai Hospital refused to see me because she would not treat someone with my diagnosis. I asked if my condition was not serious enough for her majesty, and I was told that, indeed, that was the case. It then occurred to me that I did see a breast surgeon, Dr. A. S., some two decades earlier, on account of a false alarm. He was wonderful, thorough, and friendly. Perhaps a bit old-school, putting a hand on the patient's shoulder but I did not mind. In fact, my feminist attitudes notwithstanding I was hoping for that kind of hand-holding for once. I scheduled an appointment with him in spite of his gender.

Instead of rigidly following feminist dogma, by choosing to have Dr. A. S. perform the surgery, in a way I finally allowed myself to have a good-enough father figure, the gentlemanly yet innovative physician, attentive to his patients' needs. My own father was reported to also have been kind and caring with his own patients, many of whom held him in high regard, even if sadly, he was not able to consistently maintain such an attitude towards me and the rest of the family.

On Wednesday, December 11, at the crack of dawn, I traveled to Dr. A. S.'s office on the far East Side of Manhattan (an endless journey) and he was just as terrific as ever. For starters, he recognized me or at least my name after twenty-two years! Really?! Is he human? He said that the diagnosis based on the imaging seemed correct and the surgery I needed was going to be "a walk in the park." "Not much, a 15-minute procedure," after which I was supposed to be as good as new. I scheduled the surgery, an extensional biopsy in contra-distinction from a lumpectomy, a term, it turns out, is reserved for removing a malignancy. The date was December 20.

The day started early, there was nil per os after midnight, I did not want food but my mouth was dry, I asked for a sip of water or at least some mouthwash but was denied. There were a lot of interventions: more needles, more sonograms, pills, consultations. I could not wait to be wheeled into to OR and be put out of my misery. At the end of the hallway I was taken off the stretcher and instructed to walk (to preserve whatever was left of my dignity?) to that gleaming sanctuary of modern medicine, with at least half a dozen professionals administering to my needs, until finally the valium drip began to circulate through my veins and I was out.

The next thing I remembered was waking up. After the obligatory post-anesthesia rest, Dr. S. came to my bedside to let me know that all went well. The surgery took longer than expected, a full 80 minutes, almost twice as long as my hip replacement surgery nine years earlier, because he needed to remove a lot of scar tissue on account of the botched needle biopsy. Supposedly, the radiologist used a needle that was way too large. I was sent on my way with an Elizabeth Pink Surgical Bra, https://mastheadpink.com/product/elizabeth-surgical-bra/, curtesy of Weill-Cornell, to better protect my bruised body. I was well enough to make a detour and go to the plant nursery and buy some Fraser fir branches to continue my habit of celebrating Christmas.

On Christmas Eve, Dr. S. called to let me know that the pathology results came back as expected: all the hyperplasia was out and there was no further treatment needed.

I am writing this in the middle of January 2020 and my breast is healing, however slowly. Last week, I had a terrible cold or the flu (or the coronavirus maybe) and for two days I could barely move. My body is beat. My friend, O, has started chemo, her face is contorted with pain. The days are getting longer but to no avail. We are in the middle of a cold wave and I am in a melancholy mood. Friends are getting sick, some are dying, some others are dead. Every new brush with death becomes more serious. In my 20s my anxieties about health and especially about survival ran from ridiculous to unreasonable. Unfortunately, the odds have changed. These days every new symptom is a potential death sentence. And even when a fatal condition is not a compelling concern one never knows when a bout with illness will usher in the irreversible decline of aging.

Forgiveness: Giving up all hope for a better past

I think I have largely forgiven my parents for their flawed humanity or at least I no longer harbor conscious resentment towards them. As mentioned earlier they were not evil, abusive people, just self-centered, inconsiderate creatures: victims of history. They have been long gone: my father died at the end of 1989, my mother at the beginning of 2010. While there is much I miss about them, it is also easier to forgive without repeated exposure to their most aggravating features, which, sadly and as a rather unflattering reflection on me, I found difficult to tolerate till their dying days.

What about the monsters of history, Hitler and Stalin, and their henchmen? Can they be forgiven? Specifically, is it even for me to continue to nurse resentment or to forgive? I cannot hold onto grievances or forgive for the savagery committed against my parents and the other many millions. It is exclusively the victims' prerogatives, who are, along with their perpetrators, mostly gone, that is, dead by now. I can cultivate my grievances over the destruction of my family and my parents' tormented souls and twisted characters but who can sort out the blame? And whom would I be directing my hatred against? An army of dead people? A culture, the cultures, and historical decisions that gave rise to a system of calculated brutality (Harries, 2003; Subert, 2019; S. Wilson, personal communication, October 8, 2019).

Perhaps a more useful approach towards the monstrosities of historical and sociopolitical developments is witnessing and acknowledgment. The many Holocaust museums, whether they be in Jerusalem, Washington, D. C., or Budapest, are exactly that: establishments dedicated to remembrance and possibly atonement, not to vengeance or forgiveness that is disingenuous and hollow.

While in the past several decades the Shoah and the Gulag have come to represent the evil empire, it is essential to remember that this state of exemption (Agamben, 1995/1998; 2003/2005), the reversal of habeas corpus, that hallmark of Western Civilization (with its otherwise often questionable merits) is, sadly, not exceptional at all. Some sovereign power with its absolute rule over the subject reducing, at will, said subject to, what Agamben terms homo sacer, deprived of the rights of citizenship and reduced to bare life, has been the norm, the de facto experience throughout much of human history. Just think of the colonization of Africa and Asia, the systematic annihilations of the native populations in much of the Americas, chattel slavery in the United States and elsewhere, the Armenian genocide, Guantanamo, to name some of the most documented examples. The exercise of sovereignty extends to the rule over life and death, the decision over who can live and who must die (Mbembe, 2003). From time-to-time humans, post-agriculture and post-settlement (for all we know prior to those developments some ten thousand years ago there was a golden age of hunter-gatherer cooperation and equality) made efforts to have social contracts that diverged from ruling by sheer force or manipulation, at least for the elites, but those constructs tended to be fragile and relatively short-lived. Are the establishment and the maintenance of rights for the mostly white ethnic male populations in the so-called developed world a convincing argument to the contrary?

Vengeance: Who benefits?

Kurt Vonnegut (2011) was an American prisoner of war at the time of the bombing of Dresden towards the end of WWII. In an introduction to his novel, *Slaughterhouse-Five*, based on his experiences at the time, he wrote:

> The Dresden atrocity, tremendously expensive and meticulously planned, was so meaningless, finally that only one person on the entire planet got any benefit from it. I am that person. I wrote this book, which earned a lot of money for me and made my reputation, such as it is. One way or another, I got two or three dollars for every person killed. Some business I'm in.

Let it be said that Vonnegut's position is controversial. There are many who believe that the destruction of Dresden may have accelerated the fall of the Nazi power and if it saved just one of their victims, it was justified. Others argue that by February 1945 the war had already been won. True, but the inmates of the camps and the soldiers on the front were still dying.

My concern about revenge and retaliation is not primarily about compassion for the perpetrator, even though with over two million people, mostly men of color, behind bars in this country, that is a supremely relevant perspective. My preoccupation is chiefly about the damage it does to the body and the psyche of the avenger. Sue Grand, who has written extensively about evil and its impact, both in her book, *The Reproduction of Evil: A Clinical and Cultural Perspective* (2000) as well as in various papers, accepts that "after atrocity, vengeance is a natural lust" (2019, p. 149). Yet she also warns us that it is an insatiable, dangerous, and dissociative process, a manic defense which will not heal any wounds and will not facilitate mourning.

Still, there is such a thing as the "obscenity of understanding" (Lanzmann, 1991), the empathic stance towards perpetrators of radical evil, such as the members of the SS and the KKK. While we all have a dissociated perpetrator in us and we all have the capacity to dehumanize, we are not all potential murderous monsters. To prevent moral slippage distinction needs to be made between destructive potential and radical evil (Frie & Grand, 2019).

Psychoanalysis in the time of plague

Much has been written about the challenges of the coronavirus experience in the world of psychoanalysis. There has been tremendous anxiety for the well-being of our patients, colleagues, family members, and ourselves. There has been loss, the loss of personal contact, the cocoon of the office, the physical environment as an extension of our personalities, the décor, the view, the material manifestation of the holding environment, so carefully designed over the years. I was also worried about my beloved plants, four of them to be precise. How long would they survive? A colleague was generously watering them for a while but I could not expect her to continue indefinitely, nor did I really want her to. I felt guilty for accepting. As much as I love my plants, I am sure that my heightened concern for them was a displacement of terror about and anticipatory grief for the people at risk: my potential body count.

Then there was the adjustment to remote work, starting to see patients in an alternate space. Those who could, left town, and set themselves up in less densely populated areas; some were re-configuring their living quarters to carve out a private corner suitable for confidential communication. Some still went to an office, especially if they were able to walk there; some scrambled. Some people, especially those new to teletherapy, struggled with the technological learning curve and with the impact of technology on the analytic relationship and the transference-countertransference matrix.

There was a silver lining, however thin it may have been. I must say that I am blown away by the speed and ease with which, as a group, we, psychoanalysts, transitioned to the new reality. Based on my rather unscientific survey in New York City, on Friday, March 13, 2020 most of us went to the office and saw patients there. Then by Monday, March 16, the majority worked from someplace else. People who claimed to have barely known how to open a computer were communicating via Zoom, Skype, FaceTime, you name it.

More importantly, the question of whether this is psychoanalysis seems to have been settled at least for now, and I sincerely hope once and for all: It is! On various listservs I read the occasional clinician bemoaning what they refer to as the dilution of the transference, the degradation of the frame, but by and large psychoanalysts, certainly in this country, even if perhaps less so over the rest of the globe, have come to accept that this is the best we can do at the moment, the new normal. The unspoken implication seems to be that if a trained psychoanalyst works with a psychoanalytic mindset, that is with the willingness and ability to engage the transferential processes, that is psychoanalysis, regardless of whether the work takes place in the office, at a country estate, or in a bunker; regardless of whether the patient is lying on the couch or sitting face-to-face; regardless of whether we are in the same physical space or on Zoom or Skype.

Personally, I prefer to work with patients on the couch. I find that it facilitates reverie (even though I can stare out the window and watch the clouds in the sky with a patient sitting across from me all the same), but, in my experience, it is not always richer or deeper that way. With some, yes; with others, face-to-face communication can prove to be a treasure trove. What does the patient's facial expression communicate? What about their gestures or mine? What do they see in me that I am not aware of? This aspect of the work is further accentuated through video. We can both see a lot of detail, a blow-up. Just like in the 1966 Antonioni movie of the same name, on the enlarged copy we notice details that previously escaped attention. I learn so much! I also get a glimpse of the environment: the meticulously arranged furniture or the disarray; the poverty or the wealth of the interior.

In my opinion, the greatest flaw of remote work is the patients' lack of access to the office and the waiting room. They frequently contact us from their homes where they do not have sufficient privacy, surrounded by their customary environment, reminding them of their daily responsibilities. There is no commute, whether it be a five-minute walk or an hour-long train ride, an extension of the analytic process.

I hope that this unmitigated catastrophe will ultimately usher in a period of increased awareness of our fragility as a species, including our susceptibility to climate change, ruthless exploitation, and also a move toward a more democratic and egalitarian era of psychoanalysis. I hope that virtual therapy is here to stay and will remain a viable option for candidates and experienced practitioners alike. I hope that we can expand the reach of analytic treatment to underserved communities, members of which may not be able to trek multiple times a week to a desirable practice location, and facilitate the establishment of community psychoanalysis.

"But it is not psychoanalysis" has always been the battle cry of the elites, of the groups with the most power, who would tenaciously guard the gates of their professional affiliations to keep out the uninitiated in order to secure their continued prestige and financial rewards. Much has changed in this regard over the past few decades, but not nearly enough. I am looking forward to a post-corona, post-apocalyptic expansion of psychoanalysis for the people, by the people. I hope I will live to see the day.

Throughout my training and analyses, through teaching and writing, through discussions with colleagues, family, and friends, over time I have come to the conclusion that the defining historical event of my life was the Shoah, which had, in fact, concluded, at least in practical terms a decade before I was born. Every disappointment, every injury, all doubt, and despair were, however remotely, connected to that devastating and shameful period. I am not so sure anymore that this will continue to be the case. The coronavirus 2019 pandemic, the economic collapse, and the attendant shift in social awareness have ushered in a still-unfolding new paradigm.

The coronavirus has exposed the structural inequalities and exploitative nature of the human sphere across most of the planet. The process of depleting natural resources began some ten thousand years ago, with the arrival of settlement and agriculture. Nomadic hunter-gatherers and to some extent early settlers had respect for their environment and were aware that taking more than what they needed, including small amounts of sacrificial goods to appease their gods, would, in the end, damage or destroy the source of their sustenance. That respect has been long lost. Whatever dim awareness of the symbiotic interconnectedness between the human and the nonhuman lingered, was shattered by the advance of capitalism, especially its more ruthless, dissociated American manifestations.

During this pandemic the rich can shelter in luxury, members of the middle-class, whatever it exactly is, have enough comfort to work from their home or at least have access to safe transportation, the poor may perish. Through the Spring of 2020, in the New York area, where I live, at 7 pm sharp, people would open their windows, walk to their front doors, sit on the stoop, and hoot and clap in celebration of the workers deemed essential, who kept marching to their job-site, in spite of the enormous risk to life and limb. Initially, I enthusiastically joined the ranks of the clappers: this is the least I could do. But as it became increasingly obvious that, with the exception of some health care professionals, the people we were celebrating tended to belong to the lower ranks of society, often working for minimum wage, barely able to make ends meet, I came to the conclusion that this celebration was mostly a feel-good exercise of the privileged. All our clapping and banging our pots and pans in gratitude have not changed the structural inequality and lack of genuine concern. In fact, it may have helped alleviate our guilt over our participation and prevent more mutative action.

My whiteness

The acclaimed Nigerian author Chimamanda Ngozi Adichie reportedly stated that she did not identify as Black until she came to America. She became Black in the United States. She is not alone. Her sentiments are echoed by people from much of Africa, who have also lived in the United States: They did not think of themselves as Black until their arrival. They were Hausa or Igbo, or Yoruba, not Black. It is the historically determined racist social order, with all the discriminatory implications of a rigid caste system, that designated them Black.

Well, I had not known that I was White either until I landed on these shores. I was Hungarian and a little bit Jewish; a short, freckled woman with some further attributes. Having grown up in a largely monochrome society, I never thought of myself as White.

I have to assume that I was perceived as White upon arrival but this perception was lost on me at the time. In fact, it has taken me a long while to recognize and understand my whiteness. I grew up with what I assumed to be a progressive, fiercely egalitarian mindset, which eventually proved to be ahistorical, decontextualized, and inadequately suited to understand contemporary US social reality, particularly race relations. In retrospect, I wonder if this mentality was truly progressive, even in Hungarian, Eastern-European contexts. Denial of race relations allowed the long-standing ethnic tension in the region go without being addressed. Beyond virulent antisemitism, and the marginalization of the Roma, there were plenty of hostilities among Hungarians, Slovaks, Romanians, Croatians, etc.

I did not know about my white privilege either, nor did I think I was privileged, especially, not during all those years of poverty and odd jobs. Nor did I think I was privileged when I started social work school at New York University, where most of my classmates were white and monied women. There were bright-eyed and bushy-tailed 20-somethings, dedicated to saving the world, at least until they settled down in their suburban homes to have their 2.3 children and a dog. Then there were older, second-career or post-marriage, post-children ladies who financed their education with their trust funds, previous finance job savings, or their divorce settlements. How was this environment going to help me reckon with my whiteness and its attendant advantages? Yet, I was privileged all the same. And it wasn't just my whiteness. I came from a stable, educated family, my parents' pathologies notwithstanding. I, myself, had a university degree. I could afford all those years of slumming because instinctively I knew that, at least if I did not wait forever, I would have a lot to fall back on.

My racial education did not start in earnest until my Jewish Board days. At the clinic I had clients and colleagues of color, I had a couple of Black superiors. I was routinely drafted into cross-racial, back then referred to as multicultural, trainings, some outstanding, some less so. I wish I could say that I was a quick study but unfortunately that was not the case. Having been force-fed socialist PC lingo growing up, with the indoctrination starting in grade school, if not earlier I had (and still do) a great deal of aversion to having my language policed. Otherwise, I was good. I did not stop to consider that there was no otherwise. The language keeps the score, encrypting socio-historical heritage. Let me be clear, I am not even referring here to racial slurs, which would have never ever occurred to me to use; I am talking about the language of power, opportunity, subjugation. A case in point, is an evolution of terms from black to African American to Black, with a capital B. For years I questioned the utility of these changes, arguing – along with ever so many supposedly well-meaning liberals, mostly immigrants, who tend to be completely clueless about racism in the United States – that calling people African Americans will not change the basic racist social structure. Gradually I realized that I was wrong. Referring to groups of people in one way or another may not fundamentally change society but it has an impact, mostly by empowering versus disempowering. Besides, simply out of respect, every person needs to be addressed as they wish, whether it be Black, Latinx, queer, or they/them.

It's been a work in progress ever since. For a long time, I used to think that I was interpellated into whiteness: I did not come to the

United States because of its history of slavery and racial violence, I came IN SPITE OF IT. Except that this narrative conceals another truth. I came here because of the kind of country this is, or at least used to be, vast, rich, somewhat democratic, somewhat equalitarian. Which it was but not for people of color and especially not for Black Americans. Nachträglichkeit yet again: I chose to participate in a universe, which proved to be much more brutal and sinister than I had imagined. Like it or not, when I got off the plane at Kennedy International Airport, on September 16, 1980, I inherited four centuries of slavery and racialized brutality, with all the advantages afforded to me, as well as the guilt and the shame that come with this terrible legacy.

It is ironic that just as soon as my work at the Jewish Board helped me realize that I was a second-generation Holocaust victim/survivor, I had to start reckoning with my unwitting participation in a racially oppressive caste system. At first and for many years I believed that my own intergenerational trauma history allowed me to have an empathic understanding of the suffering of people of color, including Black Americans. And to a large degree, it did, and while I was naively un-self-aware, I did a good enough job with my Black patients. Recently though I have become more conscious of the unbridgeable experiential reality, what Knoblauch (2020) calls the socially constructed "uncanny gap" (p. 304) in the dialogue between Black and White. There are limits to my empathy and recognition. In this acknowledgment there is a kernel of hope: I can cede power and, in the end, perhaps I can develop a better-tuned ear.

The scene of the crime

Whenever I return to Budapest, I visit my parents' grave. I find the Jewish Cemetery there a beautiful and peaceful place. There are a lot of old, untended graves, much vegetation, bugs, not many people. I am very fortunate to have most of my family, including my parents and grandparents buried there. Only my uncle's body is missing: he was murdered in the Holocaust. Amongst the Hungarian Jewry, that is considered fortunate, and indeed, I am grateful.

The cemetery in Budapest with all its missing bodies is the representation of the original crime, perpetrated all over Europe during the 20th century, in Auschwitz, Mauthausen, Stalingrad, the Gulag, at the ghettos in Warsaw and Budapest, just to name a few fields of terror personally meaningful to me.

This is the crime scene I have been investigating all my life, with and without awareness. As I commented elsewhere (Csillag, 2014), the Bible's claim that God visits the iniquity of the fathers on the children to the third and fourth generation is what we mean by transgenerational transmission these days. It is an old concept in new clothes: in some cultures it goes by such names as fate and karma.

Bion (1992) tells us that the goal of psychoanalytic writing is not to report and describe, but to create an emotional experience in the reader that is very close to the emotional experience of the writer/analyst/analysand (Ogden, 2005). In these pages I have attempted to follow Bion's injunction and transmit a sense of my emotional states as analyst and analysand as well as a private and political citizen at various historical moments.

Note

1 The author gratefully acknowledges permission to republish the following material in this volume:Excerpt from "One Art" from POEMS by Elizabeth Bishop. Copyright © 2011 by The Alice H. Methfessel Trust. Publisher's Note and compilation copyright © 2011 by Farrar, Straus, and Giroux. Reprinted by permission of Farrar, Straus, and Giroux. All Rights Reserved. From *Complete Poems* by Elizabeth Bishop published by Jonathan Cape. Copyright © Alice Helen Methfessel 1983. Reprinted by permission of The Random House Group Limited.

References

Abraham, N. & Torok, M. (1984). "The lost object – Me": notes on identification with the crypt. *Psychoanal. Inq.*, *4*, 221–242.

Agamben, G. (1998). *Homo Sacer: Sovereign power and bare life* (D. Heller-Roazen, Trans.) Stanford, CA: Stanford University Press. (Original work published 1995)

Agamben, G. (2005). *State of exception*. (K. Attel, Trans.). Chicago, IL: The University of Chicago Press. (Original work published 2003).

Alvarez, A. (2006). Some questions concerning states of fragmentation: unintegration, disintegration, and the nature of early integrations. *J. Child Psychother.*, *2*, 158–180.

Apprey, M. (2014). A pluperfect Errand: a turbulent return to the beginnings in the transgenerational transmission of destructive aggression. *Free Assoc.: Psychoanal. Cult. Med. Group Pol.*, *66*, 15–28.

Baranger, W. (2009). The dead-alive: object structure in mourning and depressive states. In M. and W. Baranger, *The work of confluence: listening and interpreting in the psychoanalytic field* (pp. 203–216). London: Karnac.

Bass, A. (2014). Three Pleas for a measure on uncertainty, reverie, and private contemplation in the chaotic, interactive, nonlinier dynamic field of interpersonal/intersubjective relational psychoanal. *Psychoanal. Dial.*, *24*, 663–675.

Bion, W. R. (1962). *Learning from experience.* London: Tavistock.

Bion, W. R. (1967). *Second thoughts.* London: William Heinemann Medical Books limited.

Bion, W. R. (1982). *The long weekend: 1897-1919 (Part of a life)*, Bion F. editor. Abingdon: Fleetwood Press.

Bion, WR (1992). *Cogitations.* London: Karnac.

Bishop, E. (2008). *Poems, prose, and letters* (p. 166). New York: Farrar, Straus and Giroux.

Boulanger, G. (2004). Lot's wife, Cary Grant, and the American dream. *Contemp. Psychoanal*, *40*, 353–372.

Csillag, V. (2014). Ordinary sadism in the consulting room. *Psychoanal. Dial.*, *24*, 467–483.

Csillag, V. (2019). Impasse: dead souls. *Psychoanal. Q.*, *88*, 53–74.

Csillag, V. (2020). Dangerous liaisons: the time is out of joint. *Stud. Gend. Sex.*, *21*, 27–37.

Csillag, V. (2020). Esperanza and the melancholy of otherness: a discussion of "A country of two: race and social class in an immigrant therapeutic dyad". *Psychoanal. Dial.*, *30*, 102–109.

Davoine, F. & Gaudilliere, J. (2004). *History beyond trauma.* New York: Other Press.

Eigen, M. (1993). *The psychotic core.* Northvale, NJ, London: Jason Aronson.

Eng, D. L. & Han, S. (2000). A dialogue on racial melancholia. *Psychoanal. Dial.*, *10*, 667–700.

Etkind, A. (2009). Post-Soviet hauntology: cultural memory of the Soviet terror. *Constellations*, *16*, 182–200.

Fairbairn, W. D. (1952). *Psychoanalytic studies of the personality.* London: Tavistock Publications Limited.

Ferenczi, S. (1929). The unwelcome child and his death instinct. *Int. J. Psycho-Anal*, *10*, 125–129.

Freud, S. (1930). Civilization and its discontents. *S.E, XXI*, 57–146.

Frie, R. & Grand, S. (2019). Meeting across history. *Psychoanal. Dial.*, *29*, 151–158

Goldberger, M. (1993). "Bright spot," a variant of "blind spot". *Psychoanal. Quarterly*, *62*, 270–273.

Gonzalez, F. (2017). Iteration and homologies of difference: a discussion of Veronica Csillag's "Emmy Grant: Immigration as repetition of trauma and potential place". *Psychoanal. Dial.*, *27*, 480–486.

Gorney, J. E. (2004). *Division 39, publication of psychoanalysis* (pp. 43–45). American Psychological Association.

Grand, S. (2010). *The reproduction of evil: a clinical and cultural perspective.* Hillsdale, NJ: The Analytic Press.

Grand, S. (2019). Excitations of vengeance: the we-ness of history. *Psychoanal. Dial.*, *29*, 143–150.

Green, A. (1997). The intuition of the negative in *playing and reality*. *Int. J. Psycho-Anal*, *78*, 1071–1084.

Green, A. (1999). *The work of the negative* (A. Weller, Trans.), London: Karnac, Free Association Books.

Green, A. (2011). *Illusions and disillusions of psychoanalytic work* (A. Weller, Trans.), London: Karnac, Free Association Books.

Gumpel, Y. (1998). Reflections on countertransference in psychoanalytic work with child survivors of the Shoah. *J. Am. Acad. Psychoanal.*, *28*, 343–368.

Guralnik, O. & Simeon, D. (2010). Depersonalization: standing in the spaces between recognition and interpellation. *Psychoanal. Dial.*, *20*, 400–416.

Haraszti, G. (2006). Trapez a lejton. In: *Paper presented the Oktatas, elitek, zsidosag a 19–21. szazadban Conference*, Budapest, Hungary: December 15th, 2006.

Harris, A. (2019). The perverse pact: racism and white privilege. *Am. Imago*, *76*, 309–333.

Harries, R. (2003). *After the evil: Christianity and Judaism in the shadow of the Holocaust.* Oxford, UK: Oxford University Press.

Khouri, L. Z. (2012). The immigrant's neverland: Commuting from Amman to Brooklyn. *Contemp. Psychoanal*, *48*, 213–237.

Kovacs, A. (2008). *A masik szeme.* Budapest, Hungary: Gondolat.

Knoblach, S. H. (2020). Fanan's vision of embodied racism for psychoanalytic theory and practice. *Psychoanal. Dial.*, *20*, 299–316.

Lanzmann, C. (1991). The obscenity of understanding: an evening with Claude Lanzmann. *American Imago*, *48*, 473–495.

Layton, L. (2019). Transgenerational hauntings: toward a social psychoanalysis and an ethic of dis-illusionment. *Psychoanal. Dial.*, *29*, 105–121.

Levenson, E. A. (2017). The purloined self: interpersonal perspectives in psychoanalysis. *Edited by Alan Slomowitz*. London & New York: Routledge.

Lijtmayer, R. M. (2001). Splitting and nostalgia in recent immigrants: psychodynamic considerations. *J. Amer. Aced. Psychoanal.*, *29*, 427–438.

Lobban, G. (2006). Immigration and dissociation. *Psychoanal. Perspect.*, *3*, 73–92.

Machado, A. (1912). *Campos de Castilla* [Fields of Castile.] (V. Csillag, Trans.), Madrid: Renacimiento, p. 80.

Mbembe, A. (2003). Necropilitics. *Pub. Cult.*, *15*, 11–40.

Meszaros, J. (2010). Progress and persecution in the psychoanalytic heartland: antisemitism, communism and the fate of Hungarian psychoanalysis. *Psychoanal. Dial.*, *20*, 600–622.

Mitchell, S. A. & Harris, A. (2004). What's American about American? *Psychoanal. Dial.*, *14*, 165–191.

Ogden, T. H. (2005). On psychoanalytic writing. *Int. J. Psychoanal.*, *86*, 15–29.

Ogden, T. H. (2007). Elements of analytic style: Bion's clinical seminars. *Int. J. Psychoanal.*, *88*, 1185–1200.

Ogden, T. H. (2019). Ontologycal psychoanalysis or "What you want to be when you grow up?" *Psychoanal Q.*, *88*, 661–684.

Rozmarin, E. (2017). Immigration, belonging, and the tension between center and margin in psychoanalysis. *Psychoanal. Dial.*, *27*, 470–479.

Saketopoulou, A. (2014). To suffer pleasure: the shattering of the ego and the psychic labor of perverse sexuality. *Studies in Gender and Sexuality*, *15*, 254–268.

Saketopoulou, A. (2019). The draw to overwhelm: consent, risk and the re-translation of enigma. *J. Amer. Psychoanal. Assn.*, *67*, 133–167.

Seligman, S. (2014). Paying attention and feeling puzzled: the analytic mindset as an agent of therapeutic change. *Psychoanal. Dial.*, *24*, 648–662.

Spielrein, S. (1995). Destruction as a cause of becoming. *Psychoanal. Contemp. Thought*, *18*, 85–118.

Stein, R. (2008). Why perversion?: 'False love' and the perverse pact. *Int. J. Psychoanal.*, *86*, 775–799.

Subert, M. (2019). Motives and legacies behind 2008-2009 Hungarian Roma murders and apologies. *Contemp. Justice Rev.*, *22*, 3–22.

Sullivan, H. S. (1947). *Conceptions of modern psychiatry*. New York, NY: William Alanson White Psychiatric Foundation.

Symington, N. and J. (1996). *The clinical thinking of Wilfred Bion*. Chapter 7. London: Routledge.

Tolstoy, L. (1877/2001). *Anna Karenina*. Translated by R. Pevear & L. Volokhonsky, New York: Viking Penguin.

Vonnegut, K. (2011). *Novels & Stories 1963–1973* (pp. 804–805). New York: The Library of America.

Winnicott, D. W. (1949). Hate in the countertransference. *Int. J. Psycho-Anal.*, *30*, 69–74.

Winnicott, D. W. (1969). The use of an object and relating through identifications. *Int. J. Psycho-Anal.*, *50*, 711–716.

Chapter 4

Numbers, poetry, psychic truth: a journey from East to West, from mathematics to psychoanalysis

Katalin Lanczi

Generations

On a glorious spring morning in April 2018 I am standing on the top of a hill in the county of Zemplen, Hungary. This is wine country, home of the famous Tokay wines – and my father's birthplace. The views are as stunning as he had longingly described. We have walked up to a large statue of Christ, pride of the village; it is well signposted and visible from afar.

But there is an absence: the village synagogue. On a spring day in 1944, several hundred Jews were herded like cattle into the small building, crammed, barely able to breathe, to be transferred the following day to the ghetto in nearby Satoraljaujhely. From that ghetto they were, together with my grandparents, deported to Auschwitz. Most perished there, a few returned. Then, during the uprising of 1956, the synagogue was set on fire and the remaining Jews ran for their life – again. It lay derelict until recently when someone bought and rebuilt the ruins, creating a seasonal gallery. We are unable to find it: no signs, nor a presence on Google Maps. I note my fear of asking villagers for direction.

On descending from the hill we finally spot it behind high fences, its garden overgrown. I strain to read the barely visible plaque that briefly describes what happened in 1944. The contrast with the other monument is as stark as it is illustrative of contemporary Hungarian reality.

Aged four, I become friendly with a little girl in kindergarten. For some unfathomable reason neither her parents nor mine encourage the relationship. I feel hurt and baffled; very unusually, my parents

DOI: 10.4324/9781003306542-4

do not give an explanation. Only many years later do I realise that her family's name was a well-known far-right/aristocratic one. There was mutual recognition between the two families: we were on two sides of history.

I shall explore, *après-coup* as it were, my experience, mostly incomprehensible at the time, of growing up in Budapest in the shadow of the Shoah, in a country where Jews and non-Jews lived side by side, together and yet divided by a starkly different experience of recent history. I felt both at home and not. It was where everything started, but it is not where I am now, emotionally, professionally, linguistically. It has been a long journey.

This journey has taken me from Eastern to Western Europe and from mathematics to psychoanalysis. My chapter will focus on these two journeys to some extent separately and thematically; there is a free-associative aspect to my account and each of the journeys will, inevitably, have its own chronology. Interspersing the account will be references to my two analyses, each in their own way having a fundamental impact on my understanding of these journeys.[1]

The author

Survival

I was born in 1955 – ten years after the end of the Second World War. For a child this seemed like a long time. As I got older, I realised with increasing pain that, for my family, the Persecution (as Grandma Stefi called it) was a recent event, seared into their memories. "Dear old Vally, she endured Auschwitz" – said Grandma Stefi, with affection and sorrow about my other grandmother. Stefi survived the German occupation of Hungary in Yellow Star houses and then the Budapest ghetto. Vally, though, bore the dubious epithet of "a survivor of Auschwitz".

Dear old Vally, she was difficult to love; she was, indeed, difficult. Argumentative, controlling, always on the lookout for a bit of persecution. Still, these days I appreciate her fortitude, her love of her plants and of nature – a greater love than of people, I suspect.

Grandma Vally, my paternal grandmother, was a survivor, with all the guilt this entailed. So were my parents and my maternal grandparents, Stefi and Menyhert. What had it taken to survive? The extended family had disappeared, without trace, great uncles and aunts, most of my parents' cousins, more than a hundred people, among them my paternal grandfather, Aladar. They "died in the war" – the specifics did not appear until later.

Survival has been a central theme in my life. A high dose of the wish to survive is necessary to flourish as an émigré and to "survive as an object" the repeated "destructions" heaped upon me by my patients (Winnicott, 1969).

Are we Jews? Are we Hungarians?

I was 11 when I "discovered" that I was Jewish, but many of my contemporaries were unaware of their origins (Erős et al., 1985, Erős, 1993).

We were not religious; bizarrely perhaps, on Christmas Eve, under the tree, we ate jellied carp and home-made challah, genuine Shabbat dishes. I can still smell Grandma Vally's fragrant, braided challah. There was no religious content, no songs and certainly no baby Jesus. Only *après-coup* did I comprehend the frisson of the forbidden and the pain of the underlying loss. It was certainly different from the celebrations, cheerful and reverent, among my non-Jewish friends.

There was no denial of our roots and, indeed, the impact of the Shoah, once my parents felt I was old enough to know. A contemporary of mine, not Jewish, recalls when I announced that "I am Jewish!". I too remember the excitement (relief? fear?). And then the stories of unthinkable brutality emerged, gradually: narrow escapes and unprocessed losses.

Besides these losses, less often remembered in the Shoah literature, was the profound loss of a culture and a way of life: the centrality of Jewish practice, the arrival of Shabbat celebrated with passion on Friday nights, the memories of joyful celebrations of the festivals, the music, the food, the colour, were all related to me with a mix of painful nostalgia, irreversible loss – and pride.

Both my parents grew up in observant, though not orthodox families in the interwar years. Most of their friends were Jews. They considered themselves Hungarian – Hungarian Jews: they spoke only Hungarian at home.

Though they remembered these celebrations with much pleasure and appreciation, my parents were militant atheists. They had both "tested God": eating bread during Pesach or sampling a bacon sandwich. *HaShem* did not respond so they concluded he did not exist.

Assimilation: an illusion?

Sunshine, an epic movie about four generations of Hungarian Jews (1999, dir. István Szabó) addresses the problem of assimilation vividly.[2] Each generation is a little more assimilated than the one before. Ignatz Sonnenschein changes his Jewish/German name to a Hungarian one when he is told it is an obstacle to becoming a judge. His brother Gustav also changes his name; as a member of the Communist Party, he feels his Jewish roots are irrelevant. In the 1930s Ignatz's son, Adam, a talented fencer, joins the top fencing club, run by the army, where the price of admission is further assimilation via conversion to Catholicism. As the anti-Jewish laws gather pace, he is expelled from the club. Even as he is taken to a labour camp, he refuses to accept that he is one of the Jews, repeating his mantra: "I am a Hungarian Olympic champion and a Roman Catholic". He is strung up on a tree, cruciform and, hosed with water, he freezes to death: the crucified Jew.

Is Jewish assimilation possible? Is it even desirable? This question remained a central problem for generations of Hungarian Jews and until the Shoah, they, like the first generation in the movie, lived out the narrative that they were Hungarians, and Jewish "by religion".

How would one understand assimilation in psychoanalytic terms? Is it imitation? Or identification? Imitation appears early in the infant's life and gradually it develops, through introjections, into more mature forms of identification. Assimilation, then, could be seen as indicating a genuine wish to belong, to identify with, to be part of the nation but other times it might represent a defensive wish to imitate or incorporate (Gaddini, 1969, Greenacre, 2011).

In the movie Adam is an example of the latter: becoming "a true Hungarian" blinds him to the reality of Nazism during the Berlin Olympics. His action represents "assimilation" demanded by the Other as the price of acceptance and success. The acceptance is, by definition, conditional, as generations of Jews have discovered throughout the centuries.[3]

I think my family believed that they could retain their Jewish identity while expressing their love for the language – their mother tongue – and the culture. In their mind, they were part of the nation. After all, even my great-grandparents were born in Hungary, or, in any case in the Austro-Hungarian Monarchy.

My grandparents were bright but not educated beyond their teens. My maternal grandfather grew up in abject poverty and at the age of 12 left school to assist his parents in their small village shop. My other grandparents came from well-to-do farming backgrounds or from families who ran small businesses. In common with many Jewish families, they saw education of their children – my parents – as the next step towards assimilation (cf. Oz, 2004).

"Get out of the kitchen – you must study" was my great-grandmother's much-repeated injunction: it was thus that my mother did not learn to cook until much later and never came to enjoy it.

My mother grew up in Budapest, though her parents had only recently arrived there from Debrecen, Eastern Hungary. She attended an academically outstanding Jewish girls' school – described earlier in the trialogue – a haven, free of the otherwise ever-growing and often violent antisemitism in state schools. The girls dreamt of becoming teachers, lawyers, doctors or artists and academic achievement was valued and celebrated. The fees were on a significantly sliding scale; nevertheless, my grandfather struggled to pay these from his small haberdashery business: essentially, he was a peddler, a travelling salesman.

My father grew up in the aforementioned provincial market town, Satoraljaujhely. The substantial Jewish community maintained primary schools but there was only one secondary school in town, run by the Piarists, a Catholic teaching order. The Catholic boys did not mix with their Jewish peers. The priest-monks, their teachers, represented the whole spectrum of national attitudes towards Jews. The virulently antisemitic Father T. regularly bullied and humiliated the Jewish boys. Characteristically, I learned this not from my father, but from one of his school friends. My father preferred to reminisce about Father R., who said, on their final day at school in June 1939, "Love each other, boys, don't look for the difference but treasure your common humanity. Our Lord Jesus commanded us to love, not hate". Most of the teachers were just indifferent to the bullying and discrimination. Appreciating what was best of the school's milieu, he had a particular sensibility towards Christian culture, church music, writers and poets whose work was deeply rooted in this, the dominant culture. He had no hope of attending university, as the "*numerus clausus*" specified the percentage of Jewish students (6%). Only Jews with connections or money would be able to attend henceforth.

My parents' Jewish identity was strong. They had passionately supported the State of Israel, a passion I, too, have retained, through thick and thin – mainly very thin these days. My mother played Queen Esther in Racine's play, staged by the school, to celebrate the establishment of the State of Israel in 1948. As a member of a Zionist socialist group, she was preparing for Aliyah. One day, aged 17, her father dragged her away from a meeting, shouting: "How could you contemplate leaving your parents and ageing grandparents? Have we not had enough losses already"? Had they not?

The hands of history: Jews and Gentiles

"I grew up overnight on 19 March 1944, a week after my 14th birthday", said my mother about the arrival of the German army. Her school soon closed, yellow stars became mandatory and mixing with the outside world was marred by a painful sense of exclusion.

By then my father had been in a forced-labour battalion for two years. Instead of conscription into the Hungarian army, Jewish boys were formed into labour battalions under the (mostly brutal) supervision of the army.

Deportation to Belsen was delayed until Christmas 1944, due to the resistance of his superior officer who declared that these were *"my stinking Jews"*. In his view they were Hungarians, and he was not going to allow "the bloody Germans to ransack my beloved Christian Hungary". After the war, the survivors of the unit gratefully invited the officer to a reunion. He declined, stating that he would not share food or drinks with Jews.

In Belsen, my father and his two childhood friends were placed in a barrack of "politicals", Dutch and German communists and partisans; those for Jews were "full". The other inmates were organised and had outside contacts; conditions were somewhat better here. Transported to Terezin towards the end of the war, he was liberated by the Soviet army – I think his politics owed much to these experiences.

My mother, her little sister, parents and grandparents ended up in the Budapest ghetto as bombs rained on the city. Their final piece of dry bread eked out to last for days now gone, they were waiting to die. When the first Soviet soldier arrived and eyed up Grandma Stefi – only 36 then – and left, they feared he would be coming back for her later. Instead, he reappeared with a bottle of apricot jam, declaring in broken Hungarian "beautiful woman", and told them to go home.

My paternal grandparents arrived in Auschwitz in June 1944. It was here that Aladar, the grandfather I never knew, was sent immediately to the gas chambers by Mengele. He vanished without a trace and I was not even able to picture him – not until the late 1960s when two photos of him emerged from distant friends. From Grandma Vally I heard about Mengele's white gloves and manicured hands – and about his magnetic, satanic power.

Nearly 70% of Hungarian Jewry were exterminated. Adolf Eichmann's efforts (Arendt, 1951) were aided by the zeal of thousands of Hungarian clerks and railwaymen, who embraced the Final Solution with the enthusiastic assistance of the police, gendarmery and army.

People my family had considered friends or friendly acquaintances turned their backs, neighbours refused to accept their greetings and watched their humiliation with glee or simply passive acceptance. They described this betrayal to me with palpable pain and anger.

Only a small number of Jews survived in hiding, mostly in Budapest; just a tiny proportion of Jews were offered sanctuary by the churches or individuals.

When the surviving members of the family returned, their homes were either occupied or had been looted. Through a devastated, ruined city littered with dead bodies and dismembered half-eaten horses, my mother staggered home from the Budapest ghetto. Here a young neighbour greeted her: "I thought you were all dead, but you are back! What a shame … ". My father, returning from the camps, discovered that a man had taken up residence in the family home. Unusually among survivors, he threatened to kill the occupier, clutching a non-existent gun in his pocket. "But how?" I would later enquire. He had no idea, but the bluff worked and the man left. The house was empty, the garden dug up and plundered.

After the war a short, heroic period of rebuilding the country followed: a multiparty system, free assembly and freedom of religious practice; however, the Communist Party gradually discredited, destroyed or incorporated the other parties and by 1948 it established a one-party, Stalinist state.

There was no more talk about the Shoah; the word "Jew" had disappeared from the public domain. The survivors – as survivors of massive psychic trauma often do – just wanted to live and not dwell too deeply on the past. In any case, no ethnic or religious groups were encouraged to organise themselves into independent community groups until well after the 1956 uprising. In that sense Jews were no exception: the Roma, religious minorities, even the main Christian churches could only operate in a restricted space until the late 1960s. There were many silences: about the losses, the Hungarian contribution to the Shoah, the Soviet army's raping and pillaging of the country and its population.

The 1956 uprising exposed the Stalinist crimes but at times also descended into ugly violence: teenagers – the "Budapest lads" – were roaming the streets with guns "liberated" from army barracks, facilitating summary executions of those suspected to have worked with the secret police.

My parents believed that, after the war, the country had changed and antisemitism was in the past, but there it was – again. It has often been stated that antisemitism was not a significant element in the uprising (Szakolczai, 2008; Kovacs, 2008). Certainly, there were no pogroms and no *official* persecution, but synagogues were burnt and Jewish apartments such as ours were marked one night, presumably to prepare for "action". Neighbours of Grandma Vally refused to return her greetings (again!), swastikas and yellow stars surfaced on the walls around the city. My mother's office at the university was defaced with a note: "Jew, go home!". (Home? Where exactly?) During the ten days of the uprising there were dozens of atrocities registered initially and some more were added by researchers later – the "small ones" that directly involved my family and their friends were not even on the list (Standensky, 2000).

The second generation

Prolonged experiences of helplessness, humiliation, terror and hunger cannot fully be conveyed in words. It was, however, present in much of the communication of my family, in the "transgenerational at-mosphere" (Bako & Zana, 2018).

We lived in a state of readiness: in action, body and memory. *We* might have to run, *we* might have to confront those in power, re-presented by doctors, concierges, the authorities – this was the "we experience" described by Bako and Zana. Battling with the labyr-inthine "socialist" healthcare, queueing for food and, later, for better clothes were discussed extensively in the family. "Winning" these battles were shared and celebrated as *our* victories.

By then my grandfather went to synagogue on high and holy days only, but he insisted on saying a blessing over me each time I left the country on holiday. Perhaps he was unconsciously seeking to protect me – as it seems to me now – from his associations of trains and journeys and his profound death anxiety. Ordinary occurrences such as a train journey hid a dark, other reality and the "phantoms" of the past (Abraham & Torok, 1984) were, looking back now, perpetually present.

My first memory: I am three years old, on holiday with my mother and grandmother. Out on a walk, an unexpected hailstorm and ter-rifying lightning prompt them to knock on the door of a stranger. I remember the storm, the discomfort, the atmosphere of anxiety in that alien house, the suspicion and hostility of the hosts as we were made to stand in the hallway. It seems striking that this should be my first memory: being in danger, barely accepted by the world, struggling to survive in a storm.

Later I had a recurring dream that disappeared only during my first analysis. In the dream, I am running for my life, all alone, usually along the river Danube. I wake up in terror. Like all dreams, this too is multi-layered and overdetermined, but, as I later discovered, it is hauntingly similar to one of my mother's dreams. She dreamt, repeatedly, about carrying a baby on her back, running away from the river. This harked back to her actual experience of being marched to the frozen Danube. She was 14 then, but in her dream, she is a mother. There is a tele-scoping of time: her current life as a mother, her witnessing of murders as a child and her wish to protect both her own baby self and her baby, me. Her dream, never with a happy ending, was an only partially symbolised reflection of actual events.

In reality that march to the Danube, where thousands of Budapest Jews were massacred – an event that is now memorialised by the sculptures "The Shoes on the Danube Bank" (Can Togay/Gyula Pauer, 2005) – ended miraculously for my mother and her family. The sobs of her little sister, then aged eight, caught the attention of a young Hungarian fascist. Exclaiming: "Jesus and Mary, you look just like my little sister!", he let them slip away.

Massive psychic trauma: thinking about the unthinkable

Although Niederland had coined the phrase "survivor syndrome" in the 1960s (Niederland, 1968), it was in 1983, during my first psy-chotherapy training, that I discovered the growing psychoanalytic literature about Shoah survivors and the second generation (Bergmann & Jucovy, 1982) though I was already familiar with some of the literary contributions (Levi, 1959, etc). I was allocated (chose?) a presentation for a seminar on massive psychic trauma. By then I had spent a couple of years in analysis talking about growing up in a survivor family.

It gradually dawned on me that what had happened to European Jewry had cast a long shadow on my world, both internal and ex-ternal; it had become an indelible part of my identity. George Steiner eloquently describes the inescapable reality of this "black mystery" in his essay "A kind of survivor". (Steiner, 1958).

I devoured everything I could find on the subject (Kestenberg, 1980, Grubrich-Simitis 1981, 1984).[4] Many of the themes seemed familiar, such as the "intensity of parenting" (Kestenberg), a central feature of my childhood. Survival could not be taken for granted and this led to symbiotic parent–child relationships (Barocas & Barocas, 1979) where the development of a separate sense of self was experienced as potentially threatening by parents and children alike. There were messages about dangers, especially of aggression and of the need to restrain any wish to challenge parents; being a "good girl" was expected and rewarded.

As babies, we may have unconsciously reminded our parents of their unspeakable helplessness and therefore became receptacles of their terrors. If "fortunate", many – including myself – also witnessed their determination to undo their traumas and provide us a childhood that was free of those terrors. The conscious wish and the unconscious projection went hand in hand.

Research suggests that parents' ability to empathically discuss their experiences was a powerful indicator of the resilience of the second generation. I feel much gratitude for my family's willingness to share, appropriately, gradually and openly what they could, although their shame about helplessness, humiliation and about what it took to survive could only be transmitted unconsciously.

Mourning and its vicissitudes

What could not be faced was diverted into a certain manic energy. The wish to live and succeed was profound and my parents, on the surface, did this quite successfully: they held down several jobs to make ends meet; they did not sleep much.[5]

My grandfather Menyhert was a workaholic too. His little haberdashery business, considered a capitalist enterprise in 1948, was taken away by the Stalinist state so he found a job with the National Press Office where he stayed until retirement. This involved the same travelling he had done working for himself and the same selling tactics. He won, year after year, the medal for "Distinguished Socialist Worker".

But loss was never far away. My maternal grandparents' home had a sense of subtle gloom about it. They struggled with psychosomatic illnesses and some hypochondria; they were rarely able to talk about the murder of siblings, nieces and nephews. At family events, with so much wonderful food, there seemed to be the haunting presence of those absent. Even though we had limited resources, there was always abundance on the table. Though this is often part of Jewish culture, I now think there were other reasons: it was as if it had been cooked for a much larger family and also as if we might starve otherwise. The habit has remained with me to this day.

I now recognise the problem of unfinished mourning, ever-present in my family and so convincingly observed among survivors in the psychoanalytic literature. Those who died in such unspeakable circumstances and could not be buried could not be gradually relinquished or mourned either. Death was experienced as defeat. Later, members of my family each struggled to face their own death and say goodbye to those dying. (Klein, 1940).

In *1945,* a recent Hungarian film (2017, dir. F Török), a father and son, Shoah survivors, return to a village from where all the Jews have been deported. Their aim is to bury religious and domestic objects and toys left behind by their murdered families. Their silent dignity, impressive as it is in the movie, does not portray the more common difficulty with mourning I have observed both among survivors and us, their children.

The villagers struggle with feelings of fear and shame and with manic denial. Most of them have benefitted from the disappearance of their Jewish neighbours: they have taken their properties, their furniture, their animals. The Catholic priest tells a parishioner wishing to confess his terrible guilt that he should just "put it behind him"; the man hangs himself. Some cannot mourn because they have not faced their crimes, those who do seem isolated, disturbed, heartbroken.

The inability to face guilt and to mourn among the non-Jewish population at large had its reasons: many lost sons and husbands, properties and livelihoods. All endured a succession of occupying armies, first German and then Soviet. The siege of Budapest left most buildings damaged, bridges destroyed; its inhabitants spent months in cellars, hungry and frightened.

The lack of mourning demonstrated in research in Germany (Mitscherlich & Mitscherlich, 1975) applies to Hungary equally. The authors propose that, although much discussion of the Third Reich had taken place in West Germany after the war, most individual Germans were unable to face their own contribution to it and persisted with a denial of their complicity in the Shoah (see also Jaspers, 1946, Frie, 2017, Fulbrook, 2018). The scale of death and destruction in Germany had contributed to their inability to work through their guilt. The undoubtable reality of the Hungarian tragedy, the destruction, repeatedly, in fact over centuries, of the fabric of society, its buildings, values and language, has, it seems to me, similarly interfered with the nation's ability to accept and mourn the reality of the Shoah and to face personal culpability (cf. Sereny, 2001).

Lies and more lies

I happened to be visiting Budapest during the first free elections in 1990. There was such excitement, such hope: posters advertising the new parties: familiar faces, the leaders of the "democratic opposition" aka "dissidents", people I had known well, beaming down from them. Back in the late 1970s we had attended the same underground meetings, read the same *samizdat* literature, hoped against hope as it seemed then, for the same changes – a democratic, European, free country. It was as if, finally, our hopes had come true. But the hope was, as in 1945, short-lived. The lack of democratic traditions seemed to prevent building our dream country, and soon there was infighting and an inability to compromise.

The rewriting of history started almost immediately (Judt, 1992).[6] The role of Admiral Horthy,[7] Hungarian complicity in the Shoah, the history of the 1956 uprising – all rewritten. Old friendships frayed as newspaper articles were published about "the Jews", and discussions about "Jews and Hungarians" became commonplace. "Jews and Hungarians ... so we are not Hungarians?" asked my anguished mother. It was as if group identifications began to crystallise in starkly different directions, increasingly separating Jews from the majority of non-Jews, the two groups interpreting history in different terms.[8] A member of the government raised "the Jewish question" in

Parliament and it became acceptable, even respectable, to wonder whether there were too many Jews in the professions, the press, the judiciary.

There were "reasons" – there always are – for Hungarian anti-semitism, among them that Jews were felt to be responsible for the Soviet occupation. Indeed, the first leaders of the "socialist" dictatorship had been Jews, newly returned from exile. They had been activists in the tiny Communist Party, the most vocal opposition to growing fascism in the 1930s and 1940s, or else they had fought in the Spanish Civil War.

Many of this small group had gone into exile to avoid arrest, torture, execution. Among them was my great-aunt, who did not return from Siberia till 1947 where she had been made to work as a nurse in harsh circumstances. She was unrecognisable: her beautiful soprano voice now a smoky tenor, her blonde hair dark and wiry, her body showing signs of a meagre diet.

Growing up, I observed examples of casual antisemitism among parents and grandparents of friends but no conscious awareness of their guilt. Facing that would remain the task of the next generation, and my non-Jewish friends made valiant efforts to understand and acknowledge this burden, but they represent only a small minority in the Hungarian landscape.

Identification and opposition

After the Shoah, many Jews, like Ivan, the protagonist of *Sunshine*, joined the Communist Party, as did my father who believed fervently that he was helping to build a new world, in which discrimination and prejudice will cease to exist, as would the abject poverty many millions endured in the inter-war years.[9]

Both my parents accepted the show trials in the early 1950s as genuine, and on the day Stalin died my mother wept. When they discovered the truth, the guilt and shame were unmistakable, but sometimes deflected with sentences like "Yes, but the communist aspirations were admirable, if utopian".

My mother never joined the Party and this contributed to difficulties in her career, but she remained committed to the best aspects of the socialist dream. My father's communist beliefs changed over the years. Never a functionary, he became increasingly disillusioned but felt that changing things from the inside was his only possible choice.

I became an enthusiastic Pioneer (the "socialist" version of the Scouts), did the marching, sang the songs. My father, though, was absolutely clear during my teenage years of enthusiasm that he did not want me to join the Party.

I got into trouble early. I was nine and Miss D, my form teacher, young and pretty, disliked me intensely. When she set us homework to write a one-page essay about "what would you like to be when you grow up" I wrote three pages about becoming an astronaut, inspired by Valentina Tereshkova, the first Soviet female astronaut. Miss D. crossed out pages two and three in red ink and my little essay was marked "unacceptable, rewrite!". My mother, bewildered and enraged, asked why, only to be told: "Your daughter does not comply with the socialist ethos. She must limit her imagination and accept reality" (Sebek, 1996). The message was clear: do not excel, restrain your ambitions, fit in. Under the gaze of Miss D., I was also mercilessly bullied for being unable to jump over ropes and vaulting tables – perceived by me, a clumsy child, as instruments of torture. While the children taunted me, Miss D. adjusted her lipstick.

My mother, always a survivor, always with the right connections, moved me to another school, Fazekas, the school where the three authors of this book met. Here, academic achievement was valued, the socialist rhetoric lightly worn.

In my teens I became an activist in the Communist Youth Association at school. Membership was compulsory but, ever a bossy organiser, I became a leader. And then I "discovered" that we had been duped: the so-called student democracy was a sham and entirely controlled by Mrs R., the Deputy Head. I began to advocate an alternative, independent organisation. Mrs R. told my parents that "youngsters like your daughter became counter-revolutionaries in 1956". My parents, united in their outrage, refused to continue the conversation.

I learnt, many years later, that my peer, the Secretary of the Communist Youth Association – who, after regime change, became a prominent member of government – had denounced me as dangerous and refused to endorse my application to university. I was saved only by the good offices of the headmaster, who insisted that I be given a recommendation for my chosen course, to study English and Hungarian literature and linguistics.

He was from an ethnic German background and, after the war, as a child, had been deported with his family to a remote corner of Hungary, for "fascist activities". He was a mathematician, and grateful that he could attend evening school in the 1950s where my mother taught him, unpaid. This was her contribution to "liberating the working class". He never forgot my mother's outstanding teaching and was equally impressed that my mother, rather than bearing grudges towards ethnic Germans, showed an ability to identify with his childhood suffering. He admitted children who had been excluded, bullied or mistreated at their previous schools. As I discovered later, he also appointed teachers whose careers had been marred by "suspicious political activities" and whom other schools refused to employ.

But the ground had already begun to shake under our feet before then, during the six-day Arab–Israeli war in 1967. For the first time in my life my parents' and grandparents' political discussions, informed by my father's accounts of banned and jammed radio stations, were at variance with the official line.

At this time, bizarrely, I witnessed the support my grandfather received from his antisemitic neighbours. Hardly acknowledging him before, they now came to shake his hand and congratulate him: "You Jews showed it to the Russkies– they could not defeat you". (This was a reference to the Arab armies, aided by the Soviet military in their aggressive invasion, now being defeated by the Israeli army, supported by the American military; a Cold War story *par excellence*.)

And then, on a dazzling August morning in 1968, the radio announced that "the glorious Warsaw Pact armies entered Czechoslovakia, on the invitation of the Czechoslovak leadership" I saw my father cry for the first time in my life.

But these events in my early teens had not yet negated my desire to fit in and contribute to the socialist dream; that came after my disillusion with school democracy. Soon after I entered university, I cancelled my membership of the Communist Youth Association, a membership that was the default position. Instead, I was now becoming involved with dissident groups, dreaming of freedom.

Sex and resistance, in that order

I hovered around the periphery of dissident groups. I went to many of the meetings and read *samizdat* literature but had neither the courage to take too many risks nor the required trendiness to belong.

The world of dissidents, though appealing and often brave, was not a particularly comfortable one. I experienced it as claustrophobic and often judgemental. During my last year at university I attended a course on radio journalism and was invited to work for TV: it was a coveted job, but the wife of one of the dissident leaders warned me that if I wanted to remain part of her world, I must not take the job. Too establishment, she insisted, too much of a compromise with the regime.

Many in this world were sexually very promiscuous. Adultery or sleeping with several people in quick succession was the norm. It was barren emotionally and, despite the sophisticated radical chic, quite enervating for men and often exploitative of women. Although the main victims were women, who internalised the demand to be "free", the men suffered too: their partners took them at their word and cheated on them, sometimes with their best friends. In hindsight, the sexual activity appears to me to have been a manic evasion of deep and pervasive depression, personal but also social. Indeed, many in the group were deeply depressed, suicide attempts were not un-common, nor were excessive drinking and smoking.

Undoubtedly, similar sexual politics operated in many circles in the West also, but alternative choices were less available to us. A friend from New York visited me in the late 1970s. He had grown up on Central Park West, in liberal/left circles and was used to the post-1960s mores there. He was somewhat surprised to observe the manic promiscuity of my world.

I taught English to a man who worked – when he was not un-employed, which was mostly – in the film industry. He had been in prison for a while after 1956, accused of "clerico-fascist" activities. Seventeen at the time, he had participated in initiatives to reopen Catholic schools. Through him I became acquainted with another alternative circle, mostly consisting of *déclassé* artists, bohemian creatives, some Catholic anti-communists and some openly gay men. This was the first time I had knowingly encountered gay people in Hungary, free within the group but absolutely hidden outside it.

In the eyes of the authorities and the public at large, at that time being gay was hardly different from being a dissident.

While homosexuals were closeted, heterosexual sex was seen by the general population as an area of "freedom". Many exercised this, the only freedom, without much restraint and yet hotel rooms could only be rented by married couples. The regime seemed to be preoccupied with the sexual mores of the people – or perhaps simply wished to control them, in contrast with the anti-bourgeois rhetoric in the early days of the communist movement.

In the 1990s, I asked to see my secret police file. After a long wait, a thin A4 envelope arrived, containing the statement of a single informant describing, spot-on, what he saw as my "regular attendance but marginal activity" in dissident circles. He did specifically mention two visits from M., presumably the person of real interest, whom he had followed to my apartment. M. had been tortured and imprisoned in 1956, accused of "anti-socialist activities". He had been a student leader but never possessed firearms. He came to my apartment twice, not to organise political activities, but to invite me to join his *soirees*, which were, in fact, orgies of a sort. I declined and he gave up: not exactly the stuff of heroic political activity.

The "West" beckons

Only a small part of my university course was enjoyable, almost entirely within the English Department, in our minds representing "Western" culture. Here I encountered a few teachers who were original thinkers. Their views were influenced by experiences while on scholarship studies in the West. A truly memorable seminar leader, A., now a friend, made linguistics, a discipline I had little interest in, a fascinating subject. American Studies was possibly the most stimulating and Prof. G., an expert in contemporary American poetry, introduced me to the work of Emily Dickinson and Denise Levertov.

I wrote my thesis on Levertov. Her interests – dreams, the internal world, psychoanalysis, mysticism, faith – appealed to me as did her ancestors, among them a Welsh mystic and a Hassidic rabbi. But, above all, not much had been written about her as yet, so I did not have to chew my way through volumes of literary criticism, an academic activity I did not relish.

The Hungarian Department was dominated by faithful party members and many of our professors were mediocre, but an important link with my future career choice emerged in my passion for the inter-war poet Attila Jozsef (1905–1937). It was through studying him that I first encountered psychoanalysis, which he linked in an original way with his interest in Marxism. He wrote several poems about his analysis and even a poem for Sigmund Freud's 80th birthday. His analyst – among many other Jewish Hungarians – emigrated to London and decades later I met an elderly colleague who had known her well.

One of the most memorable experiences in the Hungarian department was my participation in seminars on the nineteenth-century Russian novel, in the context of a course on European literature, led by Prof. E. In his late fifties, he was charismatic, charming, manipulative. He amassed a group of wide-eyed followers, hungry for discussions about Tolstoy's vision of a peasant-led utopia rather than the stale rhetoric of the "socialist" ideology fed to us daily. His explication of Dostoyevsky's focus on his characters' internal world – especially in *The Brothers Karamazov* – was illuminating and challenging. He was a faithful Catholic and spoke about this with unusual and bewitching candour. I have retained my passion for Russian literature and my appreciation of Christianity and its place in European culture ever since. Sadly, he also liked to groom young women in the group and engage them in sexual activities. I would not comply and he accepted this with grace until I complained to him about his involvement with fellow students. He labelled these as signs of my jealousy and I dropped out of his seminars.

Half-way through university, aged 20, I stayed for six months in Boston, Mass., with old university friends of my mother. Initially my application for an exit visa was turned down. but some connections helped, as was the way. My father contacted an old acquaintance at the relevant ministry and asked why my application had been rejected. "Because young women like your daughter don't return", he responded. My father commented, sarcastically, that the comrade seemed to lack faith in our socialist system – and I got the permit. In effect, the double-edged comment implied the promise that I would, indeed, return.

I loved being in the United States, "the land of hope, the multicultural melting pot" as I saw it then, its sense of freedom and opportunity. A very partial truth but, in comparison with life in the Soviet bloc, a truth nevertheless, at least for white Americans and "white" immigrants, among them generations of persecuted European Jews who gradually but not without much discrimination, became "white" (Brodkin, 2000).

I improved my English there, although on my return to university in Budapest I was told to unlearn the American accent I had acquired; we were expected to speak "the Queen's English".

In Boston I attended classes on American literature and cultural history. I also became aware, for the first time, of psychoanalytically informed literary criticism and social theory.

The US seemed endlessly exciting. I travelled by "Grey Rabbit" (Greyhound was too expensive) across the country. For three days we talked, ate and slept on the floor in a decrepit school bus with no seats.

I did not want to return to Hungary. I had the offer of sponsorship from my host, an academic, and a possible university place with a scholarship. It was truly heart-breaking to leave Boston. But how could I have left my parents behind? The old, familiar theme ... At that time, if one left "illegally" the family would be penalised for many years: no exit permits, no meetings with their loved ones.

I longed to be "free" and to see the world. Our world was restrictive: we lacked the essentials of civil society, taken for granted in the West – free press, unrestricted assembly, freedom of speech and an open culture. Still, by the 1970s we were allowed *some* travel and had the opportunity to see Western art movies, attend avant-garde theatre performances and "subversive" poetry readings. In "the happiest barrack in the Soviet bloc", often also described as "goulash communism", there were no food shortages and we could talk relatively openly about our discontent, at least in private, as long as we stayed within certain invisible walls (cf Walls (1968), film directed by Andras Kovacs). Outside the walls, vocal dissidents were mercilessly harried by the authorities.

I struggled to feel a true sense of belonging. In my early twenties I engaged in sociographical trips to collect objects of folk history. I participated in researching the life of the Roma and travelled extensively around rural Hungary. I loved – I still love – the language. I recited poetry and sang folk songs, I had friends who were not

Jewish; it was, and has remained, important to me to understand other cultures, alternative ways of life, different family atmospheres. But the more I knew the less I felt at home. It was mine – and it was not. What *had* truly been mine had been destroyed.

After graduation, on a trip to London, I met and fell in love with my future husband, a Brit and left Hungary "legally". Emigration via marriage to an Englishman assisted my acculturation. He was at home and took for granted his roots however ambivalent he was at times about them. A left-wing Anglo-Catholic, deeply committed both politically and in his religious practice, he knew a great deal about the Torah (much more than me, in fact). He was also surprisingly knowledgeable about life in the Soviet bloc, notwithstanding the fact that he had not visited it until then; *some* of his knowledge, admittedly, came from Len Deighton and John le Carré spy novels.

Once in London, I found that no one could read my accent, my clothes, my education to immediately identify my background in the way they could in Budapest. I was no longer "boxed in": I felt magically free. But I was still searching for a home.

Emigration: new life, old losses

As might be obvious by now, though I did not understand this at the time, being the child of Shoah survivors was central to my longing to leave Hungary. I felt – and this has turned out to be the case, at least until recently – that being a Jew in the UK was less complicated.

Soon after moving to London, travelling in the lift with my mother who was visiting, a neighbour, on her way to church, invited us to join her. The conversation went something like this: Me: "Thank you for asking, but I am Jewish". Her: "Oh, so you attend the Jewish church? I hope you have found one nearby". After she left my mother, visibly moved, said: "What an extraordinary experience to watch you so easily and openly being able to state that you are Jewish", unimaginable in Hungary at that time.

Developments in Western Europe and, in recent years, specifically in the British Labour Party, have somewhat shaken my sense of security as a Jew in the UK. Undoubtedly, there is no comparison with the rampant and often officially sanctioned antisemitism in contemporary

Hungary. Still, the period under the leadership of Jeremy Corbyn in the British Labour Party (2015–2020) was a disturbing one. At this time I observed that many on the left were reluctant to face the reality of *systemic* antisemitism within the party. There was a tendency to believe that the complaints about it were overblown, politically motivated, weaponised by the right-wing media. This was undoubtedly true also but the two facts are not mutually exclusive. Hundreds of Jews left the party, many more complained of violent verbal abuse and threats to their life and yet its leader hinted that perhaps Jews and the media (or Jews in the media?) were oversensitive, prone to exaggeration.

In October 2020, the Labour Party was served with an "unlawful act notice" after an investigation into antisemitism by the Equality and Human Rights Commission found it responsible for serious harassment and discrimination and a lack of appropriate procedures to deal with these. Sadly, antisemitism is part of a broader phenomenon on the left in Western Europe and I no longer feel quite the same sense of freedom and ease I had felt as a Jew when I first arrived in the UK.[10]

All this is, of course, part of a larger picture of growing antisemitism worldwide (for example, far right white supremacism in the United States, Islamic terrorism in France) and, indeed, a general increase in open expressions of all forms of racist and xenophobic ideas in the UK and elsewhere.

From Budapest to London

In the 1970s our generation, Jews and Gentiles alike, talked incessantly about emigration. To stay or to remain: this was our existential question.

Millions left the country in the first half of the 20th century and about 200,000 in 1956. Among them, always represented well above their presence in the population, were Hungarian Jews.

This dilemma was faced at various points by my family. After the war, my mother wanted to leave for Palestine, as described earlier. In 1956, when many Hungarians and certainly most Hungarian Jews considered emigration during the brief opening of the border, my parents did too. Concern about their ageing parents and me (I was sixteen months old and had measles) prevented this – but was that all? Later they both agreed that, ultimately, they stayed because, despite it all – despite the Shoah, the Stalinist terror of the 1950s, the economic hardships, the atrocities during the 1956 uprising, despite the brutal oppression of what had started as a genuine bid for freedom in 1956 – they felt Hungary to be their home.

I felt differently. But I had not fully anticipated the complexities of emigration. A graduate of English, I was unprepared for the difficulties of understanding contemporary British culture, certain accents and, indeed, many aspects of life in London. My first trip to the launderette (an institution unknown in Budapest at the time) ended in tears as I had no idea how to use the machines. I was discombobulated by the assistant's accent; in turn, she looked at me, an alien, with superiority and contempt.

My first job, in the kitchen of a pub, obtained after several months of trying, also ended in despair: I survived a whole two weeks, "preparing" meals described as homemade from frozen trays of industrially produced food, for which well-dressed office folk paid the equivalent of my daily wage. I resigned when I overheard the landlady of the pub screaming down the phone to the Job Centre: "You sent me a foreign moron – she can't understand English and she can't cook". Cooking? What cooking?

So who was I now, this "moron", aged 25, in London but not a Londoner, a Jew living outside the Jewish community, a Hungarian with some disdain towards her country of origin, a graduate barely able to hold down a working-class job, an independent woman who totally depended financially on her husband? I felt invisible.

Invisibility went hand in hand with privacy, a word that cannot easily be translated into Hungarian: possible translations in dictionaries list secrecy, seclusion, withdrawal, loneliness, words that denote a negative. But privacy in English does not imply a withdrawal, rejection or lack. Instead, it suggests a tactful respect for personal boundaries. Coming from a culture with few such boundaries, privacy offered immense relief to me.

A new émigré, I was immediately struck by the different conceptualisations of the interior space of the home: Budapest apartments – and, to some extent, even houses, though growing up I only ever came across village houses on holidays – contain interconnecting rooms or rooms arranged around a central hall. The quintessential

British suburban home in the cities, the ubiquitous terraced or semi-detached house, its design informed by the concept of privacy, separates living and private/sleeping spaces onto different floors. In apartments, rooms open to a corridor – the concept of privacy is paramount.

The English instinctively stand at a greater distance from each other than do Hungarians and a certain reticence, a slower pace, is present in relationships also. Before I learnt this, I observed people shrinking back if I moved too close, physically or otherwise.

This invisibility and the privacy, the price of freedom, were painful and exhilarating in turn. Freed from the constraints of my at times claustrophobic life in Budapest, I nevertheless found being, literally, a "nobody" painful indeed. My husband, though British, was not a Londoner and did not have a circle of friends in London either. It was just us, and a small number of his family and friends – and we were poor.

But soon I was earning *some* money: cleaning the filthy apartments of wealthy expats, clothes discarded on the floor, disgusting bathrooms, mountains of unwashed dishes. One day a group of Saudi princes and their British friends descended on the apartment and I was left alone with them while the princesses went out shopping. Unaware that I spoke English, they discussed their plans for me. I fled – and quit.

I also worked in food fairs, conducted market research on street corners, threaded beads on cheap necklaces for market stalls and, finally, worked as a bookkeeper – a comparatively comfortable job, in a warm office, where I could utilise my mathematical skills or, at least, my aptitude for arithmetic.

Then I applied for the post of administrator at a Law Centre. Waiting for my interview I noticed a copy of the *Morning Star*[11] on the table. I remarked that this was unfortunately the only English-language paper we had access to back in Budapest (except at the British Embassy, technically forbidden to visit but many of us in the English Department did, anyway) and I was amused to see it in the waiting room, indicating that I thought it was there as a joke. It transpired that the chair of the interviewing panel, D., a lawyer (and later a prominent gay rights activist), was a communist.

I did not get the job; as I later discovered, someone more politically reliable did – a surprisingly familiar story for an émigré from "socialist" Hungary. She did not stay long, as her bookkeeping skills were minimal, and I was appointed a few weeks later. I ended up sharing an office with D. and we had many discussions about Marxism and "real socialism". I came to respect her tenacity and commitment as I watched her tirelessly defend the striking miners against prosecution during the brutal miners' strike in 1984.

By now I had realised that life, values and politics were far more complicated in the West than they had been in Hungary. In Budapest, in the 1970s, there were only a few possible political positions: convinced communists, bystanders who compromised to survive professionally and personally, passive resisters who did not participate in politics at all and us – the "opposition". One did not mix much with people from the other groups – at least this is how it seemed to me at the time.

In London, by contrast, there were many political choices and complex shades of politics and it was then perfectly possible to mix with others holding a variety of opinions. I fear this is less so in the current political landscape, after the Corbyn years and Brexit. In recent times, it seems as if political differences have become too painful to discuss, as if barricades exist even between friends.

In the early 1980s it was possible – fascinating even – to have supper with a neighbour who worked for the local Conservative Association. Here one of the guests spoke at length about her weekend at Balmoral, the Queen's Scottish residence. I gave Hungarian lessons to G., a radical leftist at the time, who later became a distinguished journalist specialising in Eastern/Central Europe and who debated with me, loudly, the merits (or otherwise, as I suggested) of Daniel Ortega's government in Nicaragua.

We had drinks with a gay priest, who was passionately in favour of gay rights but rather conservative in his politics, which he expounded at length while getting us drunk on gin and tonic, rather more gin than tonic. We dined with a writer who elaborated her particular combination of, to me at the time, seemingly irreconcilable beliefs: Catholicism and feminism.

But who was I in all this? The question of identity is the émigré's overriding dilemma. What is being lost and what might have been gained in the process of leaving the homeland and establishing a life in the new country takes years – and in my case, the first analysis, to elucidate.

Budapest: my love

I knew that I loved Budapest, the beautiful, majestic city on the River Danube, the bridges, the Buda Hills with their spectacular views. I missed it painfully. London in the early 1980s was drab, broken even; its public transport intolerable. By contrast, Budapest, a small city you could traverse on foot, had efficient buses, trams and trolley-buses, good coffee, lovely bakeries – and I missed them all.

At that time London was not like other European cities: except in Soho, there were no coffee shops, not much drinkable coffee in fact and very few outdoor eateries, and even fewer serving decent food - hard to imagine now, as I write this in one of the food capitals of the world.

Being an émigré meant that I often needed to explain myself in a way people who *are* "at home" need not. My childhood in the Eastern bloc, the feel of Budapest, the language – the need to "explain" persists and yet I no longer think of Budapest as "home". It is a beautiful city where I enjoy speaking Hungarian and visiting my remaining family and friends but where, paradoxically, I am quite invisible now.

Spare Rib and motherhood – Eve, not Adam

On arrival in London feminism appealed to me immediately. *Spare Rib*, the iconic feminist magazine, was a revelation. So was the feminist bookshop and café in North London, staffed by women in dungarees. The café served cheap and delicious vegetarian food, another unknown concept for me.

On the surface, it seemed that in Budapest women were equal and, in many ways, we had been. We studied with the same fervour as the men, we planned to have a career, at least girls from professional families did. During our childhood, our mothers mostly worked full time – there was no alternative in the 1950s and 1960s, neither socially nor financially. We took for granted the apparent equality, but it was a complex situation: in some ways, women in Hungary were a generation ahead of women in the West, though misogyny and sexism existed all the same. Women earned less and carried most of the burden of domestic responsibilities, and domestic violence was rampant.

I came from a family of strong, assertive women, and even Grandma Stefi, a rather diffident personality, spoke with much feeling about giving up her deeply held wish to become a concert pianist; instead, at 20, she was expected to marry and have children. She continued to play and, for a while, teach the piano at home. Her playing was full of force, longing, frustration. My mother considered her career of prime importance – this was against the background of her own mother's sacrifice – but she also felt that as a woman and a mother she had fewer opportunities than her male colleagues. My father expected her to bear the weight of domestic responsibilities even as he prided himself on being a believer of equality between men and women – though he did always support her career.

In London, in the early 1980s, many graduate women stopped working altogether until their children were perhaps in secondary school and then returned to often non-graduate jobs. I found this astonishing. At the same time, I was also beginning to realise that motherhood had often been unappreciated in my environment, despite the existence of very generous maternity pay and conditions. This provision was, in my view, a political decision by the regime to address the extremely low birth rate, rather than representing a wish to protect babies.

Many young women of my background and generation seemed utterly focussed on making a career. I do not remember ever having a substantial conversation about future motherhood, least of all with my mother. I do not recall any serious discussions with friends about having children either, though there were some pregnancies in our social circle. But as the biological clock ticked away, my analysis began to focus on motherhood. And even before that, on being a woman. Eve, not Adam – a rather perturbing confrontation with reality.

Becoming a mother was, arguably, the greatest achievement of my first analysis and a revelation. It was – and is – the most profound experience of my life. Creating a home, domesticity, cooking, being there when the children came home from school, having a family meal every day were all of prime importance to me. Much of this only partially existed in my own childhood and I am aware of identifications that have skipped a generation. Some of my happiest memories are of watching my grandmothers pickling cucumbers, bottling tomatoes, making jam, stretching strudel, worrying over soufflés – all the while telling me about the past, about their childhood, which stretched back to the Austro-Hungarian Monarchy. I could now, luckily, take the best of my mother's and grandmothers' lives, further made feasible by working from home as a psychotherapist.

London, my love – emigration again

After 12 mostly happy though challenging years in London, for family reasons I found myself living in a small town in the county of Kent, some 50 miles east of London. It could have been 500 miles. It was another world altogether.

When we arrived, many inhabitants of the town, born and bred there, had only visited London a handful of times. There were almost no foreigners, nor ethnic minorities, in stark contrast with London: it was kind, polite – and very English. We were warmly welcomed but I felt like a Martian, unable to explain my background, my thinking, my very being. Not only had most people not met anyone who grew up in Hungary, nor even any Jews, but my profession was, at that time, hardly understood. Many a time neighbours, tradesmen or acquaintances thought I was a physiotherapist.

We got to know good people but making close friends proved to be difficult. I tried, how I tried! After a while, the cost was greater than the pain of loneliness and, slowly, I withdrew into work, solitary activities, domesticity and motherhood. I belonged to a small group of like-minded local colleagues, some of them friends; they shared my passion for psychoanalytic therapy though not my longing to be back in London. I kept in touch with my old London friends but ceased to expect similar friendships locally. On this journey of being an immigrant, assimilation beckoned with greater force, but I would not, could not, assimilate any further.

There were compensations: I discovered pleasures I had not known before – growing fruit and vegetables, having a cat and a dog, the changing seasons and the beauty of the countryside. I returned to "roots" I had never before owned – Grandma Vally's rural farming childhood. Only then did I understand the world she had never ceased to mourn. I also understood, for the first time, the intensity of love for the land, described passionately by Hungarian poets and shared by many in that essentially rural country.

I vividly recall moments of standing in the middle of my plot. I had just finished digging up the ground and adding manure; I contemplated my work. I lifted a handful of soil: it was dark, crumbly, fertile. In the spring I anxiously watered my seeds and protectively gazed at my seedlings. It was my creation; they were my babies! Cosmopolitan urban Jewry was only part of my heritage. The outdoors, the rural landscape, a source of pleasure and solace, were now mine too.

I am reminded of our first rural holiday in 1981. We stayed in a cottage which was old and damp. I was frightened. Where are the cities? Where are the people? And why ever go for a walk in the "barren" – and wet – Yorkshire Dales? That was then. Years later, no longer afraid, much as I admired the provincial rural way of life, I could not be part of its social fabric. The compromises required, the somewhat claustrophobic life of a small town, continued to be bur-densome and, paradoxically, a reminder of early Budapest times. I profoundly missed the more substantial psychoanalytic community and the world-class culture of London, its multicultural vibe and multi-ethnic colour.

The pain of this second emigration persisted. It was, indeed, much more painful than the first. Emigration always represents a loss (Grinberg, 1989) but first time the compensations had outweighed the losses: I was newly married, living in London, in analysis and training to be a psychotherapist, all within less than two years after my ar-rival. The pain of this second emigration persisted throughout the twenty-three years it lasted. London stayed in my heart and I longed to be back.

From maths to psychoanalysis

Egy belső hang – ha tetszik, nevezd lelkiismeretnek - azt kérdezte tőlem: "Minek köszönhetik a matematikusok nagy eredményeiket?" Semmi másnak – feleltem neki – mint annak, hogy a gondolkodás tisztaságát illetően olyan magas követelményeket állítottak maguk elé … .hogy megalkuvas nélkül törekedtek az igazságra, és következetesen tartották magukat ahhoz, hogy csak a világos és minden kétértelműségtől mentes fogalmakban való gondolkodás vezethet valódi eredményre.[12]

An inner voice, call it conscience if you like, asked me: How do mathematicians achieve great results? I responded that ... they demand a great deal of themselves in the service of clarity ... they aim to find truth and they insist that only clear thinking, free of ambiguity, leads to true results.

(Alfréd Rényi pp 59–60)

One of the most outstanding psychoanalysts of our times, Hannah Segal writes: " ... psychoanalysis is concerned with the mind, but specifically with psychic reality, with unconscious facets of the mind and the discovery of the truth about them; it is concerned with change, but specifically with change that occurs through truth and the development of the capacity to withstand it" (p.291).

But first it was mathematics. Beautiful, calm, exciting mathematics. Identification with my mother, a mathematician, was central to it. I was good at maths, or rather, I enjoyed using my logical mind. Having "the right answer", that there *was* a right answer, was rewarding. In hindsight, it was, in part, a way of dealing with anxiety and multi-generational trauma that could only partially be symbolised.

I was about 13 when I read a fictionalised Hungarian biography of the first significant female mathematician, Sonia Kovalevskaya (Kertesz, 1962). I recognised, instantly, my own feelings in Sonia's description of mathematics as beautiful, a kind of poetry, unencumbered with pain and suffering.[13] By the time I was 16 this was not enough. I wanted to understand the pain, I wanted to teach literature, as Mr K., my beloved – and idealised – teacher did, so I switched from studying advanced maths to studying English intensively.

Soon I wanted to study psychology at university, but my family thought it was not a respectable subject, nor one to secure my future. When I decided to return to my interest in psychology/psychoanalysis once in London, the first question my mother asked was: "but will you gain an internationally accepted qualification?". Internationally? So that I may return to Budapest if I need to, or run for my life if I have to? Security, survival, the familiar themes again.

I needed help and I wanted to help others. Soon after arriving in London I embarked on an analysis, funded, initially, by my cleaner's job.

I sought consultation with Dr C., a senior Training Analyst, to help me find an analyst. The consultation proved to be a most memorable occasion, where I observed, for the first time, the work of a psychoanalyst. The quality of her attention, her ability to make links, the intensity of the connection, her quiet and unhurried way of making sense of the jumbled mess I took to her have remained with me for the four decades since.

I wanted to train, and I knew I was not interested in Jung, or Gestalt, or many of the other options. Oh, so many options! There was no internet, not even a book that listed psychotherapy trainings. The loss of the nexus, so important in my youth in Budapest where I always knew someone who knew someone who could help – this was possibly the most painful aspect of emigration. But then a friend of a neighbour – a nexus of sorts – a counsellor, offered a xeroxed (!) list of trainings and I explored a few.

I chose Arbours, a psychoanalytically oriented organisation, much influenced by the anti-psychiatry movement. Its founders, two Americans, had worked with R.D. Laing. It was an absolute leap of faith: I had no idea how I was going to pay for it, nor whether I would be any good at it.

Arbours had an international and somewhat countercultural atmosphere. Many of the staff and trainees were foreigners like me, and, importantly, it offered the mental health experience I lacked completely. (In the UK you don't have to have a first degree in a mental health profession to train as a psychotherapist or psychoanalyst, but you do have to acquire psychiatric experience during the training.)

Arbours ran 1960s-style therapeutic communities, and the first year of training involved working with the residents, many with chronic bipolar or schizophrenic diagnoses. There was no apparent hierarchy among residents and trainees and, often with many years of hospitalisations and therapy behind them, the residents were much more sophisticated than I was. They could read me better than I could them. No white coat to protect me, just my own intuition – thrown in at the deep end.

When staying overnight, frightened and out of my depth, I observed that most residents lived at night and slept during the day. I began to discover how psychotic processes worked, the power of projections and the transference, the need for containment and the depth of anxiety and fragility typical in this patient group. The household was chaotic and not exactly hygienic; the residents either ignored me or kept me pinned to my chair in the kitchen while they complained, raged, threatened. I had good supervision and, of course, my analysis to help me survive. Unsurprisingly, I did not sleep much during those nights.

This was followed by a six months' placement in the Arbours Crisis Centre where the residents were in some form of acute psychotic state. I spent time with a catatonic schizophrenic woman who pretended to ignore me completely but went into an incomprehensible monologue as soon as I tried to move. Another resident, with a history of sexual abuse and physical violence, formed an idealised bond with me and refused to speak to anyone else, creating tensions in the clinical team. I learnt about powerful group dynamics and how the residents' disturbances were projected into the team.

Importantly, I made some close friends among the trainees: we have followed one another's lives over four decades, through further trainings, weddings, motherhood, illness, bereavement. I was extremely lucky: I found this "home" soon after arriving in London, and though poor financially, I felt the richness of belonging and the excitement of learning.

Looking back, I think the theoretical training was too eclectic; some of our teachers were rather disparaging of psychoanalysis, though others were excellent.

The clinical part of the training included work with two patients, invariably borderline, seen three times weekly, under the weekly supervision of two psychoanalysts. My first one, an anorexic woman, stayed for seven years. My second patient, a paranoid man, dropped out after a couple of months, not surprisingly, as I had no idea how to reach him nor how to contain his paranoia. He was replaced by a narcissistic man who observed no boundaries and turned up one day, outside his session time, with his young son. He did not last long either and was replaced by a young woman who had just been discharged from a psychiatric ward. She was truly challenging and disturbing, and her suicidal tendencies made me anxious. Her searing envy of me made progress difficult and her terror of another breakdown, a realistic danger, also interfered with progress. She feared, and rightly so, that I had not yet reached this area in my own analysis and this limited my ability to help her (Winnicott, 1974).

On qualification I began to build up a private practice, mostly consisting of low-fee borderline patients, a patient group highly represented among those seen in the Arbours referral service. I also began to look for further training to deepen my clinical work and theoretical understanding. I discovered that the Lincoln Centre, a more explicitly psychoanalytic organisation, offered an advanced course. I was mentored throughout the course and much beyond by a powerful and decisive character, J, a psychoanalyst.

When I told senior members of Arbours about this step, some behaved as if I had betrayed them. I had been unaware of the political battle taking place around organising the profession into a registering body, and that Arbours and the Lincoln were on opposite sides of the barricades. This was the first of many experiences of the destructive forces that sometimes surface in psychoanalytic organisational politics. It was a shock, though, that this apparently "liberal" organisation could be so illiberal. Still, I am immensely grateful for the opportunity Arbours gave me and to those who fostered my development in those years.

During the Lincoln training I developed my psychoanalytic skills considerably. The seminar leaders, supervisors and my tutor were psychoanalysts with a variety of theoretical orientations and I enjoyed a professional atmosphere conducive to intensive psychoanalytic work.

Over the years, besides clinical work, I have done a great deal of teaching of psychotherapy trainees. I lectured at the University of Kent and conducted clinical seminars in a variety of settings. I led seminars for members of the general public with an interest in psychoanalysis. Teaching clarifies what I know and reveals the gaps like perhaps nothing else does. It has also been an area of identification with my mother. I have in fact been teaching in one manner or another ever since at the age of eight I taught arithmetic to the struggling daughter of a neighbour. I stepped in to teach a new, experimental form of maths to younger children at my school when I was 14. I taught English to a large variety of adults over many years in Budapest and then to immigrants from all over the world after my move to London.

As Director of Training at the Lincoln Centre I revised and reorganised, with a colleague, the structure and the curriculum of an already excellent psychoanalytic psychotherapy training. Enjoyable and creative, this was also a huge and demanding task.

By contrast, I am not particularly good at institutional politics. I learnt this, painfully, during a politically bruising battle to retain the psychoanalytic identity of the Lincoln. I discovered that I lacked the necessary tact and political nous required for the process. I can lead but I am no good at tactical fighting. When a battle ensued and a merger with other organisations was forced through by a dedicated band of activists, I was not able to prevent what a sizable group of my closest colleagues and I saw as the destruction of excellence. For all of us, there was a devastating sense of loss. It was, at the same time, an important learning experience: I would never again take on such political roles within an organisation.

In 2007, unexpectedly, the opportunity arose to join the New Entry Scheme at the Institute of Psychoanalysis, designed for senior psychoanalytic psychotherapists. It was the brainchild of another subsequently important mentor of mine, V, and I was in its second intake. Another enriching course, with all the pain and joy of becoming a student again, then in my early fifties. Another confrontation with discovering how much I did not know. All the while, as Director of Training at the Lincoln Centre, I was carrying huge responsibilities which included judging the suitability and progress of trainees. It was a heady mix and I did not always manage it well. At times it seemed that I would fail at both, but somehow chutzpah, the help of friends and colleagues, my supervisor, my progress adviser and, especially, my husband's steadfast support, carried me through. As a result, I gained membership in a psychoanalytic society that, with all its hierarchy, group politics and somewhat Ivory Tower ethos, has finally offered a psychoanalytic home with unlimited scope for learning and development.

This was followed by a decision to move back to London after my husband's retirement: home at last.

Identity – Psychoanalytic

Earlier in this chapter, I wrote about the complexities of my personal identity. Here I am concerned with the elaboration of a fluid and yet increasingly clear sense of my psychoanalytic identity.

Much fascinating exploration has taken place in recent years, within and beyond psychoanalysis, of the multiplicity of (gender/ national/ethnic/sexual) identities. Erikson, the first psychoanalyst interested in the concept of identity, seemed to believe in the possibility, even desirability, of a continuity of character and described it in a normative manner, though he also suggested that it was "unfathomable". He linked identity with identification, stating that "identity formation ... begins where the usefulness of identification ends" (1968, p. 159), perhaps indicating that identity develops from early identifications but that an authentic identity will require a personal idiom and will be idiosyncratic.

My thinking about identity – my identities even – centres around the interplay of an ever-changing dynamic between past and present, within the broader context of a social and cultural history. I see identity as inconsistent and never unified – and when it appears to be so this may well be an illusion (Perelberg, 1999). I would suggest that psychoanalytic identity is as much a paradox as personal identity is.

Parsons (2009) juxtaposes two models of the formation of a psychoanalytic identity: one is based on complex early identifications and subjective experiences, the other on the appeal of a particular conceptual framework. Over the years my analytic identity has been formed, without doubt, along the lines of the first model, much of it based on personal experiences, my analyses and my understanding of my own history; the theory came much later. It has, I believe, a great deal to do with luck, happenstance, circumstances. I found myself in London rather than New York – or perhaps, as I nearly did, in Boston. I could not have settled in Paris; I could never master the complexities of the French language and culture.

A very British analyst

Granted, then, that I *am* a British psychoanalyst, I shall try to grapple here with the meaning of this "existential" statement within my own elaboration of my analytic identity.

Harris and Mitchell (2004) ask the question "What's American about American psychoanalysis?". They contrast American and British psychoanalysis in terms of their differing understandings of the notion of the self:

The American notion that the deepest feelings, the most personal regions of the self, find expression in intimacy with another is in stark contrast to the emphasis in other parts of the world and other psychoanalytic cultures on the privacy and ineffability of personal experience. The latter theme is especially striking in British psychoanalysis, from Winnicott's emphasis on the necessarily incognito nature of true self-experience, to Khan's writings on the "privacy of the self", to Bollas's stress on personal idiom. (p. 184).

It seems to me that the object is always present, if unconsciously, in the mind of the subject, but I have found this juxtaposition thought-provoking as it chimes with an aspect of what I recognise to be a particularly British attitude: privacy, addressed earlier in this chapter.

When my first analyst started a sentence by saying "I wonder if you might feel that … ", it was for me as unusual as it was moving: not a definite statement by another about what I felt but a tentative comment. I appreciated its implications: the privacy, the silences, the "potential space" (Winnicott, 1953) in which development could take place.

I conceptualise the human condition as based on a fundamentally private sense of ourselves. Sharing this with the Other remains, as I see it, a continuing challenge for the analyst–patient dyad. Equally, the Other as essentially different and separate will always be a struggle to perceive, thus empathy and understanding have limits, be that as a result of the "obstacles" of gender, generation, race, culture – or just because he or she is *not me*. The struggle with separateness and the Other will invariably contain the attachment experiences and unconscious phantasies of the subject.

I consider the relationship between analyst and patient, by its nature asymmetrical, much as it is based on our shared inter-subjectivity. Observing and describing, without judgement as much as possible – while being aware that sometimes this is not possible – seem central to me. Analysis in this model then is also perceived as a relationship, but the focus is on the patient's internal world and its impact on that of the analyst. The impact, undoubtedly profound, evokes conscious and unconscious affective responses.

What is the patient's response to my interpretation, tone, silence, lack of understanding? What does my counter-transference experience tell me about the current dynamics of our work? These questions are present in my mind throughout a session.

The analyst's personal views and experiences cannot be excluded from the analytic encounter but the exploration of this, for me, is on the whole an *internal* process rather than one that involves the patient. While I am called upon to investigate my countertransference continuously, I acknowledge that much of it remains unconscious and hence may lead to enactments.

Perhaps British analysts' reticence in writing about their transferences to their patients is not because of a lack of awareness. We do discuss these problems and consider essential the ongoing vigilance in monitoring our feeling states. But we may reveal less in public and less in the consulting room than perhaps our Relational colleagues do on the other side of the Atlantic. I suspect we – we? – in Britain just reveal less.

From my vantage point, the Relational model parallels Winnicott's often quoted dictum: there is no such thing as a baby, only a baby and a mother. This is a powerful Winnicottian insight, but like much of Winnicott, it is, for me, a creative challenge rather than a statement to be taken literally. After all the baby has a capacity or otherwise for survival and has inherited, genetic and constitutional features – hard as it has been to define these – that interact with but are not primarily determined by maternal care. The patient is not a baby but I do find the parallel meaningful: in my formulation patients come with their internal objects and infantile wishes and drives. While different analysts will form differing relationships with the same patient, it seems to me that certain characteristics of the patient can be described and understood both within the analytic relationship and independently of it.

Our conscious theories and underlying unconscious models do not always tally (Sandler, 1983.) My interest in this area prompted me to attend an international conference in Vienna,[14] where the focus was on teasing out these conscious theoretical models and on deciphering the underlying unconscious assumptions. Here, after we British clinicians commented on the presenter's material, she responded: "Oh you British, you are obsessed with the transference, especially the negative one, and with the frequency of sessions!". The comment does, in fact, accurately portray an aspect of the clinical stance of most members of our Society. But we/I also work with the positive transference, which can at times be just as difficult to bear. Additionally, positive transference and the erotic, Oedipal aspects of it can easily metamorphose into erotisation and thus become a destructive aspect of the analytic relationship: hate masquerading as love.

While I was a training therapist at the University of Kent, a new patient, a trainee, told me that her tutor described me as an "orthodox Kleinian, obsessed with the transference". This was a mockingly critical statement, intended to warn the patient off me. Similar "descriptions" were relayed to me by several patients subsequently, one of whom, more affectionately, called me "the Kleinian witch of the wild East".

Indeed, like most in the British scene, I do find that analysing the transference is central to my work, and Joseph's (1985) understanding of the "total situation" helps me to follow through the way internal objects are transferred in the analytic setting.

Importantly, I do not formulate this as a kind of translation, a "you mean me" type of description (Coltart, 1990). Birksted-Breen (2016) conceptualises this as "bi-ocularity", referring to two poles of analytic attentiveness: reverie and analysing. Focussing on the *here and now/you and me* goes hand in hand with "fostering the ambiguity of different times and spaces without collapsing them into the clear, logical and explanatory" (p. 25). This allows the analyst to understand and interpret defensive mechanisms while retaining another "eye" for "something else" to develop in her state of reverie (p. 26).

I believe that the internal objects patients project into the analyst have close links with childhood external objects, but they will have gone through distortions and alterations and so here the concept of *après-coup* seems indispensable (Browne, 2018). The interplay between the external world and internal psychic states seems fundamental to me and I shall illustrate this with clinical material later.

Intensive or otherwise

Another important British phenomenon is that analysts of all persuasion have a profound belief in the importance of the frequency of sessions – in four or five times (sometimes three times) weekly psychoanalysis. A much-debated issue within the International

Psychoanalytic Association, it is often perceived as British arrogance, but for me, it is not a value judgement.

Years ago I helped to set up a psychodynamic psychotherapy department in the National Health Service in Maidstone, Kent. The treatment model was once weekly, for one year. I was moved by how much the therapy meant to many of my patients and how helpful it was felt to have been, but I conceptualise it as a rather different therapeutic model in which I worked quite differently: more actively and somewhat less neutrally. Even in private practice in an open-ended therapy, this would appear to be the case. Perhaps most importantly, I started both my analyses once/twice weekly and experienced a profound change once I could attend more frequently.

Once/twice-weekly therapy on the whole, with some exceptions, seems to me just different in terms of the intensity of the transference, the patient's preoccupation with the process, the complications of the countertransference and the access it affords to the deeper layers of the unconscious. I find that the negative transference and all its manifestations – erotisation, somatisation, severe acting out, to name but a few – are less likely to lead to a premature ending. The exceptions include, in my experience, older patients who sometimes approach therapy with a sense of "now or never" and patients who have already had an analysis. But this is not to suggest that all intensive analyses work; the higher number of sessions may create favourable conditions for analysis but is no guarantee of success.

Some patients do not want or even need an analysis. For others, it seems to be contraindicated. I learnt this painfully in the first years of my career when I took literally a (borderline) patient's wish for more sessions as an indication of a wish for analysis, only to find myself out of my depth when she produced a malignant regression (Balint, 1979): her erotised, demanding transference wishes reached such intensity that, on one occasion, I had to physically hold her back lest she put her wrist through the windowpane of the consulting room in a fit of jealous rage. Conversely, I have also found that deep-seated narcissistic difficulties are unlikely to shift – if they shift at all – without high-frequency sessions.

This is a complex area but one that I mention because working intensively is a deeply engraved part of my psychoanalytic identity. At the same time, intensive work can be a deprivation: a loss of a more "realistic", more equal relationship. And there is another deprivation: financial. As not many patients can afford, for years, what would be realistic hourly rates four or five times a week, our weekly income from these patients is barely more than the hourly fees are in some other countries.

Groups/orientation(s)

Groups play a fundamental part in any organisation, and all the more so in the British Psychoanalytic Society, which – quite uniquely – has survived many internal divisions without a split.

The well-known "Controversial Discussions"[15] have led to ongoing compromise, a famous British characteristic (Perelberg, 2008). This has maintained unity but at some cost, as compromises must: like difficult marriages that do not end in divorce, partners have had to give up some autonomy. The three groups – Contemporary Freudian, Independent and Kleinian – have operated side by side both in the training of candidates and in the scientific life of the Society ever since (Kohon, 1985, 2018a)

Clearly, identification with my analysts is the bedrock of my work, and my analysts, though both Independent, were distinctly different in approach. My first analyst collaborated with and was much influenced by Winnicott. My second analyst, a psychiatrist who had worked with highly disturbed patients, though not a Kleinian, utilised more of Kleinian theory.

I did not "choose" either of my analysts. It was a given that my first analyst would belong to the Middle Group (as British Independents were called then, in the middle between Kleinians and Freudians). My consultant, the aforementioned Dr C., was, as I discovered later, a committed, militant even, member of that group. At that time, the groups and the fine details of theory carried no meaning for me, but my experience of the consultation allowed me to trust the referral. The analysis was a lifesaver of sorts; it helped me understand longstanding difficulties of a depressive kind. I made some sense of my childhood and of the multigenerational trauma I had carried throughout my life and I mourned my losses, including the sudden death of my father just three years earlier. Additionally, during the analysis I qualified as a psychoanalytic psychotherapist and began to build up a practice.

My geographical position and my circumstances (having a young family and living outside London) limited the possible location – and therefore choice – of my second analyst. The journey involved a heroic drive into London in the early hours of the morning. I knew that I needed a second analysis; the more destructive, narcissistic aspects of my personality, analysed best, I have come to believe, via the negative transference, were largely missing from my first one. There was plenty of it the second time round and the process persuaded me of the importance of a detailed exploration of such destructive elements of the personality.

Influences

Since starting my practice nearly four decades ago, I have been supervised by analysts from a variety of traditions and I value this diversity. If pushed, I would say I am broadly within the (British) Independent tradition (Limentani, 1989). Its fluidity and multifaceted nature appeal to me. Some members of this group are also members of the Contemporary Freudian group. Others are resolutely Winnicottian. Some are militantly anti-Kleinian. I think of myself as non-aligned in terms of institutional politics and, after much thought, I have resisted the inclination to be a signed-up member of any of the three groupings; instead, I find myself in a small but growing band of colleagues who have made a similar choice. Perhaps I am an independent Independent? I fear this may sound somewhat arrogant, even narcissistic, and it is certainly lonely at times, but on balance, it feels to me to be preferable to the available alternatives.

In the environment of my education in Hungary, all history was explained through a Marxist paradigm; all philosophy, aesthetics and even literary criticism were based – or at least pretended to be based – on Marxist "teachings".

My parents also tended to believe in "truths". This "certainty", partly cultural, partly psychic/internal, had survival value: in the dangerous world of their youth, it may even have been lifesaving. I prefer to be seen as somewhat woolly: it is a useful counterpoint to the part of my own personality that is prone to "knowing" and certainty. Bion's "negative capability" (1970) is a powerful challenge for me (cf. Kohon, 2019).

I am deeply sceptical about psychoanalytic "facts" as opposed to various models of the mind, each containing helpful and useful aspects of what is, in fact, a metapsychology. The developmental model of the early Freud and, later, of Anna Freud, is, to me, as useful as Klein's postulation of positions and their post-Kleinian developments. I have developed my ability to wait for the patient's associations largely with the help of Independents. I have benefitted from the attention paid to sexuality and perversion by Classical Freudians but also authors in the United States (e.g., Stein, 2005). Kleinians have particularly helped me with their focus on the minute details of the here and now. I have gained a great deal from the ongoing thinking within my Society of the impact of the external world, the political situation, questions of race and gender (Morgan, 2019).

The focus on the early relationship with the maternal person and its elaboration in the transference may have led at times to the apparent absence of sexuality from British psychoanalysis (Kohon, 2018b, Parsons, 2000) and I specifically sought out supervisors who helped me recalibrate the balance between the Oedipal and the pre-Oedipal.

I have found the work of British post-Kleinians (Brenman, Brenman-Pick, Britton, O'Shaughnessy, Steiner etc) invaluable, but I am also influenced by theoreticians from other countries and traditions. Ogden's elaboration of reverie, André Green's blank depression and the Dead Mother, Joyce McDougall's "sexualities" (in plural), to list but a few, have contributed to my understanding of the clinical situation. Kernberg's formulations helped me during assessment consultations in the National Health Service. My recent contacts with the Hungarian psychoanalytic world have led to explorations of the work of Ferro and post-Bionian field theory. In the process of writing this book I have also become interested in the thinking of Relational analysts in the United States.

Regression: from holding to containment

Over the years, I have gradually shifted my clinical stance: I draw somewhat less on Winnicott's "holding" and a little more on Bion's "containment", two concepts that are not the same but, for me are not mutually exclusive either. Ogden (2004) describes holding and the container–contained as "different analytic vertices from which to view the same analytic experience" (p. 1362). Holding is understood by him as primarily linked to "being" and the infant's relationship with time or, rather, the timelessness of early infantile experience. It is the mother's holding function that facilitates this experience. The container–contained model is, by contrast but not by exclusion, concerned with the processing of thoughts – dream thoughts in Bion's thinking – both conscious and unconscious. Containment involves transformation, holding perhaps less so.

This formulation links up with the development of my conceptualisation of regression. My first training with Arbours, due to its roots in the work of R.D. Laing, often centred around what I later came to see as a somewhat idealised picture of the curative aspect of regression. Over the years I have observed regression in patients as a route to understanding and a profound reaching out to early experience. Other times it seems to represent an avoidance of thinking: phantasies of becoming a baby of the analytic mother may be used to avoid understanding. These regressive phantasies can represent an erotisation that is, in fact, a defence against true dependence. At times patients do, of course, defend *against* regressive wishes and phantasies also.

In this context, the role of projective identification seems central. When I started my first training in the early 1980s, a seminar leader stated that "projective identification is a Kleinian myth". Of course, the concept has undergone much change and its definition is fluid and manifold, but these days it is rarely questioned as a central concept in our understanding of communication – by babies, patients and, indeed, in counter-transference enactments.

The death instinct – trauma and constitution

There are various views about the role of the environment within British psychoanalysis and without. There are differing conceptualisations of the origins of hate, aggression and envy and their relationship with trauma.

I find that the intensity of our envy varies considerably from person to person and I see this as primarily related to trauma but perhaps also, to some unquantifiable extent, to constitution. I find it more useful to think of envy as a later development than Klein posits it, but its destructive precursors do seem to me to surface in early infancy in the myriad ways in which different babies express rage, contentment, hunger, satiation.

I have found particularly useful Polmear's description of how she is helped by Kleinian ideas of the first year of life and the place of envy in the structure of the personality (Klein, 1937), while also drawing on Winnicott's concepts of the infant's total dependence. There is often a polarisation of the two theorists when in fact Winnicott accepted Klein's primitive mechanisms, though he placed them later developmentally (Polmear, 2008).

I listen closely and empathically to the traumatic memories and early experiences patients might bring but I am cautious about interpreting links prematurely and look for confirmation or otherwise in the transference and countertransference.

Understanding patients' histories and accompanying them in the development of their personal understanding plays a part in how I work, but I do not believe that these histories are exact "facts", though they represent internal truths. "It must be acknowledged that there is no simple, all-purpose life history" (Schafer, 1979).

I hold an essentially pessimistic view of the world, of our capacity for destruction – of the environment, of each other. Freud's concept of the death instinct, elaborated after the First World War, is, to me, fundamental, as is Klein's later development of it. Wars, genocide, slavery, racism and segregation, child abuse, rape – what more proof is required? The negative therapeutic reaction, such a frequent occurrence even in analyses that "go well", demonstrate to me the destructive potential in us all.

The way I work … .

So, how do I work in the consulting room?

Although the analytic relationship is a new and, hopefully, ultimately productive and life-enhancing relationship – and, as such, may be an improvement on early object relationships – I do not formulate it in terms of a "corrective emotional experience", though I note patients' longing for it to be that. Instead, I conceptualise the process as enabling my patients to explore and tolerate their internal world. I trust that, for most, analysis will prove to have been good enough, but failures of various kinds do exist, due to my limitations and/or the patient's internal rigidities as well as to some insurmountable obstacles within this particular analytic couple – mostly a mix of all three (Green, 2011; Sedlak, 2019). I find that deficits in symbolisation and an internal world dominated by perverse internal objects and inflexible narcissistic character defences are among the most intractable obstacles to genuine analytic contact.

I consider it important to hold together the envious attack and destructive rage *with* the wish to communicate, to be held and understood. I rarely interpret destructiveness without regard to the underlying anxiety, though there are inevitable exceptions to this "rule": for example, in certain thick-skinned narcissistic states of mind (Rosenfeld, 1987) sometimes only a clear statement about destructiveness towards the setting and/or towards the analyst is likely to get through the rigid carapace.

I seldom say much, if anything, in the first 10 minutes or so of the session as I wait to see where free associations take the patient. I wait to get a sense of the mood, the dominant affect and then try to address that before commenting on content. There is, in this, an essentially Winnicottian element: waiting for the moment when the patient is ready – or perhaps at times when *I* am ready.

Being in contact with the patient's affect, rather than the "correct" interpretation, and therefore the importance of pacing and timing, seems central to my way of working. When I do interpret, I try (though often fail) to say only one main thing and avoid the "on the one hand but on the other" type of interpretation, unless I am describing a conflict. I would not characterise myself as a silent analyst but I am not particularly talkative either. I prefer to follow free associations and allow their development in the patient's material rather than have an active dialogue with the patient. I have learnt a great deal from a supervisor who focussed on the nature of each interpretation I had made: why did I speak at that particular time, not before nor after? What compelled me to speak – or to stay silent?

None of this, however, is written in stone; every patient brings a unique set of new dynamics and an invitation to think and feel anew. Perhaps the most rewarding aspect of the work is the sense of discovery, the challenge of the (unconscious) meeting between two internal worlds. I find it exciting and enriching to think – and rethink – the concepts I have described in the context of each patient's internal world, without making a definitive theoretical statement about them (Britton, 1998). Ultimately, this may be a question of authenticity – whether the patient feels that I approach them in the spirit of wanting to understand, rather than from a rehearsed position.

Much of the above is an attempt to describe how I work in *ideal* circumstances. I do, at times, talk too much, get drawn into a discussion, take a partisan position, lose my analytic "cool"; I consider most of these instances enactments and seek to make sense of them after, if not during the session.

The clinical vignettes that follow are intended to illustrate the themes I have outlined. For reasons of confidentiality, these cases are highly disguised.

(Psychoanalytic) mother tongue

Much has been written about analysts and patients working in a language other than their first (Amati-Mehler et al., 1993; Antinucci, 2004). In London, it is not uncommon for analysis to be conducted in a third language, one that neither patient nor analyst speaks as their mother tongue.

Using language *per se* in analysis presents us with a dilemma. The most archaic aspects of our internal world are beyond language, so patient and analyst alike struggle to express these primitive feelings in words. Language therefore is, at best, an approximation of the earliest of experiences. Whether patients in analysis use their mother tongue or another language is important, but it seems to me to be secondary to this paradoxical aspect of psychoanalysis.

Both my analyses were in English. These days I think in English unless I am in Hungary and I probably dream in English. I read almost exclusively in English and although I speak colloquial Hungarian as a native speaker and without an accent, I struggle to express myself in my mother tongue about psychoanalysis, politics, gardening, to name but a few topics.

The internal relationship between my two languages has changed greatly over time. Learning English from the age of seven, the internal hierarchy of my languages has been in a state of flux though my mother tongue never ceases to be just that, with all its primitive resonances. A second language may have afforded me certain defences in analysis but these defences may have also provided safety in which more primitive states could be explored.

I certainly felt that, at the start of my first analysis, a safer distance from my internal mother could be utilised, at times defensively. Sexuality was just a little easier to explore in English. But this state of affairs was transient; soon resistances emerged in English, too. I have observed this with patients also: the complexity of the use of languages is endless, as I hope to illustrate in the clinical material that follows.

In my twenties English came to represent "an object of desire" as it became linked with the longing for freedom of expression embodied by "the West" (Hoffman, 1989). As I began to live almost entirely in English, the hierarchy between the two languages began to shift and by the time I was nursing my first baby, it actually felt almost inauthentic to speak to him in Hungarian, though I did sing Hungarian lullabies.

It took me a long while before I felt ready to contact the Hungarian psychoanalytic world, but, having done so, I am now in regular contact with colleagues there and have attended conferences, at times struggling to follow the conceptual framework in Hungarian. I have initiated a British–Hungarian dialogue, a working group where analysts from the two countries may meet and discuss clinical work based on their significantly different psychoanalytic assumptions. I presume that this represents a freer psychic dialogue between my two internal languages.

At a German–British dialogue in Potsdam in 2019 I was part of a panel presentation where analysts spoke about working in a second language. Some colleagues expressed surprise at the initial difficulties we described when working *in our own language* for the first time. We wondered if there might be a sharp difference between those of us whose analyses and training had been conducted in a second language and those who had had an analysis and training in their own country, and later emigrated to and now worked in the UK or elsewhere. It was as if our "psychoanalytic mother tongue" established itself in the deepest regions of our psyche and created a link with a maternal object in this second language. Still, the significance of the different mother tongues between my analysts and me, much as it was spoken about – especially in the first analysis – acquired a further meaning once I started working with Hungarian patients.

I experience English (at any rate, British English) to be a more tactful language than Hungarian, perhaps because of my conceptualisation of the privacy that it affords me. At the same time, though Hungarian vocabulary is less extensive, it is rich and evocative and its world-class poetry is dear to me though the world, sadly, is mostly oblivious of its existence.

Reading George Szirtes' poems and his book about his mother (Szirtes, 2000 & 2019) has offered me a rare gift, a bridge of sorts: he came to London from Budapest as a small child and is now a significant English poet as well as an outstanding translator of Hungarian poetry. The language of his poetry, and therefore the expression of his most intimate feelings, is English, but he has never lost his deep connection with the land and language of his birth.

The differences between the two languages can feel quite profound in the consulting room. Some reflect the many and varied cultural differences between the two countries, others the actual framework of the two languages as Hungarian is not an Indo-European language and its structure and grammar are profoundly different from their English counterparts.

There is no "he" and "she" in Hungarian so at times the language needs to be more descriptive to express a gendered idea. There are four different ways of saying "you", denoting levels of formality that need to be finely judged. My Hungarian is mostly used in informal circumstances these days, with friends and family. With Hungarian patients I had to "relearn" using the form of "you", perhaps closest to the French *vous* that seems most appropriate in the consulting room.

A deeper sense of familiarity may exist with a Hungarian patient at times as unconscious, primitive early experiences may be revived. There are experiential echoes, shared historical features – and yet I no longer feel that a Hungarian patient, *per se*, would arouse deeper resonances in me than an English-speaking one. With some the evocation of locations, smells and colours has resonated deeply. With other Hungarian patients, perhaps younger ones or from a different social and cultural background to me, this almost gut-level identification has been absent. In other words, it has ceased to be a matter of language and is now dependent more on the complexities of identifications with each patient.

Interestingly, I have had the odd Hungarian thought in reverie, but I have never said anything in Hungarian to an English-speaking patient. I have, more than once, spoken inadvertently in English in the presence of a Hungarian patient; my reverie at its deepest level is inclined towards English rather than Hungarian. So is Hungarian still the language of the more archaic layers of my internal world? Does English represent the more structured aspects of my psyche? I do not believe I can answer these questions with any certainty. English is the language in which I fell in love and nursed my children, in which I exist, and – it occurs to me now – English is likely to be the language of my last words.

Language as reality, language as defence

My patient "Sophia" was in her late thirties when she sought help after several failed relationships with married men. She lived alone and described persistent feelings of meaninglessness and a sense of isolation. Her parents - an Irish mother and a Greek father – conceived her after a holiday romance and decided to live together in London. She describes her father as domineering, at times cruel. He insisted that only Greek be spoken in the home and thus her mother spoke to baby Sophia in halting Greek. Barely a year later another, initially sickly, baby arrived and her mother had postnatal depression with a short stay in hospital.

Her father never stopped missing his homeland and made clear his contempt for all things British. Sophia's Oedipal strivings were felt to be rejected: she could not live up to the idealised Greek little girl desired by her father: modest, shy, cautious. As she reached puberty his expectations of "appropriate attire and behaviour" was at variance with contemporary British norms. Her younger sister, a more accommodating character, was Daddy's apparent favourite.

Her father was often absent for long periods due to his business interests in Greece and each time he returned, he emphasised the superiority of Greek culture.

The question of language has been central to the analysis. She chose me because of my "unusual" foreign name; she thought I would understand her experience of having "two languages inside her, competing, unresolved", but as the transference evolved, she became convinced that I could not possibly comprehend her predicament. There were, she maintained, feelings she could only express in Greek, her deepest and most genuine feelings. In English, she could only pretend: in English, she was a fake.

She longed for us to speak Greek together – though pointedly avoided seeking out a Greek analyst – and the impossibility of her desire became a source of suffering to us both; at such times the threat of a stalemate was profound, no interpretation of this predicament helped, no shared language could be found. While I empathised with her dilemma, I thought that her pain perhaps could also be understood in the context of another, even deeper, trauma, crystallised around early separations and losses.

Gradually her "demand" that I become a Greek speaker – and my "demand", as she experienced it, that we speak English – became part of a profoundly sadomasochistic transference/counter-transference constellation, where the object either dominates and wishes to take over her mind or must submit to her way of thinking. This essentially paternal transference hid an even more traumatic absence, that of an available, consistent and understanding maternal object with a secure space in her mind for her baby. It was also a repetition of the dynamics of the parental couple.

She imagined that I came from a warm, loving, idealised Hungarian family who spoke a unique language. She felt absolutely alone in the world, though she claimed this was, in fact, how she liked it.

We became increasingly aware of her difficulties around separateness and difference: unless I had an identical experience to her, I could not understand her. My accent betrayed my rootedness in another language and suggested that I acquired English as a second language later while she was "bilingual" which she felt was an incomprehensible experience to me. On occasion the sense of such concreteness and rigidity rendered me silent – I lost my ability to speak, my analytic language. My attempts at understanding what this split meant, beyond the concrete, were met by furious rejection. I realised then that I must wait and not force an early understanding of the split as this was experienced by her as my lack of comprehension of the nature of her early, as yet inexpressible, trauma.

Over time we did make progress in exploring this and her confusion about her mother tongue, in fact, her father's language. Then a further split came into sight: Greek was idealised as the location of everything that was genuine even though the paternal/masculine was felt by her to be associated with aggression and domination.

In the beginning, she often tried to script me, to "give me the language" that would help me make the "right diagnosis". She started reading psychoanalysis and invariably found that authors in learned papers were more "eloquent and sophisticated" than I was. Sometimes she critiqued my grammar; she was, unlike me, a native speaker of English (or was she?). But my repeated attempts at sensitively tuning in and yet retaining my own mind began to bear fruit: focussing on her affect was felt to be containing of her anxiety and her even greater rage. Both lessened over the years, though still resurface around holiday breaks.

In the third year of the therapy she dreamt: *I am at a party and notice two Chinese women having a conversation, in English. I am annoyed and say: why aren't you speaking Chinese? How can you make sense of one another? They look at me in that inscrutable Chinese way. I have no idea what they are feeling, but sense that they are angry about my butting in. One of them says: "we are from different parts of China, thousands of kilometres apart!"*

Her first association was that Chinese was the most difficult language in the world and added that she was aware that there were several Chinese languages, so the dream "did not make sense". There had been a Chinese community near her childhood home but "they kept themselves to themselves". She thought that she might have felt excluded in the dream but that made no sense either because, in fact, the Chinese women were speaking *her* language. The atmosphere seemed full of anxiety and I said that it seemed as if now she could not understand anything at all and that this made her feel frightened. She agreed and seemed calmer but then became silent and said she felt blocked. In the silence a saying surfaced in my mind, unusually in Hungarian: "It is all Chinese to me". Not sure that this made sense in English, now confused, I decided to wait. She continued to fret on the couch and we both seemed paralysed, as if our shared confusion represented our difficulties in communicating.

I realised that, perhaps as a result of projective identification, I had lost my ability to think in English and "forgot" the (British) English expression. Freed from the paralysis I could now formulate that the dream touched upon her feelings that I could not – perhaps would not – understand her deepest anxieties, that I was distant and that we could not find a shared emotional language. She exclaimed: "Of course! 'It's all Greek to me', isn't that what the British say?"

I said that I thought she was asking me rather than telling me, as if I was the expert, and she laughed. She now felt less anxious and we were able to think further about her conviction that communication was not possible except on a false basis (her impression of the Chinese women in the dream) and that a shared language was always a pretence, most powerfully felt at school where speaking English seemed to afford a degree of "hiding" to her. I suggested that the two Chinese women did in fact find a way to communicate and it was, indeed, in English. The sense of foreignness between us, hitherto understood by her in a rather concrete fashion as something to do with our differing cultures and languages only, now emerged as a useful means of exploring further the "confusion of tongues" of her infancy. Beyond the concrete, we could consider more genuinely and often within the transference the actual trauma of her repeated early separations and losses.

The terror of the preverbal, deeply traumatised, uncomprehending and misunderstood baby inside her now began to emerge in several dreams. She described regressive states during weekends when she curled up on the sofa, unable to think in words and I interpreted that, perhaps, her longing for me to speak Greek stands also for a longing for a preverbal merging, a state of togetherness and timelessness that requires no language.

We began to understand that she was forever anticipating the breakdown that had already happened (Winnicott, 1974), an early experience of having been, as it were, dropped first linguistically and then emotionally by a depressed, homesick and lonely mother and then by a mother preoccupied with her baby sister. The theme of powerful envy towards me came to the fore: in her mind, I had a place in the world, I had a partner and a safely established and dy-namic internal relationship between my two languages. I must have had a better childhood and a live maternal object inside me, she maintained. Exploration of her envy gradually led to an increased ability to take in interpretations. At the same time, it also enabled her to respond with ordinary anger when I got something wrong or when she felt misunderstood, rather than be overwhelmed by primitive rage that could not be verbalised.

We came to see that the parental couple in her mind had a false connection. How could they connect if they were so Other, a man and a woman, Greek and Irish? This led to a deepening understanding of her enormous difficulties in sharing thoughts and space, difficulties in "mental mixing" (Britton, 2003). She emphasised that neither of her parents were at home in London – as if her birth represented a terrible compromise, full of loss and resentment, rather than being the outcome of creative coupling. Unplanned and, in her mind, un-wanted, her difficulties with finding a partner and having a baby and her repeated attempts at joining a couple through relationships with unavailable men now made greater sense.

Working through the various strands of her difficulties with Otherness and the fundamental problem of our different languages – both actual and symbolic – led to sharing the analytic space more creatively. The actual problem of our three languages continued to appear in the relationship but with greater acknowledgement of our mutual difficulties in finding appropriate words to express particular feelings. A certain concreteness continued to figure in the therapy and after four years and to my mind not yet ready to end she decided to terminate her sessions and move abroad to a faraway country where a language other than "our" three was being spoken. This was before the existence of the internet or of cheap international phone calls. I never heard from her again and was left with a feeling of some regret about what seemed like an unfinished therapeutic process.

The interplay of external and internal reality: Brexit

At the time of the Brexit referendum, I had several patients who were deeply preoccupied with the topic – some were anxious about their own status in the UK, others were in favour of or against Brexit. It was of great significance to me, coming as I do from another European country and I wondered if my identity contributed to the frequency of the theme in the consulting room (cf. Morgan, 2016).

The national discourse during the run-up to the referendum brought out xenophobic, racist and anti-immigrant rhetoric. I noticed more than once – always outside London – a certain expression of disdain on some people's faces when they heard my accent.

There were accusations in the liberal press that all those in favour of Brexit were racists, and this was both untrue and unhelpful: the picture appeared to me to be far more complex, but positions among those in favour and those against became increasingly entrenched, as if no dialogue were possible.

Nostalgia for a never-never land

"This country has changed beyond recognition. I don't recognise the place I have known all my life. Strangers have taken over my home." Throughout his analysis, "William" would assert that this was an undeniable piece of reality: the arrival of "strangers", so different from him, would destroy his world. He alternated between seeing me, his émigré analyst, as "one of us, white, rooted in the culture of Christian Europe" and then as an uncomprehending foreigner. In the ebb and flow of our relationship, he struggled to protect from his rage what he felt to be good, helpful and nourishing in his analysis. His preoccupation with intrusion and his destructiveness, sometimes momentarily owned was, at least initially, mostly projected into the Other. Immigrants were felt to be destroying his idealised, pastoral England and developers were "overpopulating" the land around him, perceived as rightfully his. In the transference his analyst was often experienced as a greedy, possessive leech, taking away his strength, his physical prowess, his sexual drive and his independence.

Much of this was couched in a persistent nostalgia for a home that would feel safe and free of overwhelming anxiety. Longing to fly around the world, captaining his own aeroplane, alone and thrillingly independent was a leitmotif of his analysis. This struggle with omnipotence and the manic defence that underpins it continued as a preoccupation throughout our sessions.

His politics reflected this: the Brexit debate, followed by the referendum and the three-year aftermath, provided a backdrop to his analysis. In turn, the complexities of the debate and the battle for the nation's identity paralleled the elaboration of his embattled internal world, dominated by his terror.

As one of the world's oldest democracies descended into a national breakdown, followed by a paralysis threatening to create a permanent parliamentary stalemate, his analysis progressed through periods of near-breakdown experiences, manic triumphs, deep anxiety and depression, increasingly intermingled with moments of contentment and hope.

William came to analysis in a desperate state. He was plagued by suicidal feelings, chaotic and racing thoughts and raging moments when attacking his own body was his only source of relief. His periodic cocaine marathons would end in a state of abject despair. He detested his highly paid career. He was toying with the idea of becoming a psychoanalyst, though this notion was quickly discarded when he realised its financial implications and yet at times he tried to haggle about my fee. He could be puzzled about or even contemptuous of the location of my consulting room in a multi-ethnic neighbourhood.

Nostos, a Homeric word, means homecoming, and the Swiss physician Johannes Hofer added *algos* (pain) to it in the seventeenth century. He described *nostalgia* as a medical condition of homesickness, akin to depression, that had plagued troops separated from their homeland and family. Since Fodor's (1950) paper on nostalgia many more have followed (e.g., Martin, 1954, Akhtar, 1999).

Freud never specifically used the term in his psychoanalytic writings but in a letter to his absent friend Eduard Silberstein he wrote, quoting the poet Robert Burns: "A few days ago, when I … picked strawberries and raspberries on the Sofienalpe near Dornbach, I was overcome with nostalgia. Since you went away, I have been up in the mountains four times; but my heart's in the highlands, down here I find not one step is worth the trouble" (Freud, 1873). In a later letter (Freud, 1873) Freud creates an emphatic word *Erinnerungsschwelgerein* by linking up two words: *Erinnerung*, reminiscence and *Schwelgerein*, luxuriating, explained by the translator as "wallowing in nostalgia". "On transience" (1916) – a precursor of "Mourning and melancholia" (1917) – recounts Freud's conversation with the poet Rilke, just before the outbreak of the First World War, and ends, full of nostalgia, with a fervent belief in the return of a world as it had been before the war.

Sohn (1983) describes ordinary nostalgia, when it is linked to loss, as firmly rooted in the depressive position: a "state of mind that would be pained by an awareness that something that had been there and experienced, was not" (p. 203). He contrasts this with the wish to return to a phantasised situation that had never in fact existed. Instead of remembering, this latter form of nostalgia seeks to avoid all frustrations and represents a defence against reality, both psychic and external. It leads to stasis: this form of longing is interminable, without limits and with no loss accepted.

I am suggesting here that William was trapped in just such a nostalgic preoccupation, longing for a home perceived as an ideal place that had once existed, first in his early childhood in his "oneness with his mother" and then in an idealised England, untroubled by anxiety and strife. A similar longing for oneness and concrete maternal comfort, and the accompanying rage when this was frustrated, appeared in the transference throughout the analysis. On occasion, this led to endless repetitions and stasis that, in the countertransference could feel like a form of torture (Winnicott, 1975), helping me to understand and even experience the extent of my patient's suffering.

This experience of "torture" went hand in hand with my admiration for his staying power, his strong motivation to understand and his commitment to sustaining the long, exhausting journeys to my consulting room and the intense and wearying psychic work required for the analysis.

William maintained that the referendum was a democratic exercise to prioritise "the will of the people" over the "domination of the PC gang". He believed that it would magically repair the nation and provide a solution to our complex problems: it was for William a triumph of "Taking back control". Adopted by the "Leave" campaign, the slogan probably won the delicately balanced vote. Many who were seduced by it shared what I observed clinically in my work with some of my patients: the disavowal of our need for others, our dependence on what/who is outside of us (for William his partner and his analyst; for the UK, Europe). The refugee, the migrant, were reminders of the unbearable reality of this profound need and therefore had to be expunged (Rustin, 2019).

William longed for the idealised unity of the English people, within "safe" and unbridgeable borders that represented a world under his control and could be understood as a powerful manic defence. He emphasised that most migrants came in "through the back door", as if by a forceful – even anal – entry. Leaving the EU and separating from our continental neighbours was not experienced as a loss, nor was the potential breakup of the Union of the United Kingdom.

My patient harked back to the glorious victory of the Second World War. "We stood alone then, we don't need anyone now, we are an island race", he told me repeatedly. These sentiments were used to idealise, both by him and by some of the Brexiteers, what they saw as "the best of British". The "occupation" by the EU was felt to be the equivalent of the Nazi occupation the country had successfully resisted during the Second World War.

At times William "elevated" me, his émigré analyst, into a true Brit and when this idealisation and his avoidance of our separateness and our differences were taken up in the transference, his discourse could turn hostile. He would then claim that I, a foreigner, could not understand him. "You may have a British passport, but you are not British" he hissed at me. On occasion, the violence got under my skin and I would momentarily allow myself to be drawn into a "discussion". These enactments, inevitable as they seemed to be then as now, were certainly disturbing.

Other times I attempted to take up what my "foreignness" represented and his fears that I would retaliate for his attacks by excluding him from my mind or by sending him away. In the first session after the referendum he worried that perhaps I did *not* have a UK passport and thus may have to literally abandon him and leave the country. I sensed his concern for me and his powerful attachment to me and to the process.

Shortly after the referendum, following a series of particularly combative and furious sessions, he returned in an agitated state. The first name on his bill was wrong. He was devastated and I was mortified. Did I really know who he was? Or was I indeed unable to see him, to understand and care for him – these were his rapidly delivered, anguished questions. As I was listening, deeply troubled by the pain I had caused him, my first thought was that perhaps *I* had felt unseen *by him* in recent weeks as he talked incessantly about immigrants, intruders, sovereignty. The name on the bill, Timothy, did not belong to anyone I knew. And then it slowly began to make sense, through my silent associations: not long before I had watched a movie about the last hangman of Great Britain, played by the outstanding actor *Timothy* Spall.

Was it *his* murderousness or *mine* that was revealed at that moment, I asked myself? A powerful piece of counter-transference enactment, this event helped me understand further his impact on me and face my momentary inability to contain both his hatred and my murderous response.

Similarly, the Brexit process evoked rage on both sides of the polemic; compromise, mourning, acceptance of difference became elusive for the whole nation. Leavers, unable to mourn the country they had loved before the changes of the last decades, felt compelled to act destructively. Remainers found it challenging to mourn the loss of an idealised liberal consensus or, indeed, as it seemed to me at times, an idealised European Union. It was as if the country were tied up in a state of paralysis, unwilling to face the full implications of the Brexit vote and the mourning that would follow.

Sometime later, in a dream, William visited an unfamiliar but exciting room in an unknown city where he found a dead woman. He thought he might have had sex with her and then murdered her. He left the place tidy and vanished, hoping that no one would know he had even been there. However, on awakening, he felt disgust. He was visibly upset as he recounted the dream and seemed genuinely troubled by what it might reveal about him. We came to understand that, instead of mourning, he sexualised his loss and then buried his awareness – killed it off, as it were. In the process, he killed me off too but, importantly, by remembering and describing the dream he no longer needed to hide its meaning from himself and from me. Perhaps he was no longer completely identified with a murderous internal object and was more able to face the destructive aspects of his internal world and his sexuality (Steiner, 1993).

What constitutes psychic change for a patient whose internal world was, at least at the start of the analysis, so dominated by hatred of alterity and a fear of dependence? This question continued to preoccupy me throughout William's analysis. His heroic psychic journey from a tortured, raging and terrified man to a patient now more in touch with his and our shared human vulnerability, was as moving as it was impressive. His idealisation of his mother lessened and his identification with a hated and violent father diminished somewhat (Campbell, 1999).

As he became increasingly open about his attachment to and dependence on me, his need for self-harming began to diminish and occasionally a softer, more contented person emerged, though his combative style, both in the consulting room and in his home life, waxed and waned to the end.

Towards the end of his analysis, William made important changes in his personal and professional life. Working through his nostalgic preoccupations allowed him to discover that he needed to change his working and living environment radically and find ways of achieving what *was* possible rather than forever being trapped in longing for what *was not*.

The intensity of the experience and the turbulence of our relationship will, I hope, help him weather the inevitable storms life may bring, especially for a man who has endured so much pain and loss.

The interplay of external and internal reality: Covid-19 in the consulting room

"Joanne" said just before the pandemic that unless I agreed to reducing her sessions she would leave. She claimed that she had no time for "all that travelling to and from sessions". She felt triumphant that I would not be able to prevent her departure, but now, as a result of the pandemic, her reasoning ceased to offer her justification as remote sessions involved no travelling. In her mind I "imposed" Zoom to regain control; she experienced this as a form of premature and traumatic weaning.

She was young, quite happy to get the virus and be done with it: "The whole thing is world hysteria, an overreaction on a massive scale. It is just a bloody flu. I thought you were much more levelheaded, and, like me, didn't follow fashions and would not panic – now I don't know who you are", she said furiously.

I responded by exploring the painful and traumatic aspects of the abrupt change of the setting. I acknowledged that this repeated an early, devastating separation in her history. The deprivation she now experienced – the closure of the consulting room, the disappearance of the bodily dimensions of the analytic setting and the shock of being sent away by me – rocked her already fragile trust in me. After a painful and tearful response her rage gave way to desperate sadness but, as was often the case with her, the sadness was quickly defended against by further rage and I suggested that exploring her sense of aloneness was more difficult than feeling furious.

I thought that this situation had revealed that we might see things differently, and, indeed, that we might be two separate people with different thoughts, views, feelings and circumstances and, especially, differing ages. Our disagreement about the fate of her analysis had already revealed our separateness. Having a mind of my own was perceived as an attack on her integrity. But remote working also exposed a deeply held phantasy: that the couch in my warm and welcoming room was an extension of my lap, a physical space in which she could receive the warm maternal care she felt she had never had.

The patient's lack of concern, even cruelty towards me in the transference became apparent and a focal point of the analysis. Her lack of concern both for her own well-being and for her objects was now laid bare and threatened the analysis. By proposing a partial disengagement from me she also appeared to want to protect me from her hatred, thereby showing her capacity for *some* concern, but mainly her terror lest her objects return the hatred and retaliate.

This callousness and cruelty (Brenman, 2006a), at a time of such heightened anxiety did, indeed, make it hard for me to bear her presence on occasion, but our shared terror and a deep sense of loss aided our mutual identifications.

Remote working, perhaps somewhat surprisingly, has allowed us to work through her deeply buried unconscious longing for my love and the defences against it, and the analysis has continued without Joanne feeling compelled to undermine or destroy it.

Back to survival – facing mortality

"Ageing is not for sissies", warned a friend, some years older than me (quoting Bette Davis). I have often thought how accurate this is, but not more so than during a recent health scare that turned out to be a false alarm, though it confronted me with the stark reality of my mortality.

And then came the big C – not cancer, but Covid-19 that hit us all like a tornado. Our lives in London have been punctuated by news of the mounting death toll and by periods of lockdown. No bombs were falling, we were not starving. Still, we lived in a siege of sorts, at times imprisoned in our homes.

The early period of the first lockdown was a challenge, but I was "ready" when it came to the practical aspects of "survival": my second-generation survival instincts had kicked in, illustrating, yet again, my tendency for "vigilance". I had stocked up on food and essentials long before this became an ethical dilemma. Still, when lockdown came, shopping for fresh food became a challenge requiring the mentality of a hunter as I surfed the internet for delivery slots.

Out there, food banks reported a huge rise in needy people desperate to obtain food. Our street WhatsApp group was full of requests for bartering – flour, butter, eggs, yeast were particularly in short supply. Most of my neighbours reported an urge to eat more, especially sweet, starch-laden foods. There was an unprecedented solidarity in our cul-de-sac, an inspiring experience. I observed the opposite behaviour, too, reminding me of what I knew about profiteering in war time. A desperate man put in a request on a local social media platform. He had run out of toilet paper, an item nearly impossible to obtain for a while. I offered some and he wanted to know how much I would charge for it. Charge? I was astonished; apparently, several people had offered to "sell" him four rolls for up to £15!

I was working remotely, mostly on Zoom. Many of my patients adjusted, others suffered from the lack of physical presence. I had the advantage of considerable experience in remote working in recent years with patients who had moved abroad or away and continued analysis via Zoom. This meant that I was reasonably familiar with the technology, though not with the intensity of working in this way with so many patients and in a situation forced upon us rather than voluntarily chosen.

Being in regular contact with a friend and colleague in Lombardy, Italy, I knew that my personal circumstances would require me to move into remote working soon so I was able to prepare patients for this from the middle of February 2020. Most of them thought it was I who needed help as the virus at that time seemed remote and insignificant to them and when it came to closing the consulting room it was a huge shock to patients.

Analytic work presented different challenges with each patient. Most unusually, patients were required to create the physical setting. Ordinarily we analysts create – and control – the setting and then analyse the patient's use (and abuse) of it. The setting is the physical part of the frame and as such is central to psychoanalysis. "The frame is maintained and tends to be maintained (actively, by the psychoanalyst) as invariable; and while it exists as such it seems to be non-existent or it does not count" (Bleger, 1967, p 512).

The disruption of the frame was thus profound and I focussed my interpretations on patients' difficulties – or apparent and, at times, defensive ease – with creating the space for uninterrupted reverie. Equally, some patients faced genuine obstacles in arranging a safe and regular space for their sessions due to their (external) circumstances. At such an extraordinary time the existence and maintenance of my *internal* (symbolic) setting (Parsons, 2007, Green, 2011) appeared to me more crucial than ever, providing me with a framework beyond the concrete, without the bodily presence of patients.

They, in turn, responded in many and varied ways. For some, remote working brought up profound anxieties about a loss of contact, about my death or theirs, about me being, as it were, so remote as to be non-existent. For others, the less time spent travelling and a simpler way of life allowed for more space for the exploration of their internal world. One patient, a big man, felt safer to show me his rage, a feeling he had kept at bay while being in the same room, lest he caused real physical damage. Another patient revealed, for the first time, the extent and nature of his use of internet porn. As his anxiety grew about his own body – he is in a high-risk group – his need for pornography to manage these anxieties increased. He insisted on using the phone rather than Zoom as he feared that, in his mind, I would become identified with the debased women paid to perform online. Another patient revealed paranoid anxieties as she imagined that I was secretly recording the sessions or that I might be searching for food on the internet instead of listening to her. Some took delight in being able to show me their new sofa or a painting they had spoken about before, others felt exposed and intruded upon by my "looking into" their home/room/bedroom.

Some patients struggled with the technology and in each case I observed a mixture of genuine external problems (slow internet, old computer etc) and the internal states they brought to the situation: anxiety, fury, elation, resistance and so on. Deciphering the connections between these while struggling with my own anxieties and losses, most especially the loss of connection with my small grandchildren, did at times push me almost to the limits of endurance in the early months of the pandemic.

I returned to some sessions in the consulting room in the summer and autumn of 2020, until another explosion of infections and another lockdown forced me back to remote working. This return and then departure – for those patients who chose to take this up – was in itself unusual and instructive. It became an opportunity to mourn our life as it had been before and to work through some aspects of the traumatic and forced "weaning" at the start of the pandemic. I was much helped by an online discussion group with colleagues who were experimenting with similar alterations of the setting.

Brexit and Covid-19 have contributed to external environments where the complex interaction between the external world and psychic reality could be explored and understood seemingly more than ever. The problematic of separateness and the centrality of our difficulties with the Other in my clinical vignettes and throughout my elaboration of my history and identity appear perhaps particularly powerfully in these tragic times. The reality of our altered world has challenged us: patient and analyst alike face the same external threat and yet this has affected us in profoundly different ways, depending on our internal world as well as our living conditions, age and health.

Uncertainty about the future and about our lives imposed by the pandemic lays bare the reality of the human condition: our limitations, ageing and mortality.

Facing my mirror – no longer young,
the news – always of death,
the dogs – rising from sleep and clamoring
and howling, howling.
nevertheless
I see for a moment

that's not it: it is
the First Things.
Word after word
floats through the glass.
Towards me.

(Denise Levertov, Seeing for a Moment, 1981)[16]

Notes

1 Many psychoanalytic authors have similarly addressed the psychoanalyst's understanding of his/her autobiography (Greenberg, 2004, Harris, 1998, Parsons, 2009, Perelberg, 2009, Spillus, 2015 etc.).
2 After writing this chapter, my attention was drawn by a friend (Prof. J. Zeitlin) to an essay about this film by S. Rubin Suleiman (2006). She discusses the theme of Jewish identity, adding some fascinating thoughts about the debate that followed the film in Hungary.
3 The problem of assimilation has been addressed by many authors, e.g., Eng and Han (2000). Others have described the "whitening" of Jews in the US (Brodkin, 2000). Surprisingly little psychoanalytic exploration is available about Jewish assimilation in Europe but this is beyond the scope of this chapter.
4 Hungarian psychoanalytic writings did not address this topic until after regime change in the late 1980s (Virag, 2000).
5 The French psychoanalyst Gerard Szwec describes this vividly in his book *Les galeriens volontaires* (2014). (Rachel Chaplin, personal communication).
6 This was despite of the existence of Braham's detailed and devastating account of the Hungarian Shoah, translated into Hungarian in the early 1990s (Braham, 1994). See also Bohuss (2015).
7 Regent of Hungary, 1919–1944.
8 Jeffrey Murer has researched the resurgence of antisemitism and the far right in Hungary. He makes a similar point about the lack of mourning in much of the Hungarian discourse. He connects this with the concept of the abject other, which is linked to projective identification (Murer, 2009). (cf. Meszaros, 2020)
9 In his autobiography (Leo, 2009) Maxim Leo describes the participation of some Jews in the higher echelons of the East German political scene in similar terms.
10 Bernard Harrison, a philosopher, was among the first authors to identify this (Harrison, 2006). See also Perelberg, 2020.
11 The paper of the Communist Party of Great Britain.
12 With thanks to Zsuzsanna Renyi for her kind permission to publish this quote in my own translation.
13 More recently I came across Alice Munro's short story (2009) whose heroine is Sonia Kovalevskaya.
14 Comparative Clinical Methods Conference (see also Tuckett, 2012).
15 1943–1944.

16 "Seeing for a Moment" By Denise Levertov, from OBLIQUE PRAYERS, copyright ©1984 by Denise Levertov. Reprinted by permission of New Directions Publishing Corp.

References

Abraham, N. & Torok, M. (1984). The lost object – me: notes on identification within the crypt. *Psychoanal. Inq.*, *4*(2), 221–242.

Akhtar, S. (1999). The immigrant, the exile and the experience of nostalgia. *J. Appl. Psychoanal. Stud.*, *1*(2), 123–130.

Amati-Mehler, J., Argentieri, S. & Canestrri, G. (1993). *The babel of the unconscious. Mother tongue and foreign languages in the psychoanalytic dimension.* Madison, CT: International Universities Press.

Antinucci, P. (2004). I need to hide in my foreignness, will you let me? In: J. Szekacs-Weisz & I. Ward (eds), *Lost childhood and the language of exile.* London: Imago East West/Freud Museum.

Arendt, H. (1951/2017). *The origins of totalitarianism.* London: Penguin.

Bako, T. & Zana, K. (2018). The vehicle of transgenerational trauma: the transgenerational atmosphere. *Am. Imago*, *75*(2), 271–285.

Balint, M. (1979). *The basic fault: therapeutic aspects of regression.* London/ New York: Tavistock Publications.

Barocas, H. A. & Barocas, C. B. (1979). Wounds of the fathers: the next generation of Holocaust victims. *Int. Rev. Psychoanal.*, *6*, 331–340.

Bergmann, M. & Jucovy, M. eds. (1982) *Generations of the Holocaust.* New York: Columbia University Press.

Bion, W. R. (1962). *Learning from experience.* London: Heinemann.

Bion, W. R. (1970). *Attention and interpretation.* London: Heinemann.

Birksted-Breen, D. (2016). Bi-ocularity, the functioning mind of the psychoanalysis. *Int. J. of Psychoanal.*, *97*(1), 25–40.

Bleger, J. (1967). Psychoanalysis of the psychoanalytic frame, *Int. J. Psychoanal.*, *48*, 511–519.

Bohuss, K. (2015). Not a Jewish question? The Holocaust in Hungary in the press and propaganda of the Kadar regime during the trial of Adolf Eichmann. *Hung. Hist. Rev.*, *4*(3).

Braham, R.(1994). *The politics of genocide. The Holocaust in Hungary.* New York: Columbia Press.

Britton, R. (1998). The analyst's intuition: selected fact or overvalued idea? In: *Belief and imagination* (pp. 97–108). London: The New Library of Psychoanalysis.

Britton, R. (2003). Narcissistic problems in sharing space. In: *Sex, death and the superego. Experiences in psychoanalysis* (pp. 165–178). London: Karnac.

Brenman, E. (2006a). The narcissism of the analyst: its effect in clinical practice. In: *Recovery of the lost good object* (pp. 48–61). London: Routledge.

Brenman, E. (2006b). Cruelty and narrowmindedness. *Int. J. Psychoanal.*, *66*, 273–281.

Brenman-Pick, I. (2002). Dangling in uncertainty. In: *Authenticity in the analytic encounter* (pp. 177–191). London: Routledge.

Brodkin, K. (1998). How did Jews become white folks? Rutgers University Press.

Browne, H. (2018). Regression: allowing the future to be re-imagined. In: G. Kohon (ed.), *British psychoanalysis. New perspectives in the independent tradition* (pp. 209–223). London: Routledge.

Campbell, D. (1999). The role of the father in a pre-suicidal state. In: R. Perelberg (ed.), *Psychoanalytic understanding of violence and suicide* (pp. 75–86). London: Routledge.

Coltart, N. (1990). Attention. Lecture delivered on the 20th anniversary of the Arbours Association. *British J. Psychother.*, *7*(2), 164–174.

Eng, D. L. & Han, S. (2000). A dialogue on racial melancholia. *Psychoanal. Dial.*, *10*(4), 667–700.

Erikson, E. H. (1968). *Identity: youth and crisis*. New York/London: W.W. Norton.

Erős, F. (1993). The construction of Jewish identity in Hungary in the 1980s. *Revue Internationale d''anthropologie et de sciences humaines*, *42*(2), 141–150.

Erős, F., Kovács, A., Lévai K. (1985). "Hogyan jöttem rá, hogy zsidó vagyok?" Interjúk. (How did I discover that I was Jewish?). *Medvetánc*, *2–3*, 129–144.

Fodor, N. (1950). Varieties of nostalgia. *Psychoanal. Rev.*, *37*, 25–38.

Freud, S. (1873, 1875). Letters from Sigmund Freud to Eduard Silberstein, *1871–1881*, 128–130.

Freud, S. (1916). *On transience*. SE.14 (pp. 303–307). London: The Hogarth Press.

Freud, S. (1917). *Mourning and melancholia*. SE.14 (pp. 237–260). London: The Hogarth Press.

Freud, S. (1920). *Beyond the pleasure principle*. SE.18 (pp. 1–64). London: The Hogarth Press.

Frie, R. (2017). *Not in my family: German memory and responsibility after the Holocaust*. Oxford University Press.

Fulbrook, M. (2018). *Reckonings: Legacies of Nazi persecution*. Oxford University Press.

Gaddini, E. (1969). On imitation. *Int. J. Psychoanal.*, *50*, 475–484.

Green, A. (2011). *Illusions and disillusions in psychoanalytic work*. London: Routledge.

Greenacre, P. (2011) The impostor. *Psychoanal. Quart.*, *80*(4), 1025–1046.

Greenberg, J. (2004). An autobiographical fragment. *Psychoanal. Inq.*, *24*(4), 517–530.

Grinberg, L. and R. (1989). *Psychoanalytic perspectives on migration and exile*. New Haven, CT/London: Yale University Press.

Grubrich-Simitis, I. (1981) Extreme traumatisation as cumulative trauma: psychoanalytic investigations of the effects of concentration camp experiences on survivors and their children. *Psychoanalytic Stud. Chil.*, *36*, 415–450.

Grubrich-Simitis, I. (1984). From concretism to metaphor – thoughts on some theoretical and technical aspects of the psychoanalytic work with children of Holocaust survivors. *Psychoanal. Stud. Chil.*, *39*, 301–319.

Hakehillot, P. (1975). Tarcal. In: T. Levi (ed.), *Encyclopedia of Jewish communities in Hungary*. Jerusalem: Yad Vashem.

Harris, A. (1998). The analyst as (auto)biographer. *American Imago*, *55*(2), 255–275.

Harris, A., & Mitchell, S. (2004). What is American about American psychoanalysis? *Psychoanal. Dial.*, *14*(2), 165–191.

Harrison, B. (2006). *The resurgence of antisemitism. Jews, Israel and liberal opinion*. London: Rowman and Littlefield.

Hoffman, E. (1989). *Lost in translation. Life in a new language*. London: Penguin Books.

Jaspers, K. (1946). *The question of German guilt*. London: Random House.

Joseph, B. (1985). Transference: the total situation. *Int. J. Psychoanal.*, *66*, 447–454

Judt, T. (1992). The past is another country: myth and memory in post-war Europe. *Daedalus*, *121*(4), 83–118.

Kertesz, E. (1962). *Sonja professzor*. Budapest: Csikos Konyvek.

Kestenberg, J. (1980). Psychoanalyses of children of survivors from the Holocaust. *J. Amer. Psychoanal. Assn.*, *28*, 775–804.

Klein, M. (1937/1975). Love, guilt and reparation. In: *Love, guilt and reparation and other works*. London: Delta Books.

Klein, M. (1940). Mourning and its relation to manic-depressive states. *Int. J. Psychoanal.*, *21*, 125–153.

Kohon, G. ed. (2018a). *British psychoanalysis: new perspectives in the independent tradition*. London: Routledge.

Kohon, G. (2018b). Bye-bye, sexuality. In R. Perelberg (ed.), *Psychic bisexuality* (pp. 258–276). Abingdon: Routledge.

Kohon, G. (2019). The question of uncertainty. In: *Concerning the nature of psychoanalysis* (pp. 85–106). London: The New Library of Books.

Kovacs, A. (2008). *A masik szeme* (The eyes of the other). Budapest: Gondolat Kiado.

Levertov, D. (1961). Matins. In: T*he Jacob's Ladder, Selected poems*. New York: New Directions.

Limentani, A. (1989). *Between Freud and Klein: The psychoanalytic quest for knowledge and truth*. London: Karnac.

Leo, M. (2009). *Red love: the story of an East German Family*. London: Blackwell.

Levi, P. (1959/2000). *If this is a man*. London: Everyman Publishers.

Martin, A. R. (1954). Nostalgia. *Am. J. Psychoanal.,141*, 93–104.

McDougall, J. (1986). Identifications, neoneeds and neosexualities. *Int. J. Psychoanal., 67*, 19–30.

Meszaros, J. (2010). Progress and persecution in the psychoanalytic heartland: antisemitism, communism and the fate of Hungarian psychoanalysis. *Psychoanal. Dial., 20*(5), 600–622.

Mitscherlich, A. and M. (1975). *The inability to mourn*. New York: Grove Press.

Morgan, D. (2016). Psychoanalysis can help us make sense of Brexit. *LSE Business Review*; https://blogs.lse.ac.uk/businessreview/2016/10/24/psychoanalysis-can-help-us-make-sense-of-brexit/

Morgan, D. ed. (2019). *The unconscious in social and political life*. London: Phoenix.

Munroe, A. (2009). *Too much happiness*. London: Chatto & Windus.

Murer, J. (2009). Constructing the enemy-other: anxiety, trauma and mourning in the narratives of political conflict. *Psychoanalysis, Culture and Society, 14*, 109–130.

Niederland (1968). Clinical observations on the "survival syndrome". *Int. J. Psychoanal., 49*, 313–315.

Ogden, T. H. (2004). On holding and containing, being and dreaming. *Int. J. Psychoanal., 84*(6), 1349–1364.

O'Shaughnessy, E. (2008). On gratitude. In: P. Roth & A. Lemma (eds.), *Envy and gratitude revisited* (pp. 77–91). London: Karnac.

Oz, A. (2004). *A tale of darkness*. London: Harcourt.

Parsons, M. (2000). Sexuality and perversion a hundred years on. *Int. J. Psychoanal., 81*(1), 37–49.

Parsons, M. (2007). Raiding the inarticulate: the internal setting and listening beyond the countertransference. *Int. J. Psychoanal., 88*, 1441–1456.

Parsons, M. (2009). Becoming and being an analyst in the British Psychoanalytical Society. *Psychoanal. Inq., 29*(3), 236–246.

Perelberg, R. (1999). A core phantasy in violence. In: *Psychoanalytic understanding of violence and suicide* (pp. 87–108). London: Routledge.

Perelberg, R. J. (2008). The Controversial Discussions and après-coup. In: *Time, space and phantasy* (pp. 106–131). London: The New Library of Psychoanalysis.

Perelberg, R. J. (2009). On becoming a psychoanalyst. *Psychoanal. Inq.*, *29*(3), 247–263.

Perelberg, R. J. (2020). The murder of the dead father: the Shoah and contemporary antisemitism. *IPA Podcast*.

Polmear, C. (2008). An independent response to *Envy and Gratitude*. In: Roth, P. & Lemma, A. (eds.), *Envy and gratitude revisited* (pp. 63–78). London: Karnac.

Renyi, A. (1969). *Dialogues on Mathematics* [Dialogusok a matematikarol.] (K. Lanczi, Trans.) (pp. 59–60). Budapest: Akademia Kiado.

Rosenfeld, H. (1987). *Impasse and interpretation*. London: Tavistock.

Rubin Suleiman, S. (2006). *Crises of memory and the Second World War*. Cambridge, MA: Harvard University Press.

Rustin, M. (2019). Understanding right wing populism. In: D. Morgan (ed.), *The unconscious in social and political life* (pp. 39–52). Bicester: Phoenix Publishing House.

Sandler, J. (1983). Reflections on some psychoanalytic concepts and psychoanalytic practice. *Int. J. Psychoanal.*, *64*, 35–45.

Schafer, R. (1979). The appreciative analytic attitude and the construction of multiple histories. *Psychoanalytic and Contemporary Thought*, *2*(1), 3–24.

Sebek, M. (1996). The fate of the totalitarian object. *Int. Forum of Psychoanalysis*, *5*(4), 289–294.

Sedlak, V. (2019). *The psychoanalyst's superegos, ego ideals and blind spots. The emotional development of the clinician*. London/New York: Routledge.

Segal, H. (2006). Reflections on truth, tradition and the psychoanalytic tradition of truth. *American Imago*, *63* (3), 283–292.

Sereny, G. (2001). *The German trauma*. London: Penguin.

Sohn, L. (1983). Nostalgia. *Int. J. Psychoanal.*, *64*, 203–210.

Spillus, E. (2015). *Journeys in psychoanalysis*. London/New York: Routledge.

Standensky, E. (2000). Antiszemitizmus az 1956-os forradalomban. (Antisemitism during the 1956 revolution.) *Orszagos Szechenyi Konyvtar 1956-os archivum*.

Stein, R. (2005). Why perversion? "False love" and the perverse pact. *Int. J. of Psychoanal.*, *86*(3), 775–799.

Steiner, G. (1958/1967). A kind of survivor. In: *Language and silence* (pp. 140–164). London: Faber and Faber.

Steiner, J. (1993). Perverse relationships in pathological organisations. In: *Psychic retreats* (pp. 103–115). London: Routledge.

Steiner, J. (2000). Containment, enactment and communication. *Int. J. of Psychoanal.*, *8*(12), 244–255.

Steiner, J. (2008). The repetition compulsion, envy and the death instinct. In: P. Roth & A. Lemma (eds.), *Envy and gratitude revisited* (pp. 137–151). London: Karnac.

Szakolczai, A. (2008). Zsidoellenes zavargasok az 1956-os forradalom idoszakaban. (Anti-Jewish disturbances during the 1956 revolution). *Tarsadalmi Konfliktusok Kutatokozpont.*

Szekacs-Weisz, J. (2004). How to be a bi-lingual psychoanalyst? In: J. Szekacs-Weisz & I. Ward (eds.), *Lost childhood and the language of exile.* London: Imago East West/Freud Museum

Szecsenyi, A. (2017). Holokauszt-representacio a Kadar korban (The representation of the Holocaust during the Kadar era.) In: *Tanulmanyok a holokausztrol.* Budapest: Mult es Jovo.

Szirtes, G. (2019). *The photographer at sixteen.* London: MacLehose Press.

Szirtes, G. (2000). *The Budapest file.* London: Bloodaxe Books.

Tuckett, D. (2012). Some reflections on psychoanalytic technique: in need of core concepts or an archaic ritual? *Psychoanalytic Inquiry*, *32*(1), 87–108.

Virag, T. (2000). *Children of social trauma. Hungarian psychoanalytic case studies.* London/Philadelphia: Jessica Kingsley.

Winnicott, D. W. (1953). Transitional objects and transitional phenomena. *Int.J. of Psychoanal. 34*

Winnicott, D. W. (1969). The use of an object. *Int. J. of Psychoanal.*, *50*, 711–716.

Winnicott, D. W. (1974). Fear of breakdown. *Int. Rev. Psychoanal.*, *1*, 103–107.

Winnicott, D. W. (1975). Hate in the countertransference. In: *Through paediatrics to psychoanalysis* (pp. 194–203). London: The Hogarth Press.

Chapter 5

The inner touch

Julianna Vamos

Personal journey

Leaving

The train left Budapest West Station heading for Paris Gare de l'Est in November 1974, with me on board. I felt ready, though unaware of the unpredictability of this journey, and ignorant of my unconscious preparation for it. The station in Budapest, designed by Gustave Eiffel, was inaugurated in 1877, ten years before the beginning of the construction of the Paris emblem: the Eiffel Tower.

My parents accompanied me to the station. My mother's gaze showed a humble acceptance of destiny. She was brave and generous. When I hugged my father goodbye, I held him as if forever and whispered to him "you are my rock". My father stepped on the wagon with the intention of saving me a seat; I did not have a reservation. He could only make the first step. He was holding on to the bar with two hands, was stuck, could not move further. He did not have the strength to make the second step.

The transgenerational plan

Before my birth, emigration was already in the landscape. I nearly left Hungary before I was conceived. My parents tried to leave Budapest in 1949 but were caught at the border and put into jail. The family jewellery was sent to Sydney in the leg of a magnificent *armoire*. I guess it may still be found somewhere in somebody's house in Australia.

My parents' lives were saved, but not that of their first-born. My fantasised older brother – my supportive imaginary brother – died at

DOI: 10.4324/9781003306542-5

birth. This loss came after the mass deportation of my maternal family in 1944, of the grandfather I never knew and several uncles and
aunts. For most of my adult life, I have meditated a great deal on the
extinction of this huge family. I have had the wish to compensate for
this. Among these cumulative traumas, I count three transmitted to
me, and one consequent to my choice. From and through my parents,
there is the Holocaust, my parents' aborted emigration and the death
of their first child. My choice of emigration became the fourth.

Apart from these traumas, I was fortunate to have the tools and to
find the right people to work them through. I consider that my vitality
came from the over-investment of my parents in their only child – me –
after such tremendous loss. I still can feel how much their gaze was
mirrored by the unbelievable flow and force of the miracle: "life can go
on, life will continue, no matter what". This is the fate of the survivor.

The author's mother in 1943

Provisions

My parents fell in love in 1943 when my mother was in a sanatorium
for tuberculosis and my father was visiting a relative of his. My mother
telling me about the moment when she saw my father is etched in my
mind; there was an immediate sparkle. I feel how this has become part
of me. They wanted to take their relationship slowly, romantically,
taking their time. They were planning life together when my father was
deported. After liberation, she waited desperately for his reappearance.

Finally, my father came back from deportation, sick and mute. Not being able to communicate with him, my mother almost gave up and bought a train ticket to emigrate to London, as her own father had suggested to her before having been deported to Auschwitz. Before 1949, there had already been 1945: the first attempt to leave Hungary, "this damned country". She had invited all her friends to a farewell party. My father came too and stayed until the very end. By then he could talk again and invited her to the Opera to see Carmen the following night. So, she stayed, for him, with him, and never left Budapest. All my life in Budapest I lived with a couple in love.

The author's father in 1943

The author and her parents in 1958

I was a very lonely only child. I was desperately trying to convince my parents for years, with all my strength and imagination, that having another child, a brother, or a sister, was essential. I did not succeed. The numerous abortions, the customary form of birth control in Hungary in the 1950s, and my father's heart problems closed that door. So, I had no grandparents, no larger family, no siblings; we were just the nucleus: us three. There remained only a terribly damaged aunt, my mother's younger sister, with a little girl, my cousin. While I was writing this chapter, my aunt passed away.

My mother, ten years older than my aunt, was hiding in basements throughout the war, she was a "healthy" survivor, unlike my father, a deeply traumatised man back from deportation. In my adolescent years, major crises swept through our little family's life as I tried with all my strength to tear myself away from my parents. My father did not talk to me for a whole year, disappointed and desperate about how I had turned out: rebellious, autonomous and free. He wrote a nine-page testament two years before his death, of which eight pages describe how I was the only source of bitterness in his life. But at the train station, it was over, he forgot the pain of being the parent of a wild child.

This was the same father who saved me from the worst consequences of polio, which I contracted at the age of one year during the Hungarian epidemic in the 1950s. Thanks to his alertness and insistence, I received immediate care. Other than that, everything went smoothly in the tiny apartment they managed to obtain, after the loss of their *bourgeois* flat. I have never suffered of anxiety about missing anything. Looking at the one surviving photograph from before the Second World War, with the beautiful Italian armoire, the space, and the tranquillity, I adopted their internal habitat, I identified with the comfort they remembered they had, and it proved stronger than the narrowness of our reality.

I attended three elementary schools – my parents moved me to better and better ones. Of all my classmates I remember only one girl, whose name stuck in my mind: she was called Zsofi Solomon. Where could I have heard the story of Solomon? How did it stick in my mind? It certainly had a significant resonance. Until the age of ten, I did not yet know we were Jewish.

Finally, at the age of fourteen I went to high school; the first one was called "Attila Jozsef Gimnazium" named after a poet who was important to all of us. Attila József's poetry is almost unknown in France, the UK or the United States. His unique lyricism and unconscious insights transcend his words. The beauty of his poems has a rhythm and music which does not translate well because of the special nature of the Hungarian language, and I will talk about my attachment to it later.

I was kicked out of the first high school because I said "fuck off" to a teacher and he lost control and hit me. Both of us bore the consequences. They tried to put me in another high school in which I refused to even set foot. Then the mother of one of my friends managed to get me into the excellent, prestigious Fazekas High School. That is where the three of us – Veronica, Katalin and I – met. By then, I was somewhat ready to conform.

My parents provided me with all that a girl from a "good family" needs: ballet, piano, horse-riding, languages. They were different from my friends' parents: they were not intellectuals, they were not in the communist party, they did not belong to any institution, and so they did not experience disappointment with the political development of the country, as they had already felt so since the war. Before meeting this class at Fazekas, I was already deeply attached to some friends whom I had met at the age of 13, when I went to the very first party of my life. With this group of people, we improvised theatre pieces, sitting in the bathtub imagining we were in Noah's ark. We read poetry and literature together and talked about existential questions adolescence brings around. I have kept in touch with these friends ever since.

We learned something essential together in this community of our adolescence, we learned to be interconnected. We practised preserving and protecting the precious fabric that belonging gave us. In the group we were sometimes hard on each other, we contended with competition, rivalry, envy. But the secret of small-group dynamics, the "chosen family", the belonging together, was stronger than the pain. I was lucky. The spirit of this circle of friends gave me strength all along. And I was fortunate with my silent, not "regime-friendly" family background, that allowed me to be prepared to take the step my parents could not take after the war. These adolescent years gave me the contours of my identity with some special guidance as to my social taste. The quality of our network has remained a reference point throughout my life and still does today. We have remained faithful to these community values.

I was a true believer in communist values. As a "little drummer" and later a "pioneer", I belonged to these Socialist versions of scouts. I accepted – and I still do – some tenets of Marxist theory, such as the critique of capitalist production and the attendant alienation, the stuff that our heads had been filled with during our school years. And in the desire for equality, I thought how wonderful it was to be a "Working Class Hero" when I listened to John Lennon's song. Hanging out with this group of friends, my reference group, I found freedom to think. It was my "school of life".

When I got into Fazekas High School, it was the sixth establishment I was going to attend. I could not fit in there either. A few people remain particularly special to me, like Veronica and Katalin. I was only minimally involved at school. I hung out with my reference group, my circle, my future emigrant buddies. I do not remember any teacher influencing me there, nor do I remember events that could have bound us together. It was already "survival time" for me.

Essential circle

After the Second World War and the advent of the communist dictatorship, there was a small, informal intellectual group in Budapest known as the "Tribe", formed around two important personalities, both of whom I knew: the psychologist Ferenc Mérei (1909–1986) and the painter Endre Bálint (1914–1986). They belonged to my parents' or perhaps to my grandparents' generation. The Tribe began as a group of friends. They had survived all the regimes, prisons, and caesuras of twentieth-century history. The arrival of our generation in the 1970s gave us a model for being free and in contact with the world outside Hungary, even within a closely monitored socialist country. Mérei's youngest daughter was part of our community. In this Mérei *milieu,* we became immersed in a way of thinking that we kept for the rest of our lives. We learned how to elaborate our ideas freely, even in a dictatorship. Without being aware of it, I perceived that public discussions better be avoided. The absence of democratic spaces stimulated informal communication in private apartments: we were extending the borders of these private spaces to discuss public affairs. I became conscious of the danger we faced of being put under surveillance, as some of my friends had been. So, I made up my mind that for my own protection, I would not be visibly involved in politics. We entered a marginal, underground culture of musical and artistic circles. The landscape was one of poetry, happenings and homemade theatre. We hung out in the kitchen of the Mérei household, providing us with opportunities to talk and feel alive. It had the spirit of a clandestine existence, outside of Hungary's political national history. I was writing poetry back then, and I still am.

The Mérei psychic envelope

The Mérei household was shaped by counterculture. The praxis of this counterculture stemmed from the avant-garde of the 1930s in Paris, where psychoanalysts and artists worked together, forming a creative space in opposition to political oppression. The frontier was crystal clear. Spaces around these creative, free-thinking people separated us from official Hungarian socialist politics.

The Mérei psychic envelope created a special extended space for us. From this private space emerged a transitional dimension, a culture: relational-friendship culture, artistic innovation, philosophical events, psychodrama workshops and a network in which the shared experience was the priority. Lived lives, being present in all its dimensions, was more important than professional advancement. But the Mérei life philosophy provoked and demanded continuous efforts towards excellent performance and a huge intellectual investment was expected.

Ferenc Mérei and his family were Francophones. In the 1930s he had gone to live and study in Paris. He had left Budapest because of the *numerus clausus*, a limit on the number of Jewish students allowed to attend Hungarian universities. My openness to his love and longing for French literature, culture and psychology generated in me an unconscious path towards what would become my future, adult trajectory.

Transitional steps

In 1972, at the age of 18, and two years before I emigrated, my friend G. and I received what was then a big deal: an exit visa for a one-month summer holiday in England. We visited Cambridge, Oxford and London. A series of beautiful photos are reminders of our excursion. We had created a little happening in one of Oxford University's beautiful gardens. I brought out my clown soul: the sad, lost, and clumsy self that makes people laugh, jumping around and doing cartwheels.

In the 70s there was a tiny bookstore in the centre of London, where poor Eastern European visitors could get free books. I spent a whole afternoon there, and I came out with the maximum permitted five books: three by D.W. Winnicott, one by J. Bowlby, and one by R.D. Laing. I still have them in Pelican paperback. I had never heard of these authors in Budapest. At that time, I had absolutely no idea that I would end up choosing to study psychology.

On that trip I met Ian, a friend of G's in Oxford. We explained our situation to him, and having a Hungarian stepfather, he understood very well that I might need him to get me out of Hungary. At 19, I became a British subject, thanks to my marriage of convenience to him which enabled my legitimate departure from Hungary. The border was closed if you had left the country and did not return within the permitted time.

In Budapest, before leaving, I had attended the first year of a psychology course in 1973–1974. That year psychology had just become an independent discipline at the university. I wanted the challenge and a place in this highly competitive new programme. I chose it not knowing that psychology would become my passion in the future. I remained detached from university life in the same way I had done before at Fazekas High School. I did try, though. I was aware of the importance of the place, the chance, and the privilege I had. But important things happened to me elsewhere. I explored the world of contemporary music, lived with a musician from a family of musicians, and met outstanding poets and other artists, some with a melancholic streak. As always, I was with my buddies with whom we made secret plans to leave Hungary. Leaving then meant leaving behind family, friends, country and the political landscape. Back then, I had no dreams about Paris, only an appetite for new perspectives. I was not conscious of what later became obvious: that this city was calling me.

Six of us in our circle of friends left Hungary together in 1974: three boys and three girls. It was planned in secret, and all of us were yearning for Western winds of freedom and space for knowledge. The boys wanted to leave before military service. We all headed for London, as most of us were Anglophones, but we had to stop in Paris to wait for political asylum for my friends. We enroled in courses at university, and I started analysis. Studying became a lifeline for my continuity of being while struggling in menial jobs to survive. My adult life on this side of the Iron Curtain began in Paris as an unplanned transition when I was twenty years old.

I left on 1 November 1974 on my birthday … forever and yet never totally. Then my father died on the 28th of the same month and year. I flew back immediately, as I could as a British citizen, and stayed with my mother for a few months.

Paris

When I was 13, my parents took me to a Béjart Ballet in Budapest. I clearly remember the aesthetic shock and the complete immersion in the experience. It was a transformational moment. The origin of my desire for Paris was probably sowed here, in the soil of the Mérei francophone culture, my longing for art and beauty were the seeds.

Looking around

In our first year in Paris, we were audacious explorers, living an emigrant life. Finally, after a hard year there, political refugee status was granted to my friends, and we were at last ready to leave for the UK. There was an unforgettable walk in Paris with one of my friends, with whom I tried to discuss what I should do. Should I come to London with them or stay in Paris? He wisely told me that it should be my decision, and I felt the weight of my destiny and the risk of freedom. I could have easily followed my friends, remained in the group as I spoke the language and was already a British citizen … But I did not. I stayed in Paris, alone. The rainy weather in London was my conscious reason. It was not a considered decision. My psychic genera (Bollas, 2011, p. 57) came up with this unexpected choice. Later, on the couch, I gained some hint of why I needed to turn away from the original plan. I arrived and remained in Paris starting from scratch: no language, no family, no friends, no money. A nice repetition … the destiny of my parents. They lost everything and started again from nothing: I needed to do something similar. It was a child's loyalty, and I endured its harsh consequences. I learned to live a precarious life. I identified very much with Dostoevsky's characters, whose literature I had devoured in my adolescence and it now helped me sustain a state of mind of being humble, vulnerable and poor. The spirit of the Mérei household played a significant role. It has been a challenge and it remains one. Being a foreigner continues to be a struggle, even if much has worked out for me.

I managed to get a place to study psychology at Paris V-Sorbonne University, in the heart of the city on Rue Serpente. I had no knowledge of French, I had just started studying it, or more precisely, picking it up. I also needed to stay in touch with the intellectual world: I wanted to keep my identity as a studious person and not become identified with my survivor's status as a cleaning lady. I spent time in the library with my dictionaries, and oh ... I was lost. I looked around the library, and of all the people there, I picked a girl with glasses, who looked even more like a dreamer than I, and asked for her help. She became my friend, and forty-five years later we are still close. She lived near the university and sometimes took me home to her apartment on Boulevard St Michel, where she lived with her Russian father in a grand Parisian apartment. I had meals there and could be part of something which reminded me of family life.

I first lived in La Cité des Arts, an international students' hostel. A Hungarian composer-flautist friend took me in, which was such a relief. But every time I came home in the evening, and every time I went out in the morning, I had to sneak through. It felt like crossing the border before 1988, something I had experienced often until the age of eighteen. You never knew when you were going to be confronted with this violation of rules and be punished. After that year in the Cité des Arts, I embarked on my itinerant experience, moving from one "hole" to another "chambre de bonne". These tiny rooms on the last floor of every building used to be the servants' quarters. Among these "chambres de bonne" there was the unforgettable rue Vivienne, with mice, shared Turkish toilets, and only cold water; cooking on a tiny camping stove, a little window in the ceiling; improbable neighbours straight out of an old movie, observing the world from their peepholes.

Luckily, Squat Theatre as it was later called, arrived in Paris. I am reminded of a play by them. "How nice that I am not crippled" sang the beautiful young comedian, dancing rhythmically for over an hour. I had already seen it in Budapest. Then they were still called the Péter Halàsz Theatre, and performed in Péter's apartment, in Dohàny Street, near the largest synagogue in Budapest – and Europe – where my parents were married. This street brings back memories of what my family had and lost.

I hold onto the idea that no matter how hard life gets, there is still peace in our part of the world. Though I can no longer take that for granted, the way we had done in our youth. As I write this chapter, sadly, this peace – local, national, continental – feels less and less assured. I listen to devastating news of wars and falling bombs in the Middle East, of terrorist attacks in big cities, and I must acknowledge the growing instability that confronts us. Still, despite how disturbed, unjust and corrupt our part of the world might have become, I am aware that, thankfully, we are spared the horrors of war and wholesale murder here.

I was able to return home regularly from Paris to Budapest to see my mother, who very bravely tried to continue life without my father. I was faced with how immense a waste it was that my father and I had not been more at peace with each other. He was fifty-five years old when he died. I didn't realise that when they accompanied me to the railway station on that fateful day, I left Budapest, they already knew that my father's life was close to its end. I was not aware of this because he had been ill for so long. With the vitality of a twenty-year-old, I felt able to move mountains, not fully understanding sickness, age and the enormous multiple traumas they had carried all their lives. Their generosity still holds and contains me.

On one of these occasions, when I was visiting Budapest in the mid-70s to regain strength and emotional resources, I met a young man. T lived on the same street as I had in Budapest. For years, we passed each other in the street, sometimes exchanging a glance. We finally met through a friend in 1975. He became my first long-term partner in my adult life. During the year we were apart, while I lived in Paris and he in Budapest, we became a couple, planning his escape from Hungary. He could not join me in Paris because Interpol could trace him there as his father was a prominent figure in Hungary. So, he went to Sweden. For a few years, I divided my life between Stockholm, Goteborg and Paris. Sweden was very generous to us: I learned Swedish, I worked with delinquent adolescents, and my poet and I built a life together.

Unfortunately, sometime later I learnt that he was afflicted by serious addictions and mental health problems after which we separated. It is astounding that I never managed to make any close friends in Sweden, nor have I retained any connections there.

I continued university in Paris, my lifeline, to remind myself of what really mattered. I needed to stay in touch with the feeling that I had some agency over my life. Paris and my studies were initially a superficial investment, but I did it well enough to gain my Bachelor of Arts. I only remember one professor from that time, who allowed me to take my oral exam in English rather than French. I remember his kindness, his considerate gaze. He let me, an Eastern European refugee, pass with a high grade. My time at university, just like my time in high school, left me without any significant memories. Only my friend from the library, the one with the glasses, remains close. She carried a mysterious family legacy which she kept secret and to which I shall return at the close of this chapter.

In 1979, after completing my bachelor's degree, T and I decided to go to New York, to be farther away from Europe. I also spent some time in Mexico, where I visited friends and it was wonderful. At first, I thought a gap year would help me have an idea of what I wanted to do with my life. I also thought I could find financial survival there. New York touched me, heart and soul.

Because studying was my lifeline, I decided to apply to New York University and begin the administrative process to officially move, looking for an eventual immigration from my immigration, from the old continent to the new. While I was in the process of applying, I was struck by a sensation that spread from head to toe: I felt that I just had to go back to Paris. The city was calling me again. After not leaving Paris for London with my friends in 1974, I decided to leave New York and go back to Paris at the end of 1979. In 1974, the choice was unconscious and transgenerational, but this time I made a conscious decision: I wanted to be there to learn psychology and specifically psychoanalysis, which I had become passionate about. After choosing to study psychology at university to figure out what I wanted to become, it was time for me to commit to my path.

This decision to go back to Paris was a way of avoiding getting dispersed and lost. My children did something similar. One studied in Montreal and the other in New York City, but right after graduating both decided to return to Europe. I was overjoyed by their decision, as it meant that we were not too far from one another and that it was easier to see each other.

Back in Paris after my year on the American continent, I separated from T and was ready to settle down. I was finally engaging with my love objects: clinical psychology and psychoanalysis. As I had already taken the right preparatory steps with my bachelor's in psychology, I could complete my master's degree by obtaining the French *DESS* (*Diplôme d'Etudes Supérieures Spécialisées*) later called a *Master 2*. I then checked out all the doctoral programmes by going to the universities that taught psychology with a psychoanalytical approach and listening in to all the professors' lectures, without knowing much about their reputations. This is how I chose Didier Anzieu as my thesis advisor. I only later realised what an exceptional time it was to work under his guidance. My thesis was titled *"Labyrinthe d'une peau commune"* (*"Maze of a Shared Skin"*, 1986) and was about the psychic work that emerges in the process of creation by a group of artists.

Emigration–immigration

The author in 1974 outside Paris

My story of emigration was not based on rupture. I did not have to escape or lose touch with the land. Thanks to my marriage of convenience to my Englishman, I was free to travel, so I could go wherever and whenever I needed to. My friends could not do this.

Leaving legally, owning a British passport, gave me the freedom we were all dreaming of. Some friends had to hide in the trunk of western friends' cars. The lucky ones had left Hungary with a scholarship for a year and did not come back. After we left Eastern Europe behind the iron curtain, we were hanging out together, tasting freedom and all that came with it. It was an instructive time for us with new languages, an enviable wealth of culture, and a huge thirst for learning. We were learning to live in a democratic country. It also came with important, long-lasting poverty, which we had not experienced before in our privileged life in Budapest. We were vulnerable and helpless and had to learn to cope.

I lived in poverty for seven years, basically surviving on *baguettes*, working as a cleaning lady and then selling vegetables in a supermarket to earn a bit of money. My mother sent me canned food from Hungary so I could eat something more substantial. A few years later, I started working for the "Maison des Sciences de l'Homme", as an assistant in documentation for a Hungarian sociologist working on Jewish history. He knew that I did not eat well and would bring me clementines so I could get some vitamins. I was grateful to him, this substitute parent to a young adult orphan. Entering the research centre instead of the supermarket to earn money felt very uplifting. But somehow, this orphanage I chose and thought I needed, did not help me welcome positive emotional experiences.

I am surprised to call myself an orphan. Who or what did I lose to feel like an orphan at the age of 25? One of the ongoing pains, analysed for so many years between my analysts and myself during different periods of my life, is the feeling of being bare, lonely, without skin. After the Holocaust, the huge family tree became a tiny branch. The only way to keep up with this ongoing pain is through the continuous and tireless elaborations of this diminished family. I must acknowledge though that, thanks to my restorative experiences, this ongoing pain is slowly fading away and pulsating less.

For a long time, I had little room for integrating positive experiences. I was unable to recognise generous people or nurturing events. I struggled to figure out my place in the world, to overcome what I felt was an unfriendly French society, with formalities I did not understand. French social norms are still foreign to me to this day and not entirely homelike. Home would be warm, where meeting people and friendships are more important than managing everyday life. I still wonder, after forty-five years, if I will ever understand its social codes or how French people function. I love Paris because of its beauty and effervescence but without feeling completely at home. I can never fully integrate into its landscape. Still, it gives me the illusion that I am settling down. *Home is where we start from* (Winnicott, 1986) and home is where I wished to head for, without knowing what I meant.

The right place

Home is where I was born and where I would like to be buried, next to my parents. I never really stopped belonging there. It is my home, the Budapest of my childhood, where some of my dearest friends remain. I never completely left Hungary. I continued to grow there in a certain way. I learned to discern the two different environments, with its different values and perspectives. I wished to become a bridge, between Paris and Budapest, between Eastern Europe and West.

Paris is the right place for me. Here, I can be alive and prosper. It gives me a feeling of security that I will never have to leave. Paris is where I have lived for more than forty-five years, but it is not home. Home is where you take much for granted and this is not possible in a foreign land. Some lucky people can find the right place in their home country. Others can find it somewhere in the world. But there is loss in either case. If you leave, you lose the language, the poetry of your mother tongue. You are far away from your family, from the landscape of your childhood. If you stay, you deprive yourself of feeling at home in the rest of the world, in the discoveries of other cultures and all that you can learn from them. Living in the right place is being able to bear the loss that comes with it. What is the meaning of my internal sense of being at home versus being in the right place?

In our childhood home, the environment is familiar and is a given. In emigration, *you* must create this environment. One of its vital prerequisites is that you build a comfortable domain, where you can feel safe enough to rest, meditate, and hope. It is one of the big lessons I learned from my emigration. Slowly building the right environment is the basis of survival. But it is not enough for the place to be right. If you can create this habitat you can start to move and place yourself in it. In this space, you can grow, find acceptance and come through with your idiom.

Once inside one can take off the cape of security (Zorro, Superman/woman), the background object (Grotstein, 1981), and continue with the activity of symbolisation beyond primary identifications and constructions. This long and ongoing work requires precision. There is a need to highlight one's potential in a foreign land so that one can find a home for one's subjectivity and open one's creativity. My awakening aspirations were followed by carefully considered commitments.

There is no way I could have come to this point without a long personal *voyage* into psychoanalysis. I imagine I am at the gate of a beautiful garden I want to walk into, I enter hoping that it will reveal itself to be the right place, with different interconnected spaces to explore. It is a holding envelope, a secure container, inside of which my complex interior life and growth can take place. It becomes the legitimised official landscape of feelings and of exchanges with the outside world. Here, phantasies and object relationships interact with reality in an environment partially built by me.

Other people's environments meet and overlap with mine, each of them with their own thread. To be able to relax and feel some familiarity in the right place, I need to have a surrounding fabric. The fabric is the social network, better be velvety soft than rough. I weave it on my own, and we also weave it together. It is a shared experience, and it has the potential to become familiar and perhaps, with some unexpected divine help, develop the familiar feeling of home. How much importance people give to this lived-shared experience is culture-dependent, as is the need for proximity and intimacy.

I missed the familiarity of home and the intimacy I knew there. I needed a sense of belonging. In each of the more than thirty little "chambres de bonne" I inhabited, I tried to make a nest in less than twenty-four hours. I put up on the wall some beautiful fabrics that I carried from one place to another and some of my friends' drawings. I could sort of withdraw into them, but I could not relax. I felt the taste of adventure in what seemed like excitement. But as I understand it now, it was more the anxiety about whether I could find this belonging, the safety in which I can let down my guard, relax and dream.

For some time, I hoped that psychoanalysis would be a place to go to. The community and the common passion formed a potential field. In the right place, one has the right space for reflecting and dreaming. The light comes from inside, from the process of uncluttering traumatic traces, recovering internal objects, and getting rid of intrusions from the past. Immigration was the right move and analysis could be the right place. But the constant concern for the living conditions and social life remained an important factor. These processes can and do happen simultaneously.

I have settled in Paris. From its beauty, its rich cultural and intellectual life, I am nourished. I enjoy my life and my work here. I can withdraw into my beautiful apartment in the Marais. From here, the passion, the motivation, and the mission flow. But it is in my relationships that I really feel at home. My identity is no longer simply defined by roots, but also by the many enlightening and shared experiences I have had. For a long time, my life in Paris was in anonymity. Anonymity to slide into and grow at my own pace. Slowly becoming myself, no bigger nor smaller than I really am. Just the right size.

Drifting and identity

Jewish history and Judaism surround me all the time. Many in my generation are from assimilated families. Growing up we did not know we were Jewish. In the social milieu in Hungary of the 1950s, talking about the Second World War and being Jewish was taboo: in the dominant ideology, equality was a substitute for diversity. My parents took the official political line seriously and to protect me they would not air their perhaps dissident political sentiments at home.

I learned I was Jewish from a friend of my parents visiting from New York in a most unlikely place, the small elevator between the first and second floor of our apartment building on Egri Joszef Street in Budapest, where I spent my first eleven years. He said something very casual like, "Oh what a sweet little Jewish girl you are". I remember my father's face, horrified and relieved at the same time. This encounter eventually led to one of the most meaningful moments of our relationship: my father took me to Auschwitz, and we walked all over the ground, looked at the piles of clothes, the traces of daily life, papers and photographs. I was ten years old. It was not the traumatic experience my second analyst suggested it had to be. What was traumatic came before: the inability to find the way, the words, or the approach to articulate our Jewishness. This family of mine, just three of us in the tiniest of apartments, without any grandparents, aunts, uncles, brothers, sisters or cousins, without history or context, to help regulate communication. There was no larger family to help my confused parents comprehend their intense daughter.

Today, I live in the Marais, the Jewish quarter in Paris, which I enjoy. When in the early 80s my husband and I bought our then inexpensive apartment in a narrow cul-de-sac it never occurred to me that the place was in the Jewish quarter. The park where I brought up my children was not yet called the Elie Wiesel square. Nor did I used to walk by the MAHJ, *Musée d'art et d'histoire du Judaïsme* (Museum of Jewish Art and History) on the *rue du Temple*, which opened in 1998.

Jacques Frémontier, a writer, historian, and a friend gave a talk in January 2020 at the MAHJ in front of the Holocaust memorial there: an interior courtyard with a memorial on a wall by the French artist Christian Boltanski. At the MAHJ, the Holocaust is mainly commemorated by this major work, which reflects rigorous research in the archives to document all the inhabitants of the building before the war. The names of the disappeared residents were not carved in marble for eternity but glued on small posters. They wear off with rain and otherwise harsh weather, so they need regular care, just as all existential, personal and transgenerational layers in us do.

Jacques talked about his parents, who were inhabitants of the Hotel de Saint-Aignan before the war. His father's and his uncle's names, among many others', are on the wall in the museum. Jacques told us about situations when he felt Jewish despite himself.

Carrying a heavy transgenerational traumatic heritage, I came to realise that I had tried to bend history. I did not want history to determine my fate, I wanted to be the one to transform it. The wall at the MAHJ is an external material sign, the result of much internal fantasy of defence and separation: dreams and responsibilities were all reflected on its screen. Artists capture reality first, they are in the cockpit, while the rest of us, analysts included, follow in their footsteps. Now that I could finally connect a live face, that of Jacques, to the names, I understood that the lack of personal link contributed to the persistent feeling of being a foreigner. But knowing someone who lived in this building as a child when it housed a small business, his persecuted family spoke to me. Through Jacques, through his face and voice, I stepped inward and the wall in the Museum became more than just cultural heritage. In this moment, my Jewish belonging unveiled itself, like a universal fate, an enlightening event.

Shades of integration

I became partially integrated without realising it. I am less of a foreigner than I thought I was. I completed my doctorate in psychology and I am trained as a psychoanalyst. I have an apartment in Paris and a family of my own. Until recently, whenever anyone asked me who I was, I answered without much thinking, I said I was Hungarian. Never did it occur to me to state my British or later French citizenships. My French identification is limited. I feel comfortable with my accent and my relationship with the three different languages I live in. I have settled down comfortably into my outsider status everywhere. I have started to explore politics and history with a lot of caution. I was always more interested in exploring the world of interiority, even if I was aware of how much outside circumstances impact us. I am a first generational wanderer who found a place to immigrate and to belong. Time shaped the place to be the right one.

I have come to realise that I am also a part of History. There was a most unexpected moment, a massive peaceful march for the cherished values of the French Republic after the terrorist attack on the satirical newspaper Charlie Hebdo. On 11 January 2015, I was walking with millions of people in Paris. I noticed that I felt fraternity and familiarity there. It was one of the largest gatherings in the country's contemporary history. There, in the peaceful walk, I was not lonely; there were people of all ages, all origins, all classes, experiencing a moment of history in solidarity. Wherever I looked I saw pencils, even in the hand of the statue of the Republic. The pencil against guns is a symbol of fraternity against hate and against destructive instincts. At that moment, an unexpected change began to take hold of me.

I cross the Place de la République every day, as I live five minutes away. From the shared experience of the march, from civil society, in

2016, grew the movement called "Nuits Debout". For months, you could see small groups of people sitting around talking, passionately discussing philosophy, politics, art, and arguing, without any violence. In public spaces, people would stay up all night to reinvent society. This collective insomnia was like political therapy. Recent global events—ecology, politics, the pandemic—took a toll but I do not forget that we had hope then.

Paris and French culture have a tradition of hosting transitional spaces. For me *Place de la République* played this role. Space for social reverie and transitional experience not fully dominated by power facilitates a new way of being together, contemplating human existence and cooperation for the greater good.

Back then I had another incredible experience. I woke up one morning feeling like new, twenty years younger, both in spirit and body. I read in the newspaper that while I was asleep with my windows open, something surreal happened at the Place de la République, where hundreds of musicians gathered on the square to play Dvorak's "Symphony from the New World" together. Around 10,000 people showed up, silent and internally vibrating to the music. I could feel a completely new energy; an unstoppable energy no longer directed towards destroying the dominant system but toward constructing another one.

At that moment, after more than thirty years, for the first time in my life, I felt like a French citizen. Coming from a family with a history of persecution, I am prepared to resist when human conditions, structures and infrastructures break down. To be *debout* – standing upright in solidarity with others in the community made sense. In France, to be outspoken about one's ideas is integral to the culture and I have huge respect for it.

Still, French people, and more generally social life in Paris, are still a mystery to me. I participate in the French art of life of wonderful dinners and discussions. Although I prefer informal, improvised, unconventional spaces, I must acknowledge that the sustained formality of these habits constitutes the most incredible environment for discussions and a deeply inspiring intellectual excellence.

I was once invited to the home of a colleague. Two brilliant journalists were also there. They knew a lot about Eastern Europe and Judaism, and I wondered if they would be open to a personal experience that did not correspond to their overall critical view of that world. Their ideas about an imploded public sphere under communist rule did not match my experience growing up. I wish I would have told them, that severe socio-political problems notwithstanding, there was much gain. In school there was a lot to learn about emancipation, there were many inspiring revolutionary songs to enjoy. I believed in the utopia of eradicating privilege and levelling the playing field. My parents' place on the political margins, reflective of their enduring bourgeois values rather than conscious intellectual resistance, and later the Mérei subculture, my chosen community, also protected me from falling for the crudest propaganda. My preference for marginality lasted a long time. Only now have I begun to move very slowly and not without difficulty towards the main door, towards relationships with people and personalities who are not afraid of being visible in public spaces.

Professional landscape

Analysts and languages

I have never had a "French" analysis with a French analyst. Without much conscious contemplation, I chose three emigrants. The first was a Hungarian of the Ferenczi tradition, the second an American with a Kleinian influence, and the last one an Argentinian with a Freudian bent. Three analyses in three languages: Their spirit and their music infuse me. I belong to these different worlds and speak different accents. Each accent is a part of my identity.

Three analyses

Imre Herman, one of the last remaining analysts from the Budapest school, sent me to my first analyst in Paris. I did not ask myself whether it was right for me, I simply jumped into it. I went twice a week and paid for it with my cleaning jobs. This analyst, part of a French psychoanalytic association did not talk much.

At that time, I developed an infection in my fallopian tubes, and the French doctors recommended surgery which would have left me infertile. I knew I needed a second opinion, and being a British citizen, I went to London. The trip used up all my remaining strength.

I was practically down on my knees. I was hospitalised for a month. I received intensive medical care and my tubes were saved. When I returned to Paris, I did not continue with the silent Hungarian analyst. During this difficult period, I travelled back twice a year to Budapest, each time staying for a month, and spoke with an analyst every day of the week. This allowed me to rebuild my strength, so I could continue looking for a suitable analyst back in Paris. It was a fascinating process. I saw five analysts, some Hungarian – B. Grunberger, M. Török – and some French. During this period, I ventured to see a few Lacanian analysts as well. I found them inspiring from a conceptual and philosophical point of view.

I chose to work with an American woman, who was quite straightforward in telling me that she talked to her patients. So, the second analysis was in American English with a post-Kleinian analyst, trained in England and part of the *Société Psychanalytique de Paris* (SPP), a rare person to find in Paris. This work went on for ten years. Other than wanting to work with someone who would be in a dialogue with me, I needed to work through issues related to ruthlessness, abandonment and exclusion. In the course of my work with children, in a residential nursery and an adoption placement centre, my own childhood anxieties emerged.

My third analyst, whom I started to see more than twenty years later, around the time of my mother's death, was an Argentinian analyst. Our language was French. We had two years of analytical dialogue between two analysts. He had more experience and a lot of wisdom, and he was there for me while I was accompanying my mother in her last days. This period of analysis was a vital and important part of my journey.

Three languages

Three landscapes emerge out of my slightly different ways of being immersed in each language. Each one is a worldview. Does the use of a language generate a specific form of being? Do I feel the same way in English, French and Hungarian? Do I search for the same meaning?

In English I travel swiftly from one thought to another, I can express myself clearly with nuance. It appears like a forest to me, filled with the play of shadow and light, a place in which I can reflect and contemplate my internal landscapes. Veronica, Katalin and I learned this language in high school. They both studied English at University and then lived in English-speaking countries while I stayed in Paris. I lived with my partner and father of my children, an American researcher, for sixteen years. English is my children's native tongue. I love this language: I feel safe and comfortable in its spirit. My Hungarian accent permeates my speech and defines my English-speaking identity. English has the beauty and accessibility of pragmatism.

The landscape of French is more complicated to describe; it is a different kind of walk in my mind for me. It has the alternation of grand spaces and fine corners. I picked it up when I came to Paris. I had never studied it before nor learned to use grammatical gender forms correctly. I have never lived with a French person and was not acquainted with French literature as a child, so I could not achieve as much intimacy as I wished with the language, and some distance remains. In French, my accent is more pronounced than in English. It is the second native language of my children and is often spoken in my family. I find it complicated, sophisticated and extraordinarily rich. It lends itself to abstract, conceptual thinking.

The landscape of the Hungarian language is like a freshwater lake with a playful breeze rustling leaves. I enjoy its condensed word-phrases. Because of its complex grammar, the order of the words in a sentence is not set, and this allows for improvisation. It is my mother tongue, and I never realized what a treasure it was until I moved away. Unless you are a poet, a writer or a linguist, you take your mother tongue for granted. I kept a close bond with Budapest, and I never stopped using Hungarian. My children speak it very well and it is often spoken in my family. I have a deeply affectionate relationship with the Hungarian language, which provides a different path of intelligibility than French or English, a distinction I will elaborate on later.

Psychoanalytic and perinatal experiences, interwoven

Since I began my work as a psychologist, I have had two parallel passions: the analytical road and the perinatal world. I feel fortunate in the way my professional destiny has unfolded. This was due to the unlikely fact that when I immigrated to France, I came across an exceptional early developmental approach by my French tutors, Geneviève Appel, a psychologist and Myriam David, a psychoanalyst and a child psychiatrist. They happened to have integrated ideas from my home country and had worked with John Bowlby, a British psychoanalyst working on the mother/baby relationship.

As chance would have it, in the late seventies, I moved into yet another room in the south of Paris. The Iranian girl moving out introduced me to her cousin, who was working in a residential nursery and told me that the nursery was looking for a psychologist, so I immediately applied for the job. It is during the interview at the residential nursery that I met Geneviève Appell. If for no other reason than getting to know her and Myriam David, it had been worth emigrating. They had been heroes during the war, fighting for babies' rights, helping the social and health system take care of orphans, and so much more. I became their mentee, absorbing their exceptionally humane qualities which course through my veins to this day. Geneviève Appell is now 97 years old. I visit her regularly to talk about current affairs. Her moral compass points to all that is good here in France, without the elitism that sometimes comes with intellectual excellence in French culture. Learning to be a psychologist and an analyst in the residential nursery taught me a speciality that I will touch upon later.

The analytic journey is slow and deep, and I would not change it for anything. I used to fantasise about becoming a landscape architect. I love nature and structure, and I am continuously creating an attuned environment, an atmosphere well suited for free associations. *Free to move and free to be* became a film I made about my practice with babies, and I also published a paper by the same title (Vamos, 2015). What I learned from babies gives me access to archaic psychic material in adults. I feel like an assistant for the internal landscape architecture of my patients and for the analytic process.

The perinatal world

Prepared gaze

My listening is a gaze: it has been prepared, educated, transformed and filled with an image that is not theoretical, but taken in after my encounter with the babies I met in Budapest at the Pikler-Loczy

Institute. They were calm and alert in their movements, active and relaxed, collaborating with the adult. Their faces expressed an appetite for discovery and understanding.

As infant observers, we learn to read non-verbal language. Thanks to my analytic training and to the contributions of Emmi Pikler, a Hungarian paediatrician, I have a specific understanding of infants' psychic wellbeing (Pikler, 1979).

During my perinatal consultations, when I see babies and parents in extreme upheaval, I can grasp what they are going to encounter and share it with the parents. I can address the baby directly as well, I can see his face light up when he senses the meaning of my intentions, and his eyes show curiosity and intelligence. What is at work within me when I am in contact with this emotional experience? I feel that my intentions are completely understood. I find it extraordinary that I, an adult, can be in communication with a new human being. The infinite goodwill of the infant opens us to a vital inner touch, a sort of kindness, to which they respond with meaningful exchange. This goodness and the thirst for meaning constitute the aesthetic experience that Meltzer & Williams (2000) described, and establishes and reestablishes the precious communication with the infant.

I have listened to babies for the last 40 years, in a residential nursery, a daycare centre, directly with families and in foster care for adoption, and now for the past two decades in a maternity ward, in post-natal consultations and in groups. Being in the presence of newborns and their learning parents gives us the chance to be in an immediate and direct emotional experience with this primary world. Translating and interpreting that experience can contribute to promoting health and prevention. The Hungarian and British analysts had contributed much to our understanding of early development. Observing babies with the vision of Esther Bick (1964) and Emmi Pikler enables us to formulate our own ideas of these primary states and develop an original, preventive and therapeutic clinical approach to helping new parents attune to their babies.

The enlightening environment: From Ferenczi to Pikler

In the last twenty years of my internal dialogue with the psychoanalyst Sandor Ferenczi, I have come to deeply appreciate his work, as well as his ability to adapt to the unique needs of the analysands and their circumstances. His boldness to be intimate and to question our sincerity qualify as his most subversive gift. Reading the *Clinical Diary* with my perinatal implication, I was inspired by his intuitive vision of happy and satisfying childhood conditions. I was particularly interested in his hypothesis regarding the main environmental factors, which were later elaborated by other disciples of the Hungarian school of psychoanalysis, the Balints – Michael and Alice – and the Hermanns – Imre and Alice.

Ferenczi writes that there is "more evidence that the lasting effects of trauma come from the absence of a supportive and enlightening environment" (Clinical Diary, 1932, p. 210). From the beginning of his career, Ferenczi was aware that, "much unnecessary mental pain can be attributed to inappropriate educational principles that prevent enjoyment, interfering with life's natural pleasures" (Ferenczi, 1908, p. 51). In the last twenty years, I have devoted much to the creation of this "enlightening environment". This work was facilitated in the maternity ward with the help of staff, in my groups and workshops, and with parents.

What Ferenczi imagined, Emmi Pikler created. Her original vision opened space for the baby's true autonomy and a possibility for reciprocity and partnership between adult and child. The atmosphere of this world around babies can resonate with Ferenczi's reveries about the necessity for an early, caring environment provided through the adult's ministrations, which then creates an enlightening environment as described in his *Clinical Diary*.

Emmi Pikler (1902–1984) was a Hungarian paediatrician, who, after completing her medical studies in 1920s Vienna, moved back to Hungary in 1932 to work in the field of progressive education. She became a family paediatrician with precise ideas on how to accompany parents, so children could develop calmly and experience pleasure in the family. This did not mean that conflicts and difficult times were denied or not dealt with. In her weekly home visits, she would discuss any and all questions parents were asking themselves, whether about concrete material issues or more intricate psychic, emotional ones. She provided guidance, facilitating the creation of conditions for the infants' everyday lives. Her vision was that of an active, relaxed infant living peacefully with herself and her environment.

After the Second World War and the Holocaust – which Pikler survived thanks to her patients who hid her and her family – she was given the responsibility of creating a residential nursery for orphans on Lóczy Lajos Street in Budapest. This later became the Pikler-Lóczy Institute. The institute continues to be a training centre but the residential nursery has become a Daycare Center. As the French documentary filmmaker, Bernard Martino said in his beautiful film on Pikler and her work, "the twentieth century has taught us enough of the 'scientific way' to destroy the individual, there are only a few extremely rare places where one knows 'scientifically' how to help build up the individual in a setting that remains profoundly human" (Martino, 2000).

If adults can provide good-enough conditions, the enlightening environment brings light to the baby's personality, core-self, their resources and idiom. Establishing this environment is an incomparable challenge, but it is a necessary enterprise for efficient prevention. The observation is attuned and interactive, and therefore changes the environment, in which the caring adult can and becomes a transformative object for the infant. The infant then is in touch with their potential for growth and is protected from the experience of helplessness.

Dependence/helplessness

Shoring up the infant's resources by creating a good-enough environment is not developed in most traditional studies on child education. I am convinced that though humans are born biologically immature, and newborns are in absolute dependence on their environment, it doesn't mean that they are helpless. There is considerable confusion between dependence and helplessness. The term helplessness is used to denote the state of the newborn who is incapable of carrying out the specific actions required to satisfy her own needs. Building on the last thirty years of research, we now consider infants as competent and active, but we still treat them and care for them as if they were helpless. The competent child is *competent* if they can be. The old way of viewing infants, with an inappropriate educational approach, prevents us from seeing their resources and potential. When caretaking adults and family see the newborn or the infant as helpless, they act *on* them rather than *with* them.

Progressive literature on early childhood developmental research seeks to distance itself from the promotion of early separation as practised in the Western world. If the mother can keep the newborn on her body in the first hours after birth, something I have observed in the maternity ward repeatedly, the baby can and will move up to the breast to nurse, using their innate archaic reflexes. Babies have tools, programmes to help themselves. We must figure out how not to unknowingly impinge on these competencies, though this is a difficult and challenging territory.

Emancipating visions of the infant: Free movement

Unlike other comparable establishments, at the Pikler-Loczy Institute, the atmosphere between the babies and the adults was peaceful. At the institute, babies were active contributors, free to move and free to be and bodily care appeared as if it were gracefully choreographed. Babies and small children could exercise their bit of true autonomy. Learning was based on infants' and babies' appetite for exploration, facilitating an experience of being, experiencing, and learning.

In a paper, which I co-authored with Alberto Konichekis, *Being in movement* (2014) we demonstrated how movement tends to transform emotional experiences into gestural and bodily forms, and move impulsive energy into the symbolic and figurative realm. What Pikler called self-initiated motor development is a fundamental part of the baby's growth. Her contributions constitute a radical change in our view of infants and our clinical approaches in our work with them. In daily life, it means that it is best not to put the baby in a passive situation such as in a chair or walker. To move in freedom, from the dorsal position to the vertical position, allows for impulsive momentum and pleasure.

The first aspect of this proposition is the free motor activity on the floor. This autonomous movement (Roussillon, 1999, p. 68) provides a playground for the first symbolisations. We take verticality as an outcome of the unhindered development of postures with a tonic-emotional and symbolic value of the human being on the path to becoming. For the baby to stand up on his own initiative versus being made to stand up is not the same thing and does not have the same meaning for them or for the adult.

The second aspect concerns the body care situation. Free movement in the caretaking context is more complicated. It is likely impinged upon during necessary body care. Difficult as it may be, we must consider that the foundations of future collaborative relationships are laid during the provision of early childhood body care. The quality of communication in these intimate moments is embedded in the baby's body. The bodily self is a mobile self and movements are at the origin of its representations. If the adult is concerned with letting the infant build a relationship of reciprocity the infant can experience herself as a subject. She can initiate dialogue and be a partner with those who are able to cooperate.

The quality of the exchange largely depends on the object's ability to use the respectful, tactful language both in words and gestures. When the infant's spontaneous gestures are met on their own terms, then good-enough attunement to her needs becomes the language of tenderness (Ferenczi, 1982). A slow rhythm is gentle; a fast pace can be experienced as aggressive. This tenderness, with space for the rhythm of the baby's self-initiated dialogue, is the beginning of true cooperation. It builds trust in the intimate environment, in the world, and in the self. The baby can feel deeply accepted, unlike in an adult-led environment, where they are hindered in their bodily expression.

The third aspect relates to primary socialisation. Based on co-operation and adjustment the reality principle is introduced in small doses. Babies are introduced to rules and restrictions progressively without the adult's excessive demands, which do not correspond to the baby's level of maturity: this is the path to primary socialisation.

My guiding compass

I aim to create a universe for young children and adults where they can feel at ease with themselves and others. There is a delicate balance or alchemy that needs to be achieved to tend towards the creation of a peaceful atmosphere:

- Between structure and freedom: structure is not rigid; freedom is not unlimited.
- Between dependence and autonomy: dependence of the child on the adult does not imply a helpless child.

- Between close, direct adult-child and more distant indirect relationships. The close relationship is concentrated in moments of bodily care; the adult's gestures soothe rather than excite the baby.
- Between the principle of pleasure and the principle of reality: the reality principle is skillfully introduced in right amounts and at the appropriate times.
- The environment is designed with artistic and scientific sensitivity.
- The child's rate of development and its rhythm is tolerated, respected and valued.
- The relationship is closely attuned and respectful of the idiom of the child.

Even if parents and caretakers accept these propositions, it takes a long time to integrate them into practice. The infant, when secure in their own movements, robs the adult of a parcel of pleasure, that of control, which they assumed they had a right to. However, when the adult acquires this new understanding and allows the child to move freely, she becomes responsible for creating and ensuring the right conditions for infant's well-being. Willing to deprive oneself of this pleasure of control means leaving a bit of dignity to the infant (Szànto, 2016). This is a significant component of the adult's deeply redesigned relationship with the infant. Instead of seeing the child as helpless – calling her attention, urging her to move and play, teaching her new postures – the caregiver allows the child to become an active agent in their development.

Parents might also need a facilitating/holding environment for themselves that helps them experience the joy of the infant's discovery of themselves and identify with the baby's developmental potential. To put aside their own transgenerational educational model, with its conscious and unconscious concerns and demands that might lead to impingement, parents need to embark on a long and arduous journey. Such a method has been developed at my association, the Association Pikler-Loczy France, the APLF. Our principles have been disseminated to clinical and daycare centres across France and internationally (Vamos, 2015).

Les Bluets, maternity clinic

It is important to situate "les Bluets" in the history of maternity wards in Paris. It was created in 1947 by left-wing professionals, supported by a trade union and not by a state or medical institution. It was innovative from the start and it is still considered a progressive clinic. The new location of the Bluets maternity ward oversees about 3000 births per year. From the 1950s on it has been famous for its emphasis on prenatal preparation and dedication to natural childbirth. It was the maternity clinic where Fernand Lamaze introduced his prenatal classes.

I, as a psychoanalyst, alongside a team of doctors, midwives and nurses, work together to give support during the birth of the baby in a respectful and welcoming atmosphere. Facing contemporary challenges, such as medically assisted procreation, the support of same-sex parents, single parents, couples of different ethnic backgrounds, yet still adhering to its innovative spirit, the clinic welcomed my pre- and post-natal consultations, to bring awareness to the importance of this primal time during the first days, weeks and months of life for young families. I do room visits starting upon admission to the maternity ward. There are twice a week consultations after the family leaves. I also lead two baby-parent groups. The first, called *"Atelier Enveloppe"* (Envelop workshop), is for newborn babies and parents; the other group, called *"Atelier ParentAise"* (parents-at-ease workshop), functions until the end of the baby's first year.

Observation of Ilse

Mrs. C came to see me with her two-week-old baby. She could not meet me during her stay on the maternity ward, but the staff gave her an appointment for a follow-up consultation. When Mrs. C became pregnant with her second child, she learned that her mother had cancer. Her mother died a week before her delivery and was buried the same day her daughter was born. Already being an experienced mother, with a two-year-old child, she saw that her new baby made little to no contact with her. She was aware that this could be difficult and serious for the baby and for their relationship. I listened to Mrs. C share her pain of mourning her mother. The baby was asleep during the entire session. So, I suggested an appointment the next day I was there, hoping the baby would be awake. The distress of having lost her mother so quickly during her pregnancy, and the shadow it cast over the beginning of life with her new child, took up most of this first session.

Mrs. C arrived with Ilse for the second session four days later. Ilse was two-and-a-half weeks old now, and awake. Indeed, she was a little stiff in Mrs. C's arms, turning her head clearly away from her. She was withdrawn, her eyes empty. I got up from my seat, came closer to meet and address Ilse. She clearly wanted to avoid me. I continued to listen to Mrs. C's narrative. I saw that the baby remained distant, as far away as could be from what was happening. She did not turn towards me either, so I sat back in my chair.

Mrs. C and I continued our conversation. She talked about her attachment to her mother, her mother's absence, and her own suffering. *I started to realize that I would have to go through a huge wall to meet this baby.* I got up a second time, went towards them, and spoke directly to Ilse, "Hello Ilse, it's Julianna, I'm glad you came here with your mother. Now you are awake! I would love us to meet each other". Face turned away, eyes closed, no contact. I sat down again. The mother told me a bit about their daily life, that there were good moments while nursing, but that she had no connection with her baby, and her baby ignored her.

I had an idea: I quickly got up for the third time, came close but out of the baby's field of vision, so she could hear me without seeing me, and I said, "Ilse when *you feel ready and when **you** want*, I'm here and I'd love to meet you". I stayed there quietly, in touch with the vital importance of this sequence.

Little by little, the baby turned her head, found my face, stared into my eyes, then adjusted her gaze and looked at me with striking intensity. I thanked her for her trust, and I said to her, "You know Ilse, your mother has had a great, great sorrow, and she was caught up in it. It is not related to you. You are welcome to meet her, to turn towards the relationship with her". Our exchanges were fervent, she was listening attentively, her eyes were lit up and shining. Slowly, Ilse, two-and-a-half weeks old, turned her head and looked towards her mother, and the two of them dived into each other's gaze. As if at birth, the first look exchanged. It was breathtaking.

The mother was grateful. "It's the first time she has really looked at me," she says, clearly overwhelmed. "Hi sweetie, forgive me, forgive me, I was very busy with other things but I'm here, I'm here for you". This exchange was not only highly emotional but also showed the baby's incredible ability to understand the intentionality of words. I believe that it was important to give her the space and time to act when she was ready, to get into her rhythm, to let her initiate the movement herself. The mother alternated between looking at the baby and engaging with her and continuing to talk to me. The baby relaxed her body, settled comfortably in her mother's arms, and looked around a little. The atmosphere changed and the circulation of energy was restored. Mrs. C came out of her stupor and began to talk about more pleasant moments.

Suddenly I saw Ilse staring at her mother, looking more and more intensely at her with a fixed gaze. I felt compelled to get up again and enter their field of vision. I called her and she looked at me easily this time, and I told her, "Ilse, I'm the one taking care of your mother. You do not have to take care of her. Relax dear, you can be a baby" – and not a *wise* one. I saw Ilse relax again. She had a curious gaze and seemed to feel the exciting discovery of being an infant, tasting the music of our exchanges, while I held her mother in my imaginary arms.

Special frame for a special destiny: "Nés sous X but not abandoned"

In the two days a week dedicated to my work at the maternity clinic, sometimes we witness highly challenging experiences. One such case is when a mother leaves her newborn in the maternity ward to be given up for adoption. The following section presents how my pre/post-natal work creates a frame for newborns and mothers during one of life's most complex moments. A longer discussion of this process was published in the World Association of Infant Mental Health (WAIMH) Signal journal (Vamos, 2009).

At Les Bluets, in these painful situations, the staff has two goals. The first is to provide specialised care for the newborn during the time they spend at the hospital and secondly, to offer a holding and supportive framework for the mother who is entrusting her child to the care of the State. Our therapeutic approach focuses on the babies' daily emotional experiences at the hospital, rather than on the abandonment itself. Nonetheless, the abandonment issue remains at the heart of our preoccupations and constitutes a fundamental question for us in our approach to the mother. Heightened attention and solicitude are urgently needed for these infants early on, to facilitate an experience of the world as friendly enough to counteract the profound loneliness and rejection of abandonment.

The case studies we completed over the years triggered our thinking about the uniqueness of the abandonment situation, because of the intensity of the reactions they had evoked in the baby, the mother, and the team altogether. We came to realise that the absence of a solid professional framework, within which the staff can care for these adults and babies, leaves them alone to cope with their projections and impulses. This leads to disorganisation on all three levels, the baby, the parent, and the team, with possible long-term detrimental effects on the baby's development and the mother's future. As a result, we have progressively developed a new framework for care, which helps contain the emotions of both mothers and caregivers, and allows us to welcome and protect the new baby.

For babies born "*sous X*", as in babies abandoned at birth, the essential question for the maternity staff is: *What environment and relationship will facilitate the experience for the baby during their first days of existence, and what support can we give to the mother to contain her psychic state?* The special challenge for us – the psychologists and the team – is to create a dependable experience in the maternity ward at the hospital.

Winnicott's work revealed that for a newborn infant, from the moment of birth, the experience of recognising his impact on his environment is fundamental to the development of his psyche. Melanie Klein showed the fundamental need to split, that is to separate good and bad to be able to introject and preserve a good object.

In the Pikler model of psychological care expressed through concrete bodily provisions by the primary caregivers, the baby can try his hand at a type of relationship in which, beyond discovering, he can even influence his environment.

The application of these concepts to the unique situation of a woman delivering a baby that she intends to give up for adoption cannot be taken for granted. It requires a staff willing to reflect upon their daily behaviours, integrate psychological concepts and put aside their judgmental attitudes towards the mother, as well as their over-compassion for the baby.

This therapeutic model is based on the psychoanalytic reading of both the mother's and staff's inner movements, as well as on the elaboration of a here-and-now setting for the baby. This model preserves a space for the "finding-creating illusion" (Winnicott, 1951) of the baby, by containing projections and centring work on the quality of bodily care. We believe this has the potential to enhance the baby's capacity to trust themselves and their environment.

It is hard to imagine how an abandoned newborn can grow out of this fundamental negative experience and into a healthy individual. Assuming the first days of life are crucial in putting the baby on the right developmental path, we have created a model aimed at facilitating the newborn's self-organisation and openness to significant interpersonal exchanges, focusing on the behaviour of the staff, the mother, and the baby during the few days at the maternity ward. This process will ultimately support the ultimate mother–newborn separation. Though it seems unattainable to completely alleviate the pain of abandonment, it is possible to avoid its excessively traumatic effects.

We have a specific model put in place to keep mother and staff from being overwhelmed with distress and guilt, feelings inevitably linked to the act of abandonment. We have described the attention we pay to the organisation of daily care which allows the newborn infant to feel protected. Bodily care provided is a form of vital and necessary welcome. The babies are not waiting in a void and are thus empowered to meet good and protective objects, and they tend to leave the hospital open to the future.

The separate care for the mother and the baby protects both parties from destructive effects. Each moment spent at the hospital is part of the baby's personal history and is recorded in a diary. Moreover, protecting the baby has an organising effect on the mother. It can gradually help her to repair the pain of giving up her baby for adoption. Something of her parental capacity, initially unthinkable, reemerges and, as such, this sequence sometimes even results in a revision of the decision to give up the child. This revision is not the goal of our accompaniment – each woman has a right to her own life story – yet if it happens, we allow it as a by-product of the work we do with the mothers.

We have managed to transform sorrow and pity for the newborns into deep consideration for their personal resources. We have grown into being able to convey greater respect and support for mothers who give up their newborns for adoption. We believe our range of interventions contributes to the concern for this very high-risk population of women and babies. In the future, it would be necessary to conduct a well-designed study to prove its validity.

In the maternity clinic, there are other extraordinary situations that require inventive care. Becoming a mother can be a vertiginous journey. At the mysterious beginning of a new life, sometimes the parents' and babies' unexpected challenges they face call for special care and support. The following vignette is a presentation of a particularly difficult situation.

Clinical vignette: Ambre

Dramaturgy of a prenatal diagnosis on a rollercoaster

A couple learned early on during pregnancy that there were significant anomalies in the fetus. This vignette is the description of how they navigated an extremely tenuous trajectory throughout the whole pregnancy with my support. I thank them for allowing me to share our experience, which left a lifelong impression on us all. The initial scene takes place in the office of an exceptional sonographer, to which I was urgently called. The future parents were devastated. The following months were a constant negotiation between their irrepressible hope and the ominous medical reality. Together, we navigated this rollercoaster.

The series of announcements, from the ultrasound at the third month of pregnancy and up to the end of the eighth month, revealed the possibility of a poly-malformation syndrome and several developmental disabilities. The parents had to make day-to-day decisions on the medical factors. Like a mirror, I reflected their pain and maintained firm support. I kept space for them to think and reflect on an almost daily basis. This rollercoaster was inevitably shaped by the approach we all had towards life. As the parents said, from their fetus's point of view, the question was, "to be born or not to be born". Finally, Ambre, after nineteen ultrasounds and several tests of both her heart and brain, was born.

Companionship

My role throughout the pregnancy was of companionship and devotion in this clinical journey. It is best articulated with the words:

"*J'oeuvre.*" I conceive, compose and construct. I conceived a mental space around the birth: this is the description that comes to mind when I care for the one who is giving birth and the one being born.

Composing around birth means the containment of words and the creation of an environment which expresses the ancestral and human. There is an artistic dimension going beyond the realm of psychoanalysis. The manifestation is actual caretaking.

At the clinic, we construct the atmosphere, the space for open-mindedness. Our innovative prenatal childbirth classes are the specialty of my maternity clinic, Les Bluets. Being prepared is about being open to what may come, getting ready to let go of control. It also means being able to receive life or death. Most of the time it is new life: new life within the womb, new life for the parents when the baby arrives, with all the difficulty and pleasure that come with the deeply moving new experience.

It is in this conceiving-composing that the psychic heartbeat of the reverie can be created. Beyond holding a link between us, it contains the space that protects this reverie, that of the parents and mine. The atmosphere constructed thus is an evocation for dreaming of a live psychic gestation and for continued hope. This can be called psychic environment architecture: Conceiving, Composing, Constructing.

Together with the maternity team, we try to measure up to the extraordinary everyday event that giving birth is, despite the loss of rituals in our Western societies and the consequent diminishment of the holding environment. The conceive – compose – co-construct model also allows for the initiation rite for the parents. for the means also being close to something that goes beyond us: the birth of a child, this initiatory experience for parents. But how can one conceive a healthy mental atmosphere when there are doubts about the child's future?

In more ordinary circumstances, parental reverie swirls around the baby's name and around plans immediately following the birth. Parents would be thinking about the method of delivery, the creation of the nursery. Now the parents had to choose between life and death. But they did not know how to make that choice. The hospital became a hostile territory for them. In fact, there were two superimposed battles they had to face: the battle with the medical staff, and their internal battle. The medical examinations set the pace of the pregnancy. In each of our meetings, I tried to recreate, hold and keep the space of reflection and contemplation alive in the rhythm of the ups and downs of this rollercoaster.

The father writes: *"A bomb was now placed on the table, without anyone being able to say when it will explode, if it will explode. We visualized the bomb from our stance as future parents. In the subconscious, the bomb fit the shape of the belly. At least that is the image I thought of, because I was both outside and utterly involved. The mother of my child viewed things quite differently"*. (*Our translation,* Adjedj, 2016, p. 24)

The visible side

After the first meeting, on the way from the sonographer's office to mine, I had three people leap to my mind with a speed that only extreme situations can elicit.

Let me digress for a moment: for the last fifteen years, we have been organising "Seminars of the Bluets", which I lead with an obstetrician twice a year over two days. During these seminars, we use our own methodology. We choose a theme, for example the effect of the announcement of the ultrasound on the parents, which is a situation inspired by the daily experience of the caregivers. We role-play this situation. We ask the participants: "Who wants to play the mother? Who wants to play the father? The midwife, the nurse, the sonographer?" One day, I had the idea of having someone play the fetus. Every time there was a potential problem, even a minor one, the person who played the fetus explained that they felt let down and that they did not want to live anymore.

Imbued with this experience, I welcomed not only the parents but also the fetus into my office. I needed time to explore where everyone stood in relation to all these medical procedures. I felt that despite the multiple concerns regarding the baby's health, the mother did not let herself be torn away from her psychic gestation. I asked her: "How do you feel about your baby?" She replied that she felt very connected to her. Learning from the experience of the seminar, I heard myself say: "Don't let go of your baby before we know more". I pictured the fetus to be well, imagining she heard my words and felt like she could rely on all of us. When I pronounced these words to the mother, I came to understand my function as a link between continuity and discontinuity. I carried this conviction to hold onto life even when it is uncertain and felt an alliance with the mother. Her receptivity to not let go of the baby vitalised the struggle.

Today, I believe that my appeal to the mother to hold on to the baby, my conviction and my determination created a bond, a common thread among the parents, the sonographer and me. Perhaps T. Ogden would call this process dreaming up life together.

The father wrote: *"It is unlikely that I consciously perceived the full significance of this sentence, 'do not let go of the baby', from Julianna at the time she pronounced it; but I realized afterwards what a key moment it was for me, perhaps precisely because it prompted me to look for a way to hold the baby. For my partner, who from the start had been saying the baby was fine, it legitimised her instincts: someone from the hospital was telling her she was right to hold onto her child, that she was not being desperate and irrational".* (*our translation*, Adjedj, 2016, p. 25)

Resources and territory

On a rollercoaster, the ascents are terribly slow, the descents extremely fast ...

Understanding what resources parents could rely on when faced with enduring uncertainty was a challenge. The medical knowledge? The link with doctors? Our ongoing exchange? Their family, their friends? It became more and more clear to me that beyond those resources available to them, the parents themselves were a resource.

I also became aware that we needed to synergise our respective skills and create freedom in our bonds to overcome the vertigo of this story. How do we get through the endless medical interventions, tests, counter-tests, medical examinations, counter-examinations, and still stay in touch with the baby, the psychic gestation, the reverie?

Beyond the usual spaces, my office, that of the sonographer's, the hospital corridors, the cafeteria of the maternity ward became the place where the most crucial exchanges took place. We reimagined and inhabited this new territory. It was closer to life than the office – it was the environment we needed to come down from the rollercoaster.

Like the swing of a pendulum, I travelled between the stories of the parents and those of the medical team, struck by the discrepancies between the two. When the parents had just begun to hope again, the doctors shared disastrous news. When the parents were desperate the paediatric neurologist came to tell me that there was a new hopeful finding. I was the intermediary. Everything was addressed to me. There were no direct daily discussions between the parents and the medical team. It was up to me to process these extremes, to maintain the space, or else the baby as well as the parents would have had to pay an exorbitant price.

The parents did not let go of the baby, but they had to live with great uncertainty and fear concerning the baby's heart and brain. They were shuffling between the house and the hospital, these two unbearable territories. They described their struggle to survive:

> *"If the hospital is the hostile place, where we face potentially bad news, the house becomes a suspended place, almost a non-place, where caution makes constructing anything impossible ... We took the bull by the horns, we chose to occupy the field that was least familiar to us, which was also the one where everything was really happening. We decided to "inhabit" the hospital, by various means: if we could not sleep there, we could stay for lunch after an appointment. It was not only a question of place: it was also a question of faces".*
>
> (*our translation*, Adjej, 2016, p. 26)

The invisible side

Beyond the faith that the parents were a resource, I had a deep conviction that the fetus, too, was rallying. "I feel she is happy in my womb", the mother told me. This was her conviction and not a medical truth. In the configuration defined by hope on the part of the parents and the awful medical reality on the part of the doctors, I had to find a way to balance those realities and create a space where hope and reality were on the same side for both doctors and parents.

"To be or not to be" persisted implicitly. Our gazes and our exchanges revolved around the question of how we value life. The answer was perceptible in our glances, handshakes, in our greetings and goodbyes. I believed that every decision, even the smallest one, was of immense significance. This continuous sharing constituted a holding environment. The parents were able to lean on me, the baby on the parents. The baby could seize what suited her best in her intrauterine life and build herself. I trusted what the mother communicated to me, that through her own mind, she felt her baby's. That is how I came to believe the baby could know her own mind and find strength. Having the space, she could determine herself. The father writes:

> "Lowering our guard was the condition for the discussion, but as with diplomacy between nations, the relationship between us and the doctors was like a transaction where we exchanged information but did not tell each other everything. Moreover, the dialogue was multipartite: between doctors and us, between doctors, between us. In this constellation, Julianna could have been considered the diplomat of the case because she had access to all the secrets on either side. But her actual role was quite different from that of a diplomat: without revealing anything about what was being said in the doctors' meetings where our daughter had a prominent spot, she offered us a breathing space in which we could think and react together. It was after the 'resolution of the conflict', as we say in politics and drama, that we all discovered both the extent of the 'secret' negotiations and the extent of the doubts each of us had ... . We strived along this path with a bomb set on the table. But we managed to keep a relative and reasonable hope".
>
> (our translation, Adjedj, 2016, p. 29)

> "It's funny, to me it wasn't like there was a bomb about to go off", shares the mother in response. "On the contrary, it was as if I had been perpetually convinced that the ground was not full of mines. But because I was told, 'Be careful, don't walk there, it could explode', I waited for the instructions, for someone to 'check' or 'clear' the ground before continuing to move forward, that is to say, to continue to live this pregnancy and to believe in it".
>
> (our translation, Thiriet, 2016, p. 29)

Out of the womb

After months of our containing all the uncertainty and not giving up hope, Ambre was born. She looked beautiful and serene. After six days in the maternity ward, the parents could take her home. All seemed well. Then two days later, the bomb exploded. Ambre was rushed to the hospital where she had emergency heart surgery. She escaped a certain death by just three hours.

It was a Sunday and without any conscious reason or informed decision, I called the parents when I never used to. In hindsight, I told myself that our already well-established unconscious communication *was* reinforced by that unusual phone call. The father realized that though it was completely irrational, it was also completely logical that I called them. It woke them up to come back to their rêverie.

All these months on the rollercoaster lead to everyone's transformation. The parents were able to muster all the resources, theirs as well as their daughter's. I am convinced Ambre was active in this process.

We walked through time and space in the maternity ward during these months, as part of our parent/analyst relationship. I observed light and shadows, like staring at a sky that changes with the passage of clouds. It was about being present, a lot of listening, commentaries, and a few interpretations, but mainly it was about building an environment. The space for and the rhythm of facing the news together suffused our exchanges. The trust in the enlightening environment restored reverie and re-established gestating as dreaming for us all.

Ambre was saved not only because she was hospitalised in one of the best Parisian neonatal units. It was also because she had arrived in a place of true hospitality. Hospitality is more than welcoming someone: it is the focused attention, the unconscious acceptance, the ability to wait and receive what there is. The acceptance of the unexpected is part of the challenge. Ambre grasped the parental hospitality and successfully navigated pre- and post-natal complexities. Hospitality is a quality of openness even in times of uncertainty. It is a force that promotes life and can offer protection against death.

Today, Ambre is a beautiful and talented twelve-year-old girl. She is in therapy to sort out all the pre-/post-natal as well as current traumas that need to be worked through. She is learning and enjoying her friends and family.

This journey transformed both Ambre's parents and me. The parents shared with me their deeply changed relationship with the world, how they learned to weave together bonds and undo knots. I wondered how this journey impacted my psychoanalytic attitude and ethics. For me, fostering hospitality and vitality in the mental container is at the heart of the psychoanalytic process.

The extraordinary cooperation between the parents and me, the unusual degree of identification with the baby, allowed us to dream up life together. The parents kept on coming to the maternity ward for months afterwards and we all felt that we had something to offer through this shared experience. For years, I had a project in mind, I called it "Art comme l'air" (Art as Air"). We need art as we need air in human relationships. I asked the parents if we could work together. We decided to share the poetic force of our trajectory, the words, gestures and actions that helped sustain life.

"Art comme l'air" was ultimately established at the Bluets Maternity Hospital. We initiated a residency program for artists and invited them to create work around childbirth. A choreographer worked on the bodily and psychic movements in the search for contact. A video artist offered a sacred moment, as she filmed a newborn's first movement from the arms of the mother to the arms of the father. A visual artist proposed to sit in a waiting room with threads of all colours creating embroidery. Mother, father, grandparents, paediatrician, nurse sit around the cradle linking together child, family, caregiver and artist. To contemplate, to dream and to keep up with reverie.

The author in her office at the Maternité des Bluets in 2015

The analytic adventure

My perinatal work and my analytic practice have run in parallel for the last thirty years. The following vignette presents my analytic work with adults, followed by my reflections on it.

My understanding of Emma reflects a synthetised vision of psychoanalytic perspective: it brings together the many international influences that I enjoyed before my immersion in the Paris Psychoanalytical Society, SPP and its spirit as I understand it. When I reflect upon my insights on shared laughter with Emma, I find myself in touch with Freudian psychoanalytic thinking and the major importance it gives to the drives ("*les pulsionnels*") and infantile sexuality.

Emma, from deep depression to growing and playing

Pale and receding behind her glasses, dressed impersonally, Emma looked closed like an oyster. In her late twenties, she appeared deeply depressed. While in Hungary she had been on much medication for years: she had lived without any spark of life, thinking everything was grey, if not black. I did not have much space for a new patient, but she fought fiercely to get into treatment with me. I said we would give it a try. I was curious to see how we could find a way into the analytic process, how I could connect to resources within myself to keep going, and especially how to decrease her suffering from so much mental pain. I sensed that, even if we were not especially engaged in our first encounter, I could rely on my intuition that analysis was worth the adventure of discovery-recovery.

We spoke in Hungarian. Back then this did not carry any special value for me. Because my own analysis in English was so much more meaningful than the one in Hungarian, I believed that the native tongue was not as crucial as the personal style of the analyst, as his/her presence, unconscious communication, and ability to understand beyond words.

Emma comes from a big family of five children, of which she is the third. Her parents, grandparents, brothers and sister all live together in a large family house outside Budapest. Emma's childhood was an immersion in family life, one imbued with repressive religious structures. She played with her siblings and stayed close to her mother. She did not like to be separated from her and often clung to her.

When it was time for her to start kindergarten, she froze and could not engage with her classmates. It was a traumatic experience for her to be away from her family and especially her mother. Now, she wanted to be as far away from them as she could – her sad father, exhausted mother and too many rival siblings. She obtained a diploma in Hungarian and French literature from Budapest University and left for Paris in 2012 on a scholarship. Since her arrival in Paris, she had lived with a man, Fred, a researcher, who took very attentive care of her.

We started analysis three times a week in 2013. Emma was the most depressive person I have ever met and treated. The first years were challenging and hostile: she was mistrustful, resigned and indifferent to my efforts. Her self-deprecation was omnipresent, she experienced herself as a prisoner in empty depression, and she had no social life. When she threatened to kill herself, I made it clear that we would not be able to work in this way. Understanding her threat of suicide as a provocation and as her crying out so that I would save her life, helped me get through to her. A new dimension of transference was emerging she had been using the couch, but now, lying on it was too "dangerous" without the holding gaze, so I suggested that she sit up and work with me face to face. We struggled for three years like this.

In my analytic work, I maintain a clear frame and firm boundaries. When I saw that Emma was too distressed to lie down, I had her sit up and face me for several years, until she was truly ready for the couch. With Emma, who for a time suffered from grave depression and a loss of interest in life, I maintained a strong empathic presence and invited her to engage in a journey of discovery. I am interested in instilling curiosity in the patient about the links between early experience and current difficulties. My unwillingness to tolerate her suicidal fantasies had a positive effect; ever so gradually she moved into life and connection with others.

The dominant themes in her life were her lack of sexual satisfaction and almost non-existent social life. Every day she conveyed to me these needs, feeling repeatedly empty and useless. Sometimes I could associate her story with a line from a children's song. We had these few moments of connection when we relaxed a little. I was just hanging on in there, supporting the endless complaint and complacency, showing her, whenever the material permitted, how powerfully the depressive part of her was overwhelming her life instinct.

In 2016, something important happened: she started to get off her medication, began a master's course to become a translator, and started to make friends for the first time. When she returned to Budapest for her first internship, she began to enjoy and appreciate her family and the background it gave her, and to feel the love she received.

The last two years of psychoanalysis were quite different from the preceding seven years. Emma discovered excitement in object relationships, her sessions were much more about outside events and, finally, internal transformations made life livable and her image of herself became less negative. She began to dare to "dream big", something that she felt she did not deserve before. This was a breakthrough which made it possible for her to ask herself why she did not dare to want a circle of friends, love, and work, which she so very much desired. She always put the brakes on enjoying life, leaving her with a severe and constant feeling of being destroyed and empty inside. She was attracted to the intense and safe pain of not being anybody. Nowadays this narcissistic suffering shows only for a few short moments: it does not swallow her up anymore.

In 2019, while she was doing her second internship abroad, she risked much more investment in her relationship with Fred. In the absence, she felt more desire for him. Her sexual desire began to emerge, and she accepted his proposal to get married. When she was away from Paris for months for her internships, we continued by phone, something I had already practised with patients who travel because of professional obligations.

This second internship took her out of the routine of her ordinary life. There she learned to get involved and become integrated into group life without too much anxiety, something that she had long desired. Back in Paris, she got married to Fred because she felt that the *relationship was now strong enough.* She got a job offer from a small group who had asked her to work for them specifically because they recognised her organised and precise approach. Her self-experience was safer, she had some security now, and she did not collapse, nor fall apart whenever she dared to venture into new territory.

At the centre of these changes, she felt that for the first time in her life she was brave because she was listening to herself, following her heart's desires. She felt almost audacious. She fought against comparing herself to others and she stopped creating scenarios that threatened failure. For years, the smallest interactions, like a lunch with colleagues, were thought of in terms of victory or failure: "I had lunch with X, and it was successful". She even started to think that she would be happier not just working as a translator but wanting to write fiction.

As she became more in touch with herself, she realized that after all she was not content and satisfied in her marriage. She weaned herself from her husband's devoted care. She moved out, got a new place, and became more autonomous. This is when the months-long lockdown started due to the Covid-19 pandemic. The moment of lockdown, taken very seriously in France, was obviously a huge challenge. After coming out of her internal lockdown, she was shut*off* in a new apartment all alone.

We continued our work by telephone without any interruption. The closing-in was so extremely hard for Emma that she resorted to taking medication again. After a few weeks, her capacity for vitality accelerated and I saw that she felt more alive and dared to breathe more freely. I reminded her that no matter how hard it was to live with fear, pain and solitude, she was not in survival mode anymore, that living was not all about survival. Her relational world was no longer about managing her encounters successfully, avoiding risks, controlling each move towards another person. She said in French that this was a period of being "*soulagée et libérée*", relieved and free. She had never spoken in our sessions in French before. It had been a slow change, slow and deep throughout all these years of analysis.

This is when I realized how languages and the double culture worked for Emma. Hungarian opened important infantile spaces, while the French language granted access to new development. It allowed us to climb out of boredom and depression. Some sessions were becoming very alive, as we were playing with words and being creative and imaginative in our languages.

In the last week before the summer holiday – sacred in France – Emma came to the session with a strong image of how she had felt for years. She said it was as though she had been in a huge block of ice, and that finally felt there was an axe cutting through it. Unexpected cheerfulness had bubbled up. She asked herself if she would be able to hold onto it, despite the holiday coming up and a pause in our sessions. She started a little notebook, writing down on one side all the attacking monsters, and on the other, all the tools she had now found to fight against them. Then she came up with the image of Sleeping Beauty: like her, she had been trapped in a long, frozen winter night. I suggested that Sleeping Beauty had had a long, long way to go to figure out how to dare to wake up. She could rely on analysis, so the ice had started to melt. Once out of the frozen state she could have dreams, share them, listen to them and accept to depend on the process and on me.

I asked myself if doing this analysis in a language other than Hungarian would have made a difference. Focusing on understanding could have been done in French, but the melting of the ice was partially due to our exchanges in Hungarian. Beyond the more nuanced expressions that our mother tongue offered to both of us, it also provided its sensorial qualities, childhood rhymes, and early imprints. In Hungarian we felt we knew better which register to be in. We could enter the meaning of a word more precisely. She once remarked: *"In Hungarian, I can kick into the exact register where it is happening"*.

In the last session before the holidays, Emma was in a good mood. She said she felt that she did not need to be perfect to feel good and that, somehow, spaces had opened for her lately. She had even initiated communication with a man, Benjamin, whom she was interested in without being too anxious or worried about his reaction. We talked a little bit about how fear closed such spaces, and she remarked on how reality was very different from the phantasy land where she had been struggling with all her destructive phantasies. She had become open and receptive to reality and that made her feel more like an actor in her life. She talked about her gratitude for Fred, her ex-partner, who had been helpful and kind to her. Without him, she would not have been able to come this far, psychologically and emotionally. Now she had to figure out what might come next.

I have included an excerpt of a session, seven years into the analysis with Emma, because I think that we had been heading towards this moment since the beginning of treatment, without being able to formulate it. Having my most depressed patient become a "funny one", laughing together and thinking of her present and future, was a privilege. We have both been working hard for many years.

Clinical vignette: Emma, her heart's desire (October 2020)

Emma said a little prayer in the morning before coming to her session. She said she did not pray for good things to happen to her anymore, but that whatever happened was a good thing. She had been reading in the metro and felt good. She thought about freedom, how things had become less complicated, less stressful, just a while ago. A few days earlier she had been able to organize a farewell meeting at a bar after work to say goodbye to her team.

E: *I don't have to fit in with other people's expectations, I feel liberated.*

JV: Like in your prayer. You don't ask for freedom, but you ask for being able to be present and experience whatever life brings around. To be alive and have feelings is not menacing.

E: *Yes, I was afraid for so long, that if I felt things, l would be destroyed. The image I had of myself was so bad.*

She went on to describe an issue with her friend Olga who had cancelled their dinner arrangements. Emma was instead trying to join her new boyfriend, Benjamin, but he had other plans. He texted her that it would be difficult to include her at the last minute and sent kisses. At first, it was a small shock to her, and she didn't reply. She guessed that he had sensed her feelings were hurt because he sent a few more messages about the rain and other matters.

JV: He tried very delicately to keep in touch, to invite you back into an exchange.

She had managed to exit quickly out of the feeling of being abandoned or excluded and wished him a good time.

JV: Without making him feel guilty? Could you contain the small disappointment, the feeling of being excluded? It looks like you were two adults who could solve a situation.

E: *I am happy I could come up with those few words and was ready if it didn't work out, without being devastated like before.*

JV: Your prayer has been listened to ... .

E: *That God listened to me?* [She laughs. I too laugh a little.]

JV: Yes, you have been listened to in your internal world.

Then she told me that when she was very uptight, people stayed away more. Perhaps it was not because they did not like her, but that they did not know how to relate to her. She now appreciated relationships much more and felt closer to others; she had close friends and family now. Her vision has changed. She was not so alone anymore, and this gave her self-confidence.

[Silence.]

E: *What I have also recognized in myself, if ... Well, the question of humor is subjective, who likes what. [She continues in a funny voice.] I think I am very funny.*

We found ourselves astonished by her comment, which claimed something authentically positive about herself, after so many years of self-deprecation.

JV: [I burst out laughing.] This is good news, what a relief!

Then she had an association that enabled her to say that she was a "funny guy". She laughed and I did too.

JV: Humor has found you. Humor has knocked on your door.

E: *It is not like telling jokes, it's more the way of linking things together, associations. Irony, self-irony. Not everybody likes it, but I do.*

JV: If you are not paralyzed by anxiety and hate, thoughts and feelings can flow. It can be deep or funny, in humor it can be both at the same time.

Our communication had changed significantly. I felt that she could enjoy her life and experiences, and that by experiencing the present and accepting it, a dynamic energy could begin to circulate between us and within her.

E: *It feels good to be natural, because in life there is nature, rather than play a role like in a theatre, instead to be more like plants and animals.*

There was a long silence, a particularly good silence, one of reverie.

E: *Perhaps Benjamin could understand that I felt bad because the day before he told me about his own feelings of being excluded, and I said that sometimes I still felt this way, but that I didn't let it overwhelm me. I dared to tell him that I had been depressed for years. He didn't move away from me, which had been my big fear.*

Reflections on the session

After seven years of struggling with depression, constant denigration of herself, with suicidal feelings and an unsatisfactory sexual life, Emma is in a new relationship, living life with its ups and downs, sexual love, intimacy, and her new work situation. Sometimes she must face her old fears, but she can think about and contain them, without falling apart. After years of experiencing cold indifference, hatred and distance towards, and from, her objects – which she transferred onto me – she opened up to her family, made friends and expressed gratitude for the analytic process and her analyst. There was an important turning point in our work when in the fifth year of analysis Emma left Paris twice for six months as part of her training as a translator. Translation was a platform for transformation, a tool with which to symbolise depressive affects.

The lockdown, just after she had moved out from the safe marriage with Fred, closed her in again, and her recently and shyly opened relational field disappeared. Our work together was a long struggle and perseverance had its benefits. The atmosphere of our sessions, the respect of her "oysterness" and finally *our common* background bore fruit. When we started, Emma was afraid of coming to life. The fact that I respected her defences for a long time must have allowed her to open up.

The session starts with the narrative of the morning prayer which I understand as a meditation. It represented a change in perspective, the lightening of the grip of the superego: Emma said, *"Instead of praying for good things to happen, whatever happens is good"*.

Her prayer spoke of a capacity to relinquish her infantile and magical belief that enlisting the help of a higher power would ensure that her wishes would be granted. She instead trusted her idealised all-powerful Mother/Analyst would be able to transform her suffering, giving it meaning, and thereby making it good.

When I replied "You don't ask for freedom" I was interpreting the patient's dependency on her analyst. As I continued: "... but you ask for being able to be present and experience whatever life brings around" I was acknowledging her breakthrough.

Emma's insight in the metro, about having the taste of freedom to be herself, revealed her capacity to enjoy the present moment, and indeed free herself from the omnipotent mother and from her long-standing submission to her objects. Its full meaning became conscious to both of us as an "après coup" effect in the session.

The episode she mentioned also shows that she had gained more autonomy. After her girlfriend cancelled their plans and her boyfriend is not available, Emma does not fall into anxiety at abandonment as she did for years. My comment about her boyfriend wanting to *"keep in touch"* with her, messaging her delicately, transformed her demands into desire and acceptance. This was also the fruit of long-term internalisation of patience, respect, care and attention within the analytic process, which allowed her, at last, to be able to perceive, tolerate and receive care from others.

Not feeling guilty to be alive, contrary to what her fierce superego had dictated for so long, allowed her to let go of her *"pulsion d'emprise"*, her stranglehold on her objects. This instinct to master (Freud, 1920) the need to control, made it impossible for her to enjoy emotional flexibility. Now she can increasingly experience what a relaxed and calm psyche may offer her.

The first little laugh – when she said: *"I am funny"* – embodied an encounter between us, allowing elaborated feelings of complicity and friendliness after all the difficult years of destructive wishes. It brought a marked relief of tension.

But the second laugh of shared excitement was more "uncontrolled", showing a shift from a depressed, lost person to a funny, entertaining one, from isolation to social contact. It also illustrated a

shift in Emma's perception of the relationship between a shy analysand and a less feared "mother figure". The excitement expressed
itself in robust laughter and joy and was a very moving experience of
warm affection and circulating libido. The triumph of life over depression, humour was the pearl the closed-up oyster now produced.
The silence which followed signified peace, and the internalisation of
a capacity for intimate sharing. Emma talked about linking things
together.

At the end of the session, she said: "*It feels good to be natural,
because in life there is nature, not play a role like in a theatre, instead to
be more like plants and animals*". It felt like she had walked out of her
tense and nervous child self and found a natural adult one. In the
Freudian model, this creative energy that bubbled up and flowed in
her was the result of the vitality of infantile sexuality.

Her very last words in the session, "*I dared to tell him that I was
depressed. He didn't move away from me, which was my big fear*" shows
her awareness of her fear of being abandoned, and her successful
struggle to manage it. She felt daring because she told Benjamin that
she was depressed. She feared she would lose him, but she felt triumphant and relieved when he stayed. There still is work to be done.

The oyster image I had of her showed how closed she was, but it
seemed that it was also a defensive ploy, a sign of some hope.
Defences may well protect against intrusion, but they also protect
against fears of what it is to let go and open, let passions and aggression out. Our laughter was a bonus because it put us in a specific
emotional state, getting inside each other's internal world and accepting this shared non-controlled state. The relaxed open spirit of
shared humour and laughter expressed our intimacy.

Threading a needle in a hurricane suggests trying to make the impossible happen. This session showed a breakthrough, life becoming
livable and even sometimes enjoyable. Emma's cold heart progressively became a passionate one, and her feeling that it was dangerous
to be fully alive could be tolerated.

I burst out laughing with an elementary force when Emma said in
the session that she now considered herself funny. We shared a joyful
moment laughing together. It was with the same elementary energy
that I burst out crying when I shared this session with my two colleagues. Both times it was not only a surprising emotional experience,

but an understanding of the strength of the energy that had finally started to circulate in her and between us. These two events mark transformative moments in the psychoanalytic journey. The experience of Emma escaping from depression or from the destructive grip, the "life drive" triumphant over depression, engendered extraordinary emotions. Experiencing love and passion for the analytic adventure is a huge pleasure and privilege.

Thoughts on becoming a psychoanalyst

I believe that what made me want to become an analyst was my "*fêlure personnelle*", or personal wound and my persistent curiosity and thirst to understand psychological development, my own and that of others. At the age of five, I took a long look at my parents, staring at them, and remembered every detail of how I became aware that *they didn't understand me*, despite their love. How can love and not understanding come together? I was later able to put words on what I also felt, *I did not understand them*. My deep desire to figure out this enigmatic link (Laplanche, 1987) which existed between them must have been the main factor that set me off on my analytic adventure.

Languages

Languages, both verbal and non-verbal, play a significant role in my relating and reflecting. I developed the ability to communicate non-verbally fairly early in my life, but my practice with infants and young children helped me develop that skill further. It had certainly been growing since my adolescence through my engagements with different contemporary art forms: music, dance, painting. My patient Emma and I often communicated non-verbally. I felt her primary emotions and her frozen state deeply. Containing the anxiety which came with its slow melting was not through words alone: gazes, handshakes, the rhythm and the tone of interactions all played their part.

Then there is the world of verbal exchanges. With Emma, our mother tongue, Hungarian, played a vital role, connecting us to our bodies and drives. Hungarian has such a different intelligibility and logic than English or French in the nuances it makes, the freedom it gives to people who share the language. Hungarian has the ability to signify an entire sentence in a single word. It uses a grammatical process of agglutination which does not rely on gender or time. The Hungarian language with its figurative and agglutinative quality is capable of arousing in the speaker a perceptive-hallucinatory experience that allows spontaneous expression. The Hungarian language lends itself to the making of more metaphors in which conscious and unconscious are closer to each other than in English or French.

The three languages I use, English, French and Hungarian, are part of my professional identity and journey. I am aware of not being perfect in the two languages I learned later in life. But just as the words cannot capture all the richness of sensations, emotions, and unconscious movements, being imperfect does not feel like a disadvantage. My relationship to my own history and unconscious is bound up with the different states of mind that belong to these different landscapes as I described them previously.

Some intimate moments with my patients occur when we are searching for a word and feeling free to move between the different possibilities in our two or even three shared languages and their landscapes. For both analysand and analyst, this freedom can help to capture the message that is waiting for expression. Such a walk around languages plays a part with my Japanese, Latin American and Eastern European patients. The patient and I are both living in and discovering a foreign land.

The family sphere

At the midpoint of my journey through life, I imagined a tree with one branch only and felt that it would not fully grow and mature. I withdrew from professional life for a while. I then turned towards what carried meaning for my partner and me as a couple and there I, we, grew. I gave birth at home and stayed on for six years raising my children. I found those years to be as challenging as a few years of psychoanalysis. It was a time outside professional business but very much inside an essential aspect of my life and vocation: I was in touch with ordinary urban solitude with young children in a foreign culture, with no family nearby. We had to reach for our innermost resources to provide us strength. It reminds me of one of my dreams that I found in my dream journal: I was a turtle sunken in asphalt. Starting a family, my analysis and the chosen environment made the turtle emerge and slowly advance towards the sea. This development came from our appropriation of all the accumulated challenges of life, the vital social fabrics we could weave, and the nourishing taking in of the arts and, for me, psychoanalysis. Much later I wrote a book about mothering with a midwife colleague (Roy et al., 2018) and I have been involved with the World Association for Infant Mental Health (WAIMH) for twenty-five years.

Raising my children in an environment quite different than what I had come from opened up unexplored territories. Other than this fundamental and life-changing experience, I have been exploring all kinds of new therapies, body work, and I have been engaging with psychodrama from the Mérei-Vikàr approach. This approach was introduced by Ferenc Mérei as an original way of practising psychodrama on the soil of the Hungarian psychoanalytic spirit.

Professional development

I have attended several international conferences and presented in IPA colloquiums, where I enjoy discovering other perspectives and horizons. But my participation in small working groups has been the most satisfying learning experience in my psychoanalytic adventure.

There have been many and varied such experiences for years and years: a discussion group on observation led by Genevieve Haag, G. Williams; an English language reading group of the International Journal of Psychoanalysis; an ongoing seminar on René Roussillon are but a few of such groups.

Régine Prat, one of the original thinkers at the SPP, leads an exciting and unusual group. Freudian psychoanalysis, contemporary authors, developmental research, and neuroscience, are all brought into dialogue with each other, followed by two-hour clinical exchanges. She and I share perinatal work and facilitate a seminar: The dialogue between Esther Bick and Emmi Pikler.

I regularly go to Brussels to the European Psychoanalytic Federation (EPF) to Christophe Dejours' "Work Related Suffering" seminar, exploring new forms of servitude (Déjours, 2015).

I participated in "Psychoanalysis and Politics" meetings led by Lena Auestad, a Norwegian philosopher where I met Joseph Dodds and since then have become deeply interested in psychoanalysis and ecology.

Clinical theories

I asked the group I was facilitating last week on a *Dialogue between Bick and Pikler*: How would you define infant observation? How would you describe your own internal state of mind when you are observing? While the participants were considering the questions, I wrote down to myself: to observe is to listen to the vitality, to the baby herself and to the infant in me. It is to create an envelope around the axis of attention and give value to what is there, and what is on its way to coming into being. I oscillate between wonder and pain, between hope and reality, between spontaneity and knowledge, between balancing and falling, between close attention and reverie, between gentleness and gravity. This is my state of attention for observing the beginning of life, though it is not far from how I listen in my sessions with my adult patients. We are in a dialogue. I am aware of my intentions, my stamina and commitment, trusting the process and composing with our unconscious communication, trying to perceive and "play with" transferences. I learned observation from Gianna Williams who came to Paris from the Tavistock Clinic in London, and from Geneviève Haag in Paris, who had studied with Esther Bick. G.Haag has a unique understanding of our psychic constructions on all levels, from the sensory and motor to oedipal.

I often mention Ferenczi, to whom I am most strongly attached. His sincerity in his desire to heal, and his therapeutic approach serve as basic reference points for me. In Paris, in the 1980s, I explored the different Freudian and Lacanian theoretical approaches – they did not enthuse me as much as Melanie Klein did. I became familiar with Klein through my second analysis and through my twenty years with the GERPEN group (*Groupe d'Études et de recherches psychanalytiques pour le développement de l'enfant et du nourrisson*). This group was created by James Gammil, my supervisor for child analysis, a direct heir to Klein. He introduced Melanie Klein to correct a caricatural and deformed vision on her approach. For twenty years, I did not miss a single meeting and case discussion with Donald Meltzer and Martha Harris. After 2010, other very influential creative analysts were invited, among other: Christopher Bollas, Antonino Ferro, Gianna Williams, Stefano Bolognini, Joshua Durban. I established my analytical identity through Kleinian and Meltzerian thinking.

Another influence came from my university background. I discovered my doctoral supervisor, Didier Anzieu in the same way I had discovered Winnicott in the London bookstore. I feel impregnated by his clinical and theoretical ideas. My thesis was on connecting his lively and inventive thoughts on the creative process and small group functioning. I embraced his skin-ego concept, his work on artistic creation and group analysis. I found a group of artists to observe in their creative project. I observed five phases in the process of creation Anzieu described in individual work in this group: creative grasp, becoming aware of the unconscious psychic representation, the organising code and its bodily existence, the composition of the creation itself and making the artwork live outside its own context of creation.

In terms of groups, the idea of the skin-container took on a life of its own for me. Anzieu's influential concept of the psychic envelope in *The Skin-Ego* (1994) is another basic point of reference in my adult and perinatal work. His metaphor of the 'Skin-ego' as a psychical wrapping that contains and consolidates the subject is an essential contribution to our contemporary vision of the psyche. I am grateful now as I realise how much I was influenced by Anzieu.

I have remained both an insider and an outsider in the Paris analytic society, which functions with a strict hierarchy and where I never felt especially welcomed. Friends and colleagues close to me have felt the same. This probably resonates with my apprehension of institutions. I had escaped a country under the control of a dominant ideology, where personal thinking had not been encouraged. Nevertheless, my entering *the Société Psychanalytique de Paris* for training at the beginning of the twenty-first century was the right choice and happened at the right moment. The training was extremely valuable and belonging to this highly demanding analytical society was important to me. I had good experiences and supervision, though my research and curiosity are off the beaten tracks. I found the seminars on Freud and other authors deeply involving, I understand the challenge of fully assimilating the concepts of the drives, the transference and infantile sexuality. I see infantile sexuality as a source of desire and permanent creative activity, with an active presence in the unconscious psychic life of adults. In this context, René Roussillon is an extraordinarily knowledgeable, open-minded analyst with a contemporary view. He teaches Freud whilst drawing also on the current development of psychoanalytical contributions.

The infant in the analytic encounter

Emmi Pikler's work makes me think of Winnicott's impact on everyday practice and on different psychoanalytic schools. His theory is based on observation, on ideas of good-enough health and well-being, on playfulness and creativity. His thoughts on surviving hate and envious attacks, the relationship between true and false selves in our psychic structure are cornerstones of psychoanalytic theory and practice. Relying on *playing* in Winnicott's conceptual framework connects us to the infant within. Winnicott considers psychoanalysis a highly specialised form of playing as communication and a way of maintaining creative aliveness in the session. When there is no communication, vitality fades.

I have an intimate relationship with the infant in us, with a brief past and a long future. In the transference, the past is the present. The potential for the patient to come into being and develop his/her idiom is present in each adult and I hear in each the need for meaning and development. "The infantile is the only part of oneself that is flexible enough to transform itself, malleable enough to learn from experience, loving enough to forgive, passionate enough to sacrifice, bold enough to take on impossible challenges, young enough to hope" (Guignard, 2021).

The work of liberating the infantile requires a tender caring approach within the framework of our analytical setting. (In France we talk about psychic bisexuality.) In adult analysis, there is the chance for patients to transform and reconfigure their object-relational world. Sometimes adult patients will have a long and difficult trajectory to find their unique singular psychic home. Similarly, as it takes time for patients to find their idiom analysts also need time to create their own psychoanalytic idiom. It was through Donald Meltzer that I came to understand how my own state of mind can shape the space with the patient in the analytic encounter. Meltzer states that it is the family who hopefully endows the child with essential psychic capacities: to engender love, promote thought, contain depression, sustain hope (Meltzer & Harris, 2013). Given that the family sometimes fails to engender these capacities in the child I like to think of my work as an environmental psychoanalyst who creates the environment that generates these potentialities and maintains the conditions to foster development, trusting in the process and knowing that results can be imperfect.

Intimacy: My core preoccupation

The cultural and psychoanalytic perspective I carry, follow, and hold onto is that of Ferenczi's. I continually have an internal dialogue with him. The Budapest intellectual community cultivated by poets, writers, artists and analysts, the informal, close, and deep personal relationships and the Hungarian language connect me to him. As I lately discovered, my parents took me regularly to the same two places Ferenczi had frequented: Cafe New York and Restaurant Royal. My relationship with him and his contributions feel intimate, characterised by his warm, open, caring and non-dominating personality. Ferenczi's vulnerability is his strength, his honesty is his integrity, and his clinical insights show his exceptional talent. In his searching and looking, and not necessarily finding, and in admitting his mistakes, Ferenczi continually revealed himself.

I rely on the Hungarian school of psychoanalysis in my analytic work. It provides me with a balance between the classical Freudian theory and Ferenczian care. I think that in the Hungarian school there is more space for regression, for consideration of needs and kindness towards the bodily and psychological care of adults, and the child in them. Michael Balint, Ferenczi's heir, wrote about primary love, and, with his wife Alice Balint, was already early on theorising about the psychology of infant care. It is because of my clinical concerns that I have thought a lot about the "primary landscape". I wrote about "primary harmony" for a Balint congress, and about the "primary environment" in the twenty-first century in the *American Journal of Psychoanalysis*. One of my main clinical interests has to do with the nature of transmission and the roots of co-operation in the primary object-relation. It is one of the main themes of the training I conduct for childcare specialists.

All this amounts to a subtle alchemy that has distinct cultural roots. To put it simply, I am more "at home" in what I have internalised as the ambience of the Budapest psychoanalytic school than in the classical Freudian theories that we study and continue to refer to in France.

I wonder if it is more difficult to be intimate in Western culture or if intimacy comes in a form in the West that I have not yet been able to discover, even though I consider myself well-adjusted after my immigration forty-five years ago. Intimacy does not seem to me to be appreciated and valued to the same extent or in the same way that it is in Hungary. When my colleagues in the SPP started working on the telephone during the lockdown, they complained that this contact from ear to ear was much too close, too intimate. When I showed them my little film "Hello Baby" – a collaboration between the filmmaker Valerie Winckler and myself – which shows the first minutes between mothers, parents and babies, at a scientific meeting, the intensity of the moment provoked discomfort in some colleagues. Too much intensity was felt to be too intimate. It is my personal experience that the space for intimacy in the social sphere is less present in French culture, because the vulnerability that comes with it is probably too frightening, even though Julia Kristeva, of Bulgarian origin, added the value of vulnerability to the French national motto, "*liberté, égalité, fraternité, vulnérabilité*" (Kristeva, 2016).

Intimacy is a private psychological space where one can communicate with oneself. If this is in place, then looking from inside towards the outside can make communication with another alive and creative. Resonance with the other, psychological hospitality, knowledge and ignorance are all part of this quality called intimacy. The condition for daring to be truly intimate requires some psychological and physical integration, the embodiment of the self.

Other sources of creativity

All that is important in development or trauma, in beauty or pain, come closer to being understood when evoked through art. I rely on art, of whatever form, to reflect the poetic depth of inner upheavals. From those who use words, the reverie and unconscious wisdom in the poetry of the little-known Hungarian poet Attila Jozsef have been a constant presence in my mind. While writing my chapter, one particular line evoked and contained my whole experience with immigration: "*Distance, glass marble of the skies, you will achieve in all your ways*" (from his poem *Lullaby*). Its oneiric quality implies to me that if you go the distance, you can achieve what you dreamed of.

Then there are more widely known others, who nourished me like Fyodor Dostoyevsky for his compassion, Franz Kafka for his perceptiveness, Samuel Beckett for his unpretentiousness and deprived language which reveals an inner truth, and many other contemporary authors who touch on our universal challenges: all are ongoing resources in my life and practice.

In a discussion following a theatre piece, Julia Kristeva asked the question: What good are poets in times of distress? She goes on to explain that "for me, the poet is above all a musician of language, he overwhelms the mother tongue and/or national language because he grasps its nerve - the tuned voice and senses, and he excels in what the early Stoics called the 'inner touch', the oikeiois; this impalpable sensation that connects each person to the most intimate part of himself and the other, thus constituting the first sketch of what will be called a 'conciliation', an 'amor nostril' and later 'humankind' and 'brotherhood'. The poet is at the root of this 'inner touch', he is the carrier wave of incarnated universality. Why the poet? Because by readjusting the senses and the sensible, by articulating unspeakable passions, the poet crosses identities, borders and foundations, and makes co-presence with others shareable. I am telling you that the alchemy of the poetic verb is an inseparable lining of the fraternity that impelled this evening's meeting. It was therefore inevitable, indispensable that when humanity collapses, the poet should be sought out and asked, and he should be asked first, not, to be or not to be, but simply to start over. For without him there will be no more 'inner touch' that can be shared, there will be no more humanity" (Kristeva, 2016).

Poets grasp the music of language, the adequately tuned tonalities, connect us to our most intimate selves and give us hope for conciliation. The mystery stays with us: what is the next chapter of our human destiny? Our immense challenge is finding the vitality needed for ecological healing. How to create worldwide cooperation, solidarity? Who sees ahead? Who envisions how?

Whose portrait is it?

My friend with the glasses, from the library in Paris, once told me the story of a portrait of Franz Hellens, her grandfather, painted by Amadeo Modigliani. The story takes place two years before Modigliani was to die tragically. At the time, he was still living in poverty and made portraits to earn some money. That is how he met Franz Hellens (1986), the writer, who asked him for a portrait. Modigliani came to the appointment, bought two bottles of wine and started to paint.

Modigliani painted with a dream-like quality. Concentrating hard, with an intense gaze, he worked for a few hours, and then they went out to smoke a cigarette. The two men did not speak much.

When they came back, Modigliani finished with just a few more strokes. When he declared it was ready, Hellens came to look at the portrait for the first time. It was a great piece of work, but he could not recognise himself in it. He showed it to his wife, who did not see him in it either. He paid a small sum for it and sold it for a little bit more soon after. Before he let it go, Hellens had it photographed and tucked the photo in a book. The book was relegated to the bottom of a drawer and forgotten for a long time. He later heard that the painting had been sold from one person to another and had gained more and more value with each sale.

Twenty years later, he was curious to see the portrait again – or rather the photograph – and searched until he finally found it. He was plunged into even greater amazement. He was certain that neither he nor his wife, nor friends, nor anyone else had been mistaken about whether this portrait resembled him. *It did not.* But seeing this photo now, what a shock! What do you expect he saw this time? There was no doubt: the portrait he had just found was that of his son, his youngest child.

Final thoughts

The author in Paris in 2022

I started this meditating-reflecting-writing journey from Budapest to Psychoanalysis with this sentence in my mind which an immigrant friend of mine once told me. Talking about how the exiled becomes conscious of not being more than *"his own walk without a road"*, it is precisely at that moment that the revelation of exile can take place. In the end, instead of the pain of loneliness, I appreciate the freedom of it: I am my own walk. I have my family and friends with me and I can tell you my story from it. People come to analysis because they do not know what they ignore. Artists ignore what they know, as in the story of the Modigliani portrait. The unconscious and the infant are promoting creativity. I started with a train and finished with the image of the child. The train in my story is not the train that took my father to Auschwitz; it is the train that has taken me to the Right Place, Paris, where I could grow and become the analyst I am today. My parents accompanied me and let go of their only child, which allowed me to embrace my destiny.

References

Anzieu, D. (1981). *Le corps de l'oeuvre* [The body of the work]. Paris: Gallimard.

Anzieu, D. (1994). *Le penser: Du moi-peau au moi-pensant* [To think it: From skin-self to thinking-self]. Malakoff, France: Dunod.

Appell, G. (2019). *Les premières années du bébé: Son bien être et ses compétences jour après jour* [The baby's first years: His well-being and his skills day after day]. Toulouse, France: Erès.

Arendt, H. (2015). *La langue maternelle* [The mother tongue]. Paris: Eterotopia, collection Rhizome.

Bick, E. (1964). "Notes on infant observation in psychoanalytic training". *International Journal of Psycho-Analysis*, 45, 558–566.

Bion, W. R. (1962). *Learning from Experience*. London: Tavistock.

Bollas, C. (1987). *The shadow of the object*. London: Free association Books.

Bion, W. R. (1986). "Paris séminaire". *Revue Psychothérapie Psychanalytique de Groupe*. Paris: Érès.

Bollas, C. (2011). *The Christopher Bollas Reader*. London and New York: Routledge.

Cassin, B. (2013). *La Nostalgie: Quand donc est-on chez soi?* [Nostalgia: When are you home?]. Paris: Autrement.

Cioran, M. E. (2009). *De la France* [Of France]. Paris: Editions de l'Herne.

David, M. & Appell, G. (1968). Lóczy ou le maternage insolite [Lóczy or unusual mothering]. Paris: Edition Scarabée.

Déjours, C. (2015). *Le Choix: Souffrir au travail n'est pas une fatalité* [The choice: work related suffering is not a fatality]. Paris: Bayard Éditions.

Dimitrijevitch, A., Cassullo, G. & Frankel, J. (Ed.) (2018). *Ferenczi's influence on contemporary psychoanalytic traditions: lines of development, evolution of theory and practice over the decades*. London and New York: Routledge.

Dodds, J. (2011). *Psychoanalysis and ecology at the edge of chaos: complexity theory, Deleuze/Guattari, and psychoanalysis for a climate in crisis*. London and New York: Routledge.

Ferenczi, S. (1985). *Klinikai napló* [Clinical Diary]. Budapest: Akadémiai Kiadó.

Ferenczi, S. (1995). *Journal clinique* [Clinical Diary] (Equipe du coq heron, Trans.). Paris: Petite Bibliotheque Payot. (Original work published 1985).

Ferenczi, S. (1932 [1995]). *The clinical diary of Sándor Ferenczi* (J. Dupont, Ed., M. Balint, Trans. & N. Z. Jackson, Trans.). Cambridge, MA: Harvard University Press, 1988 (second printing, 1995). (Original work published 1985).

Ferenczi, S. (1968). *Oeuvres completes, Tome 1: 1908–1912* [Complete Works, Vol 1] (J. Dupont, Trans.). Paris: Payot.

Ferenczi, S. (1970). *Oeuvres completes, Tome 2 1913–1919* [Complete Works, Vol 2] (J. Dupont, Trans.). Paris: Payot.

Ferenczi, S. (1974). *Oeuvres completes, Tome 3 1919–1926* [Complete Works, Vol 3] (J. Dupont, Trans.). Paris: Payot.

Ferenczi, S. (1982). *Oeuvres completes, Tome 4 1927–1933* [Complete Works, Vol 4] (J. Dupont, Trans.). Paris: Payot.

Freud, S. (1920). *Beyond the pleasure principle*. London: Hogarth Press.

Freud, S. (1927). Civilization and its discontents. *S.E.*, XXI, 57–146.

Gamill, J. (2007). *La position depressive au service de la vie* [The depressive state at the service of life]. Paris: In Press.

Guignard, F. (2021). *L'infantile et le psychanalyste en séance* [Web conference presentation]. IPA webinar, January 24, 2021.

Golse, B. (2009). Le droit des bébés à disposer d'eux-mêmes [The right to self-ownership of babies]. *Psychiatrie Française*, 40(4), 97–110.

Golse, B. (2010). Communication in the symposium "Infancy in Times of Transition" at the *12th World Congress of the World Association for Infant Mental Health*, June 29–July 3, 2010, Leipzig.

Green, A. (1999). *The work of the negative* (A. Weller, Trans.). London: Karnac, Free Association Books.

Grotstein, J. S. (1981). "Primal splitting, the background object of primary identifications and other self-objects". *Splitting and Projective Identification* (pp. 77–89). New York: Jason Aronson.

Haag, G. (2018). *Le Moi corporel: Autisme et développement* [The bodily self: Autism and development]. Paris: Le Fil Rouge.

Hahn, R. (Ed.) (1994). *Sincerity and other works: collected papers of Donald Meltzer*. London: Karnac.

Harris, A. & Kuchuck, S. (Ed.) (2015). *The legacy of Sandor Ferenczi: from ghost to ancestor*. London and New York: Routledge.

Haynal, A. (2002). *Disappearing and reviving: Sandor Ferenczi in the history of psychoanalysis*. London: Karnac.

Hellens, F. (1986). *Modigliani, Le voyant* [Modigliani, the psychic]. Bruxelles: Jacques Antoine. (Original work published 1937).

Jabès, E. (1987). *Le livre de partage* [The book of sharing]. Paris: Gallimard.

Jozsef, A. (1999). *The iron-blue vault: selected poems* (Zs. Ozsvath & F. Turner trans). Hexham: Bloodaxe Books.

Klein, M. (1975). *The writings of Melanie Klein: love, guilt and reparation 1921–1945 (Vol 1)*. London: Hogarth Press.

Klein, M. (1975). *The writings of Melanie Klein: envy and gratitude and other works 1946–89 (Vol 3)*. London: Hogarth Press.

Konicheckis, A. & Vamos, J. (2014). "Être en mouvement: Les fonctions psychiques du mouvement éclairées par les enfants de l'Institut Pikler-Loczy" [Being in movement: psychic functions of movementenlightened by the children of the Pikler-Loczy Institute]. *Le bébé en psychanalyse* (pp. 81–98). Paris: Presses Universitaires de France.

Kristeva, J. (2016). *Je me voyage: Mémoires* [I travel myself: Memoirs] (J. Vamos, Trans.). Paris: Fayard.

Laplanche, J. (1987). *Nouveaux fondements pour la psychanalyse* [New Fundamentals for Psychoanalysis]. Paris: Presses Universitaires de France.

Levinas, E. (1967). "Langage et proximité". *En découvrant l'existence avec Husserl et Heidegger* (pp. 218–235). Paris: Vrin.

Martino, B. (2000). *Loczy, une maison pour grandir*. Association Pikler Loczy France. DVD (170 min).

Meltzer, D. & Harris, M. (2013). *The educational role of the family: a psychoanalytical model*. London: Karnac, Harris-Meltzer Trust.

Meltzer, D. & Williams, M. H. (2000). *L'appréhension de la beauté, le conflit esthétique, son role dans le developpement, la violence, l'art* [The apprehension of beauty, aesthetic conflict, its role in development, violence and art]. Larmor-Plage, France: Editions du hublot.

Mérei, F. (2006). *Tanulmányok* [Studies]. Budapest: UMK.

Meszaros, J. (2010). Progress and persecution in the psychoanalytic heartland: antisemitism, communism and the fate of Hungarian psychoanalysis. *Psychoanal. Dial.*, 20, 600–622.

Nechtschein, L. (January 2020). Personal communication.

Ogden, T. (2012). *Creative reading: essays on seminal analytical works.* London and New York: Routledge.

Pikler, E. (1979). *Se mouvoir en liberté dès le premier âge* [To move freely from the beginning] (A. Szanto & M. Geffré, Trans.). Paris: Presses Universitaires de France.

Prat, R. (2008). *Maman-bébé: duo ou duel?* [Mother-baby: duo or duel?]. Toulouse, France: Erès.

Roussillon, R. (1999). *Agonie, clivage et symbolisation* [Agony, splitting, and symbolization]. Paris: Presses Universitaires de France.

Roussillon, R. & Golse, B. (2010). *La naissance de l'objet* [The birth of the object]. Paris: Le Fil Rouge.

Roy, A., Vamos, J. & de Wailly, D. (2018). *Devenir maman pour les nuls* [Becoming a mother for dummies]. Paris: Éditions First.

Stern, D. (1989). *Le monde interpersonnel du nourrisson* [The interpersonal world of the infant]. Paris: Presses Universitaires de France.

Szànto, A. (2016). *L'enfant qui vit, adulte qui réfléchit* [The living child, the thinking adult]. Paris: Presses Universitaires de France.

Szekacs-Weisz, J. & Keve, T. (2012). *Ferenczi for our time.* London: Karnac, The History of Psychoanalysis series.

Szekacs-Weisz, J. & Ward, I. (Ed.) (2004). *Lost childhood and the language of exile.* London: Karnac: Imago east-west, The Freud Museum.

Vamos, J., Adjedj, P.-J. & Thiriet, A. (2016). "Dramaturgie d'une diagnostic prénatal en montagne russe" [Dramaturgy of a prenatal diagnosis on a rollercoaster]. *Empathie autour de la naissance* (dir. M. Dugnat) (pp. 19–32). Toulouse, France: Erès.

Vamos, J. (2009). Nés sous X, but not abandoned. *The Signal, Newsletter of the World Association for Infant Mental Health*, 17(1–2), 6–12.

Vamos, J. (2015). Free to move, Free to be. *The American Journal of Psychoanalysis*, 75(1), 65–75.

Vamos, J. (2018). *Primary Harmony* [Conference Presentation]. Freud Museum Convention on Balints, December 8, 2018, London, UK.

Vamos, J. (2018). Hello baby: welcoming a child into a contemporary family. *Ferenczi's Influence on Contemporary Psychoanalytic Traditions* (pp. 262–268). New York: Routledge.

Vamos, J. (2019). A primal environment for the 21st century's 'Naissance': thoughts on the language of tenderness in Ferenczi's footsteps. *The American Journal of Psychoanalysis*, 79(4), 594–600.

William, S. G. (1998). *Paysages intérieurs et corps étrangers: Les troubles d'alimentation et d'autres pathologies* [Interior landscapes and foreign objects: eating disorders and other illnesses]. Larmor-Plage, France: Editions du hublot.

Winkler, V., & Vamos, J. (2018). *Hello Baby*. Vimeo (7 min).

Winnicott, D. W. (1949). Hate in the countertransference. *International Journal of Psycho-Analysis*, 30, 69–74.

Winnicott, D. W. (1951). Transitional objects and transitional phenomena. A study of the first not-me possession. *International Journal of Psycho-Analysis*, 34, 89–97.

Winnicott, D. W. (1986). *Home is where we start from: essays by a psychoanalyst*. London: Pelian Books.

Chapter 6

Afterword: Three voices, interwoven lives, distinctive pathways

Adrienne Harris

Introduction

Reading and thinking about how and what to write in reaction to these biographical essays, I found myself equally bound into history and into the present moment. In the context of a global pandemic, we are all revisiting history, trying to find our bearings in a transformed/destroyed world and, in some cases, trying to retrospectively understand how this could have happened, considering all the unpredictable and differential fates people are being dealt.

The three women writing these retrospective and reflective accounts, Veronica Csillag, Katalin Lanczi, and Julianna Vamos, have been friends since adolescence. I introduce them now, by their full names and in alphabetical order (by last name) but will refer to them by their first name, going forward in this essay. As they reflect and revisit three full, engaged, and interesting lives, we can see remarkable similarities and remarkable differences. Eerie resonances, like the potent role that psychoanalysis has played in their formation as people and in their professions, interact with intriguing differences in their links to culture, to politics, to different literatures and cultural passions.

All this reflection is presented and discussed in the context of a shared background of deeply traumatic events in the 20th century in Eastern Europe, specifically in Hungary. These stories are of both lives that one must acknowledge as haunted and lives of great creativity, enthusiasm, and determination to live, love, and work. These are the stories of challenging and fully actualized lives, trauma and triumph, sober and sad reflections, and deeply felt commitments to

DOI: 10.4324/9781003306542-6

ideas, to work, to service to others. Above all, one feels the commitment to witnessing, carrying, and representing traumas and wounds that are cross/inter-generational.

These essays are very unique contributions to the genre of autobiographical narratives, particular to time, place, and generation. They also very skillfully and convincingly build an argument for the power of a psychoanalytic lens on the complex histories of women, of emigrants, that are challenged with massive and unprepared-for changes. The stories that unfold in these essays reflect on how culture, ethnicity, religious prejudices and practice, gender, access and rights to sexuality, and perhaps most acutely, on how the decision to emigrate (in a variety of ways and contexts) transforms, inevitably and unexpectedly, a life, a family, the memory of history and of genealogy.

What I would want to underscore in this Afterword, is that while each of these stories is set in a context of extraordinary anguish and danger, what is most apparent in the writing and in the thinking is a deep sense of spirit, of ambition, of determination, and in different but also overlapping ways, an openness to the unexpected, the chance meeting, the group experience that suddenly opens an intellectual universe, an encounter with the arts and the *avant garde,* and a path to creativity and mobility. All three have different and complex experiences of relational choices, migration and career, and life paths. In overlapping ways, these stories also chart the layered and unpredictable pathways to love and family, pathways that require the complex negotiation of new countries, new passports, love, sexuality, and convenience and strategy in unusual and often daunting situations. But this is perhaps not entirely foreign to women operating and growing in less extreme conditions of change, danger, unpredictability, and the dark hand of history. Strategy and passion interweave in the personal odysseys of all three of these women, coming of age in the 1970s, determined on freedom in ways familiar and novel to both younger and older readers.

Each author has her own strategy as a writer, Veronica having perhaps the most performative, sometimes cynical, and also playful style. All three, operating as adults with deep formations in psychoanalysis, write openly and candidly. I think it is important to note here at the outset of my commentary that the narratives, stylistically quite different, despite many overlaps in life challenges, are describing the normal trials and tribulations of love and profession, and family, but that these "normal" developmental challenges are lived and weathered in, and ultimately transformed in powerful ways, by staggering circumstances.

While many of the issues raised in these essays are familiar to me, in my own experience of writing and growing within psychanalysis, I want to start with what I learned and what I felt about the collective view the three essays give of the context and beginnings of these three lives.

Early history: Beginnings

The three writers here were all born in the mid-1950s in Budapest, Hungary. Their formation, childhoods, and adolescence were spent in what stands as one of the most systematic periods of multiple traumas that I can imagine, even in our current deeply challenging circumstances. Their lives unfold, as the families and people around them take in, metabolize, and inevitably cannot process, the horrors of the war and the Holocaust. The intergenerational transmission of trauma and specifically the trauma of genocide and the Holocaust knows no geographical or temporal bounds. In this essay going forward, I will refer to this traumatic experience as the Shoah, a term all three authors use. This horror, its formation, and its aftermath are foundational to all three narratives and manifest in conscious and unconscious forms. But I do think it is worth contemplating the close immediacy of horror (past and present) in the childhoods of these writers. All three narratives chart the unsettling experience of living amidst the systematic and determined erasure of thought and reflection and discussion about the Shoah. It is crucial to notice, in these narratives, that the complex, troubled metabolism of the Shoah is almost immediately burdened with the processing of Soviet domination and invasion.

For all that the stories of these three have much common ground both in the terrifying and violent history and in the determination to thrive and survive, the tonal differences have really stayed with me. Katalin immerses us immediately and frighteningly in the destructions and deportations and murders of the 1930s and 1940s, the Shoah. It was only on a second reading that I realized that she had spent about the first quarter of her essay, locked into the history, the violence, the unresolved mourning, and the deep virulence of antisemitism. Veronica begins her essay already in the new world, looking back. She often writes with an intensive, one might say "gallows humour," her analytic understanding of her history is sharp and clear. While it is true that each writer is reflecting in the present about their and their families' past, Katalin is deeply present in registering trauma and unmournable loss, even as she will write of her escape to Western Europe and psychoanalysis with a gleeful magical intensity.

Juliana's essay begins at the moment of her emigration to Paris in 1974. She understands and deeply conveys how layered this moment is with dangerous departures, exile, deportations, and death. But the paragraph is also a stirring and compassionate exploration of the complex ambivalence of migration under the extraordinary conditions of these three women's lives and their cultural and traumatic inheritances.

I am not wanting to suggest so much that the histories of loss and trauma were so different but that some important and divergent coping or writing styles are at work. Family dynamics, the specifics of loss and danger, the differing roles of religion, culture, and identity are woven into stories that are interlocking, interactive, and distinct.

As adolescents and young adults, the three young women take on politics, the allure, and complications of radical political thought, and perhaps most troublingly, Marxism, because it would be encountered in the context of a virulent Soviet regime. They were growing into adulthood in an intense and often contradictory time in which sexual rebellion and an opening of consciousness are interwoven with political repression, political surveillance, dissidence, and at the same time, an intense period of intellectual expansion for these young women. Their interests and passions were different but passion, whether intellectual, personal, or sexual, animates these narratives.

I am about a half-generation older than these writers and I remember the period of much Hungarian migration to Canada where I grew up. That migration, the occasion being the 1956 Uprising in Hungary, was often idealized in Canada. Public discussion of the uprising and the arrival of Hungarians was offered in a spirit of self-congratulation in the context of the Canadian policy of a more open door. Surely, at that time, there was a radical underestimating of the trauma to those leaving their country and family.

In all three narratives in this book, with very distinct and individual voices, these accounts of the leave-taking from Hungary tell a much more complex story than the more superficial accounts in the Canadian-based narrative that I remember. The moments of migration, often a goodbye or farewell at a train station are full of complex and contradictory emotions: guilt, excitement, fear, pain. Acceptance and fear from the parental generation: pleasure, hope, and uncertainty in the young people starting their complex and inevitably emergent experiences.

At a particular point in each of the three accounts, the period of late adolescence, the complex worlds of sexuality, culture, and politics come into focus. It was both familiar and different. I thought of the comparable period in the late 1960s in North America, where radical thought and protest were transformed into more violent forms. North Americans of my generation, becoming politicized, as each of these three women do in different ways, did not have the complex history of Marxist and anti-Marxist thought that these women had to metabolize. The history of the Shoah, the deportations and battles of the World War II, and of the excesses and dominating intrusion of the Soviet period all had unique and complex effects on each of these women. And yet, happily, what is very present in these narratives, which will be familiar to Western European and US readers, is the delighted encounters with sexuality, with freedoms of the body, often entangled with intellectual freedom in its various forms. What is important to notice in these accounts, is their differences and their subtlety. Freedom is not idealized in these narratives. The social and political surround of their adolescence and young adulthood was often toxic and frightening, but these essays also chart the delights of growth and increased sophistication alongside the horror of surveillance and totalitarian controls. These contradictions and connections leave a very unique and particular flavor to the stories.

What is powerful and so clear in all three of these accounts is that while we can see and hear how traumatic and challenging the Hungarian world they were born into actually was, their narratives are not about victimization. They are, rather, all three, the narratives of ambitious and determined women, certainly of the generation influenced by second-wave feminism and the personal and familial consequences of migration which were clearly a challenge. These narratives have a quite distinctive tone: frank, thoughtful, and the lives they recount have such a clear mixture of determination and unexpected emergence. Why am I focused on this aspect at the onset of this essay? Because the stories are both familiar and not, bound to history and generic. For me, these narratives chart a particular trajectory of questions, determinations, fears, and choices that are very particular to women, perhaps more women of mid-century than contemporary women but many of the particular pressures on women still persist. Ambition, it has always struck me, is not ever entirely easy for women: the focus on one's own individuality, the determination to be visible and to matter, the focus on self. I particularly like the clarity and self-possession in these narratives, always also with a deep sense of the ordeals and challenges.

I have been in Hungary twice, for events organized around the work and career of Sandor Ferenczi. On both occasions, I spent part of the time in Budapest. Reading these essays, I have both associations with and images of the Dohany Street Synagogue and its archival rooms, with evidence of the war trauma and the Shoah. I also found myself visualizing the space along the Danube where Jewish citizens were executed. That space was the site of terror and genocidal activity, although the memorializing is fairly recent. Yet it is hard to be reading these essays and not to imagine the complex visible and invisible haunting of their environments. Katalin's nightmare of running along the Danube seems infused with this history, as she herself deeply understands. Veronica's narrative describes the experience of her mother, eight months pregnant, also on the line to be executed and thrown into the Danube. The haunted histories here are deeply challenging and painful to read, and hard to hold onto, but it is one of the imperatives of this project that the writer and reader face these histories.

These are also stories of migration and add an interesting set of observations to this complex and multiple configured experiences. I read these essays with my own migration story, seeing points of identification and difference. And as is so often true, the deeper understanding of these choices and their particularity comes long after they have played out. Veronica, in the Trialogue, notes the surprising (and in their peer group, unique to them) progression towards and then deeply into psychoanalysis. Their particular place and commitment to psychoanalysis are both overlapping and distinct and, emerged in three strikingly different psychoanalytic and cultural contexts. Her observation about this seemed right. How much did the turn these young women took into a theory and practice of uncovering the unknown, the unremembered, the unrememberable emerge from their histories, their intergenerational transmissions of one of the most taxing periods and contexts in 20th-century life?

This set of writings has made me think about the unconscious forces that play out for all of us and the mixture of chosen and unchosen in our pathways and arrival points. Like all three writers, I started with an interest in culture, the theatre, and literature, also embedded in a strong desire to leave home. Reading these narratives, I remember my own longings to be able to get away from home. From the already prescribed into excitement, England and the United States were always my targets. Reading these stories made me rethink my own, no matter their differences and wonder about the particular challenge for women of their and my generation to exercise or even own ambition and adventure.

In thinking about how to approach these complex and deep narratives, I decided to focus on several distinct questions/issues. How does each writer start her narrative? What is the emigration/immigration story that each tells? How does each writer situate her relationship to psychoanalysis?

Julianna begins in a dramatic complex moment, sitting on a train as her parents see her off to another country, another life. Parents, who are such a complex mixture of liberating empowerment and suffering and abandonment fear. These terrors that haunt several generations are set in play in the first page. Reading all these narratives, I kept thinking of Maurice Apprey's (2014) concept of the pluperfect errand, the tasks one undertakes in a life that turns out to be inscribed in the lives of others, in other generations; tasks that are both chosen and given. Apprey's concept, really helped me live in the complex temporalities of these essays. The term "pluperfect" is crucial. The errands are both potentially liberating, set up perhaps generations before, and can hold in tension the impossible and necessary demands that each generation makes on the next ones.

Julianna's scene on the train evokes many associations. The trains of deportation, the trains to freedom, the vitality of ambition and openness to something yet to be encountered, the exciting newness of ambition, alongside the muted and struggling parents who empower and attempt to have mourning that does not compromise the future.

In each of these narratives, the frame is history, the dashed hopes of the post World War I period of the 1920s, the trauma of the Second World War, in particular, the Shoah, and the growing recognition, in each of the writers, that they arrived into families in which extended family has been wiped out and immediate family are left to carry trauma that, in the case of Julianna's father, is literally unspeakable. And yet, in her narrative, it is equally believable that childhood and development were also open and energetic. There is rebellion and conformity, opportunities to grow intellectually, and aesthetically. This is for anyone a recognizable inwardly mobile, education/culture-driven exploration. For Julianna, there is a huge importance of community, of a particular group of intellectually and culturally curious young people given life and wings and projects by an earlier generation of intellectual mentors. This mentoring and the group experiences that held her and her comrades, endowed her with the kind of intellectual openness and awareness that makes the arrival and subsequent life in Paris, seem utterly expectable and the outcome of conscious and unconscious roots. French culture and French speech seem almost inevitable outcomes of the adolescent pleasures she describes in the Essential Circle. It has cultural and counter-cultural cachet. What could be better?

By contrast, Katalin's movement from adolescence into adult occupations set in the context of the intergenerational transmission of trauma was cast within some different narrative choices. The extensive impact of antisemitism from the 1930s carried forward is prominent. The massive dislocations and extinction of a large and extensive family, occur over the period of deportation and the Shoah. While all three writers live as secular persons, I thought that Katalin's history and her narrative described growing up more culturally Jewish than Julianna's or Veronica's. Katalin's account, for example, has a more extensive and more closely observed concentration on the presence and impact of antisemitism, at many levels of cruelty.

Early in her chapter, Katalin brings in a psychoanalytic lens to think about intergenerational trauma. Now of course, all three writers construct their narratives as mature adults, with minds and characters, deeply invigorated by psychoanalysis. But it was interesting to think of when and how the explicit psychoanalytic approach enters each person's narrative.

Katalin is linking a dream of hers to a similar one of her mother's. In both cases, the dreamer is running along the Danube River, trying to escape. But from what? In the mother's dream, she is carrying a baby on her back.

She tells us:

> There is a telescoping of time: her current life as a mother, her witnessing of murders as a child and her wish to protect both her own baby self and her baby, me. Her dream, never with a happy ending, was an only partially symbolized reflection of actual events. In reality that march to the Danube, where thousands of Budapest Jews were massacred, had a miraculous ending: a young Hungarian fascist let them go after he spotted my sobbing eight-year-old aunt, exclaiming: "Jesus and Mary, you look just like my little sister!"

The near-misses, the danger. Bridge story. I believe what she is describing is the series of murderous events that are memorialized in a sculpture along the Danube where many Jews were murdered. It is a powerful example of the intergenerational transmission of trauma and for me, also an evocation of Apprey's pluperfect errand. Veronica's essay has moments of eerie resonance with these states of mind.

Veronica writes a related but also a distinct account of beginnings. Politics, internalized almost reflexively at first and then creatively and joined with cultural as well as ideological pre-occupations and projects, is significantly more important than Jewish identity. There are powerful continuities and discontinuities in these biographies that also record development, gender problems and solutions, and a tumultuous social-political surround. Veronica retrospectively learns about surveillance and betrayal, and one might appreciate here how the common occurrence of such developments contributed to the speed with which she aims for departure and freedom. It is also true that she is the earliest to marry, but also to divorce and enter adult life and relationships with an intensity that perhaps the other two engage only later on.

In these narratives that chart the early development and the emergence of a wish for change, for transformation, for a future, we see part of the complex intergenerational transmissions. Yes, future, growth, freedom. But also, the repair of the past, which is always a mix of mourning and melancholia, and is always both a wish for repair and for rewriting and for undoing. One of the complex transmissions in all three involves Jewish identity, which by the time of their generation, is cultural more than religious.

Migration

This process unites this trilogy of stories but the differences, the patterns and the solutions to flight, and the need for growth and change are interestingly different. Veronica's voyage is aided and undergirded by a connection to a theatrical company, Squat Theatre, which became well known and admired in the United States as a captivating ensemble of experimental theatre. It seemed to me that there are deep intellectual and cultural currents in all these migratory choices.

Julianna was inspired by cultural studies and readings and education from her adolescence and it was not surprising to me that she was drawn to Paris, to French speech and French Culture. Katalin's migration to England seemed more about some personal experiences but also about language and culture. Like many stories of our development, sometimes the pathways seem crystal clear and sometimes enigmatic.

I listened to and read these accounts of migration (whether as escape, choice, inclination, history, or unexpected relational configurations) thinking of the mix of determination and emergence. Thinking also of my own migration, a decade earlier from Canada to the United States, imagining consciously that I needed to escape a culture that seemed tedious and conforming and uninspiring. But, to reiterate a feeling I have had about these narratives, each person's pathways are in the context of a cultural, community, and political structure, that had generational and intergenerational trauma at a deep and extreme level. I felt, in these narratives, each writer's sensitivity to family trauma and the inevitable family difficulties and the complex pain and hope that migration stirred in the extended family.

In fact, if there is some (delicate and self-reflective) emotion, it is regret about the departure and emigration from family. This felt familiar to me in regard to my own emigration from Canada. Conflicts within family, intergenerational tensions, and needs for difference and for emancipation are the complex backstory of these three narratives, alongside history and political repression. The intergenerational piece felt deeply familiar to me.

Veronica has the most unsettling and tumultuous migration story, with often volatile and sudden movement: marriage, separation, moves, the complex emotional demand of labor and work so beneath her capacities and history. She takes quite some time to settle into the productive, intellectually demanding, and satisfying work of psychoanalysis. All three do end as psychoanalysts and psychoanalysis in varying ways saves many a day. As it does for all of us.

Again, I find myself tracking my own story of the encounter with psychoanalysis via the study of literature, theatre and a romance with acting as each of these three women find their footing and their ambitious reach through the theory, the clinical experience, the practice of psychoanalysis, and psychotherapy.

Inevitably, for me, thinking of women's career trajectory takes me into many feminist bypaths and pre-occupations on how ambition functions and sometimes eludes women. Some of Veronica's run-up to her career feels like a saga that almost makes her distinguished work-life an accidental outcome and that can often be the woman's narrative style and self-experience. But I think taken as three complex stories, ambition is both pre-destined, and emergent from the protagonists' psychic strengths and determinations as well as the press of history. Sometimes one is aware of the costs and demands of self-assertion in women's narratives. Sometimes, the courage of these three writers is profound and deeply individual.

Katalin's narrative brings psychoanalysis into the story early. I felt that the significance of the traumatic losses in her family, the intergenerational transmission of trauma, the loss of extended family, were operating on her determination to leave and find a different space. Here, in particular, though it is in all three stories, I feel the migration as a pluperfect errand, something demanded and for-bidden. The specter, past and present of antisemitism, the Jewish children in this generation, like Ferenczi's unwanted child (Ferenczi, 1929), are both called to leave and survive and flourish and to retain and conserve history. The West beckons. But so does the past.

Veronica's essay records the most challenging and disrupted de-velopmental trajectory. At a certain point in her narrative, when she is settled in New York City and has formed but also fully supports a family she contemplates her experience: "I find it difficult to re-construct how I went from a tornado-just-hit-me, utterly miserable to less miserable and then eventually finding solidifying ground under my feet" (p. x). She has described a difficult and contentious family life, as a deep understanding of the complex betrayals and compro-mises that Jewish citizens of her parents' era endured and struggled with in the context of Soviet life and its required compromises. She names the invasion of Czechoslovakia and the collapse of Prague Spring as a moment of emotional anguish, perhaps the stirrings of the need to leave, to escape. If Katalin and Julianna were drawn to cultures and worlds where more was possible, Veronica's passage to emigration and a new world comes more clearly from a need to es-cape in order to survive. Betrayals, existential dread, surveillance, fragmenting of her family and a complex road to stability in America are at the heart of this brave story.

The road to psychoanalysis

One of the perhaps eerie, certainly potent synergies in these narratives is the pathway each woman has found to psychoanalysis. For all three, the psychoanalysis they found was distinct to the culture they were living in, but in all three cases, the finding of psychoanalysis and the joining of psychoanalytic communities and institutions were both personal salvation and an exciting opening to vocations and profes-sional identities.

Encountering psychoanalysis is often a complex process, at times a move to safety and protection and at times an opening into new and potent forces of change. Growth occurs both in security, in states of determination and in moments of raw courage. These narratives made me think of my own move into psychoanalysis via developmental psychology. I think it was a move towards security and conformity, away from the more tempestuous and radical forces of 60s politics and a life in theatre and acting. Katalin's encounter and evolution as a therapist and later psychoanalyst begins in London where she describes going into analysis and becoming trained in a very interesting setting. This center, influenced by R.D. Laing (1965), would have occupied and produced an intense atmosphere both about healing and radical change.

Julianna moves from an exciting exposure to literature and culture, particularly French culture in an adolescent group built around an important and charismatic figure. It seemed from that experience very clear why she would move to Paris. Less predictably, she begins to work in psychology as an undergraduate and continues an interesting route to psychoanalysis. Recently, in 2021, I heard her speak about her work in Paris on adoption and early infancy and abandoned or traumatized infants. She speaks from a fascinating point of intellectual and psychoanalytic conjunction: attachment studies and the work of the Budapest school, Balint, Ferenczi, and Hermann, among others. Her contemporary psychoanalytic bent is quite uniquely, I would say, both generic to her origins in Hungary and contemporarily part of the English-speaking psychoanalytic world, from London and the United States via Bowlby, Ainsworth, Main, and others.

Katalin describes a strong and demanding undergraduate education, a mixture of English and Hungarian literature and language, including some classes in comparative literature and philosophy and the like. Her move to London comes after some exciting experiences in North America and, in a move that is a familiar aspect of many life changes, falling in love and marriage is part of the mixture. The life she describes in England has its own migrations, London to Kent and back to London as well as a migration within psychotherapy and psychoanalysis from the more radical work influenced by R.D. Laing through clinics (Arbours) and institutions increasingly focused on psychoanalysis. She has had a distinguished career in the Institute of Psychoanalysis in London, after what sounds like wonderful training and supervision, and the freedom to be eclectically independent (other forms of migration).

In addition to her leadership role in her institute, Veronica's psychoanalytic career has involved writing and teaching. It is interesting to encounter her narrative of her early life and the tribulations of university years and the counter-cultural projects and sexual explorations of her young adulthood in the light of a strong and intellectually and clinically anchored contemporary experience. One of the most moving parts of her narrative was her account of work at the Jewish Board, as she notes, one of the most important and deeply useful mental health clinics of the time. There she both gets training and deepens professionally, but also comes to understand the intergenerational transmission of trauma and its potent presence in her own life and history.

In all three stories the transitions from student life, from life in family and cultural security in Budapest to the professional psychoanalytic communities of the United Kingdom, the United States, and France, including a transitional period of work in the kind of labor that can trap a woman forever. Domestic work, house cleaning and child care, jobs, and pathways away from professional and financial security occupied each of these women during the transition and working through migration. Again, I found myself feeling the difference in the security of my own 'migration.' I can identify a lot with the longing to leave home, to leave constriction, and be in motion – personally, socially, professionally. But the migratory voyage in my case did not change class or economic positions. Like Veronica, I moved from a focus on the theatre and cultural life to psychoanalysis and did so via a route through academic developmental psychology. The migration that for me was both more demanding and more perilous was the movement from a less politically conscious sensibility, via feminism and the 1960s, to a more radical political and social vision. Working on this essay I thought a lot about my own history. As each of these writers, I think that psychology, academic life, and then psychoanalysis saved me from many of the excesses of the 60s. Having children was another stabilizer for me. I have a sense of that as an aspect within this generation.

Haunting

Trains are everywhere in these narratives. They lead to freedom, and they lead/led to deportation, to death, to the endless task of carrying the Shoah. They are a way out but the evocation of history haunts all generations. I think of the moment, early in Julianna's narrative when her family accompanies her on the train to Paris. Everyone is brave and loving and heartbroken. Her father, who will die later in the same month wants to get onto the car Julianna will travel in and save her a seat. He cannot take the second step up. Memory, aging, sorrow, and the deep continuation of parental love. Likely all of the above.

Psychoanalysis, as a profession, a practice, and a theory is well suited to the experiences of haunting and being haunted. I speak as a psychoanalyst and as a person deeply carried and nurtured by psychoanalytic work and thought. It was interesting for me to read the migrations and trajectories within psychoanalysis and psychotherapy that these three analysts took. I feel most identified with Katalin who starts and then moves on from a more radical theory of psychoanalysis. My turn to more conventional psychoanalytic training, although also relational, came after early forays into politically radical forms of treatment. This threesome's interests range over wide differences. Katalin becomes affiliated with the Lincoln Center where she does administration and training before becoming a member and then a Fellow of the British Psychoanalytic Society. There is Julianna's work in Paris on the theoretical and clinical understanding of family disruptions, such as adoption and early loss and Veronica's practicing and writing in the spirit of relational/interpersonal theory in the United States, along with leadership and administration in her Institute. Psychoanalysis and psychotherapy define the mature work of all three, though their pathways are very particular to each. Now as this book is written, we have three accomplished and productive psychoanalysts, continuing to contribute and develop in their fields of interest and expertise.

Working as an analyst and being a patient are processes in which ghosts and demons of many kinds are conjured up and hopefully transformed (Harris et al., 2016) In a daily and hourly way, one sits with a variety of ghosts. And, as contemporary analytic theory is now suggesting (Ogden, 2019), this creative and transformative process must befall the analyst as well as the analysand. So, I am speaking with a strong sense of identification in suggesting that the migration in and through psychoanalysis, both links these writers and friends, and is a link for this discussant, and is a fundamental part of reparation and processing of haunted subjectivities.

Last words

Each writer ends her essay in their particular way. Veronica visits a grave, Katalin opens up her perspective from the personal narrative and contextualizes her trajectory from Budapest to England by calling us to think about Covid-19 and about Brexit, a worldwide and a local event that creates defining experiences for her, however, focused and intent she has been on work and personal life. Julianna, in her ending, meditates on the complexity, the ambivalence, and also the triumph of migration and exile. She conjures up two trains: one goes to Auschwitz carrying her father, one takes her to Paris, to freedom, to "her own walk."

Veronica's essay ends with a visit to the cemetery in which her parents and ancestors are buried. She notes, with some anguish and deep feeling, that the fact that only one family member is missing makes her family among the fortunate. But we are also with Veronica in the cemetery, noticing that her uncle, whose body is missing, had been deported to Mauthausen. As she says, and it is an aspect of all three of these memoires, this is the crime scene always under investigation, always present, always haunting and whether, as Veronica notes, your source is Biblical or psychoanalytic, it is the intergenerational transmission of trauma. Traumas in these stories are longstanding and whether witnessing silently or loudly exclaiming, I would say that all three writers are haunted. I feel, as a reader and commentator, that it is imperative to encounter, take up and meet these hauntings.

I see in the essayists' choice of endings the way that this threesome is linked and distinct. Any one of them could have written any of the three kinds of endings each one selected. Veronica says this early in the trialogue: this threesome is very different and very linked and similar at the same time. Affinities and differences have made these autobiographic essays and my task of commentary, very fascinating, and for me and I believe, readers with both echoing and very different histories of growth and evolution, very moving.

References

Apprey, M. (2014). The pluperfect errand: a turbulent return to beginnings in the transgenerational transmission of destructive aggression free associations: psychoanalysis and culture. *Media, Groups, Politics*, 77, 15–28.

Ferenczi, S. (1929/1994). The unwelcome child and his death instinct. In Ferenczi, S. *Final contributions to the problems and methods of psychoanalysis* (pp. 102–107). London: Karnac Books.

Harris, A., Kalb, M. & Klebanoff, S. (2016). *Ghosts in the consulting room.* Relational perspectives book series. London: Routledge.

Laing, R. D. (1965). *The divided self.* London, England: Penguin Books.

Ogden, T. H. (2019). Ontological psychoanalysis or "what do you want to be when you grow up?" *Psychoanal. Quarter.*, 88, 661–684.

Index

Page numbers followed by 'n' refer to notes.

For Product Safety Concerns and Information please contact our EU
representative GPSR@taylorandfrancis.com
Taylor & Francis Verlag GmbH, Kaufingerstraße 24, 80331 München, Germany